EARLY MARYLAND IN A WIDER WORLD

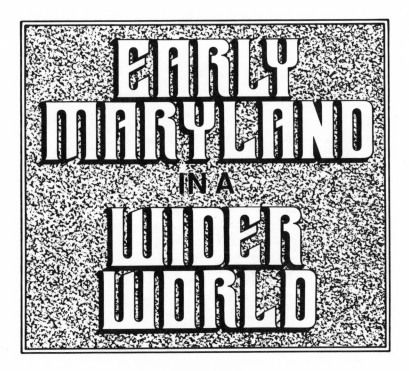

Edited by
DAVID B. QUINN
St. Mary's College of Maryland

WAYNE STATE UNIVERSITY PRESS • DETROIT, 1982

Library of Congress Cataloging in Publication Data
Main entry under title:

Early Maryland in a wider world.

Includes index.
Contents: Ships and sea / Melvin H. Jackson—
Spain and its empire in the sixteenth and seven-
teenth centuries / J.H. Elliott — The Spaniards in
eastern North America / J.H. Parry—[etc.]
1. Maryland—History—Colonial period, ca. 1600-
1775—Addresses, essays, lectures. I. Quinn,
David Beers.
F184.E16   978.2'02   81-13071
ISBN 0-8143-1689-1   AACR2

This volume is published with the financial support of
St. Mary's College of Maryland.

CONTENTS

Contents

FORGING THE CHESAPEAKE WORLD

CONTRIBUTORS

John Bossy, Ph.D. Professor of History, University of York
(England); formerly visiting fellow, Institute for Advanced
Study, Princeton. Author of *The English Catholic Community, 1570–1850* (1976).

Lois Green Carr, Ph.D. Historian, St. Mary's City Commission. Author of many papers on Maryland history; editor
(with Aubrey C. Land and Edward C. Papenfuse) of *Law,
Society, and Politics in Early Maryland* (1977).

William P. Cumming, Ph.D. Emeritus professor of English
literature, Davidson College. Author of *The Southeast in
Early Maps* (1958); author and editor, with others, of *The
Discovery of North America* (1971), *The Exploration of
North America, 1630–1776* (1974), and other publications.

Richard S. Dunn, Ph.D. Professor of history, University of
Pennsylvania. Author of *Puritans and Yankees* (1962); *Sugar and Slaves* (1972); *The Age of Religious Wars* (2d ed.
1979); and other writings.

J. H. Elliott, Ph.D. Professor of history, Institute for Advanced Study, Princeton; formerly professor of history,
King's College, University of London. Author of *Imperial
Spain* (1966); *The Old World and the New, 1492–1650*
(1970); and other works.

G. R. Elton, Ph.D., Litt. D. Professor of English constitutional history, University of Cambridge; formerly president of the Royal Historical Society. Author of *The Tudor
Revolution in Government* (1953); *England under the Tudors* (2d ed. 1969); *Reform and Reformation in England,*

7

1509–1547 (1977); and many other works on British and European history.

Melvin H. Jackson, Ph.D. Adjunct professor of history, St. Mary's College of Maryland; formerly curator of maritime history, Museum of History and Technology, Smithsonian Institution.

Francis Jennings, Ph.D. Director of the Newberry Library Center for the History of the American Indian. Author of *The Invasion of America* (1975) and many papers on relations between Indians and whites.

Russell R. Menard, Ph.D. Associate professor of history, University of Minnesota. Author of a number of papers on early Maryland and Virginia; contributor to Land, Carr, and Papenfuse, eds., *Law, Society, and Politics in Early Maryland* (1977), and Thad W. Tate and David L. Ammerman, eds., *The Chesapeake in the Seventeenth Century* (1979).

J. H. Parry, Ph.D. Professor of oceanic history and affairs, Harvard University; formerly professor of history in the University of the West Indies; principal of University College, Swansea (University of Wales). Author of *The Age of Reconnaissance* (1963); *The Spanish Seaborne Empire* (1966); *The Discovery of South America* (1979); and other works.

David B. Quinn, Ph.D., D. Lit. Professor of history, St. Mary's College of Maryland; Andrew Geddes and John Rankin Professor Emeritus of Modern History, University of Liverpool; sometime visiting professor, College of William and Mary and University of Michigan. Author of *England and the Discovery of America, 1481–1520* (1974); *North America from First Discovery to Early Settlements* (1977); editor of *New American World: A Documentary History of North America to 1612*, 5 vols. (1979); and other works.

PREFACE

The quest for the origins and early history of Maryland and of its place in the Chesapeake world of the colonial period has made great progress in recent years, but it has lacked a synoptic account of the background and early development of the colony in relation to its English background, the exploitation of the Atlantic Ocean, and the influence of Spain and its empire. Moreover, so far many of the earlier stages in its development have been insufficiently studied. St. Mary's College of Maryland, on the site of Maryland's first capital (and at the center of the work of the St. Mary's City Commission), has felt a special obligation to emphasize the colony's early history in its widest historical context. The present volume originated in a series of lectures given during 1977 and 1978, inspired by Dr. Renwick J. Jackson, Jr., president of the college. It appears with his blessing and assistance.

To Professor John M. Hirschfield, chairman of the Division of Social Science and History, belonged much of the labor of selecting lecturers and arranging the series. We were fortunate in having the close cooperation of a distinguished team of English, American, and Anglo-American scholars, whose lectures are published here substantially in the form in which they were delivered, although in some cases subsequent revisions have been incorporated. To Professors J. H. Elliott of the Institute for Advanced Study at Princeton University, G. R. Elton of the University of Cambridge, J. H. Parry of Harvard University, and John Bossy of the University of New York, whose European backgrounds have done much to prevent the series from becoming narrowly regional, we are profoundly grateful. Professor Richard H. Dunn, Dr.

9

Francis Jennings, and Emeritus Professor W. P. Cumming, distinguished authorities in the field of American colonial studies, have enabled us to add much that is novel on early Maryland. Professor Melvin E. Jackson and I represented the St. Mary's College faculty in this gathering.

In order to place the lecture series in a more general context, I have added an introduction that I call "Prelude to Maryland," and I have also been very fortunate in persuading Dr. Lois Green Carr and Professor Russell R. Menard to develop a short study dealing with the Lords Baltimores' objectives and achievements in the social and political sphere. Their contribution incorporates in summary form the results of Professor Menard's wide research in English and other sources and Dr. Carr's unrivaled authority on the records of Maryland itself. Their collaboration has been most fruitful, and we are proud to include their study in the lecture sequence.

We are grateful to many persons for help along the way: Professor Frederick Fausz; Mrs. Betty Knight and Mrs. Myers of the St. Mary's College secretarial staff; Alison Quinn for helpful criticism and for making the index; those who have given the necessary permissions to reproduce materials; and Mr. Richard Kinney, Mrs. Jean Owen, and Dr. Sherwyn T. Carr of Wayne State University Press for their effective help and cooperation at every stage in construction of this book. But final thanks are due to the distinguished group of lecturers, who not only delighted their original audiences but have allowed us to use their lectures as the basis for what we hope will prove an effective introduction to the prehistory and early shaping of one of the more interesting and exciting experiments in early English colonization.

David B. Quinn
St. Mary's College of Maryland

INTRODUCTION:
PRELUDE TO MARYLAND

David B. Quinn

Maryland as it was founded in 1634 was intended to be a new type of colony. In some respects it can be seen as a continuation of that tobacco-based Chesapeake settlement which had been painfully emerging in Virginia. Indeed, Maryland and Virginia were to take their place in a unique society, a Chesapeake world which well into the eighteenth century distinguished the shores of the great inland sea from the other European communities of eastern North America. But Maryland also represented a place of refuge for one of the nonconforming English communities, the Roman Catholic one, as distinct and separate in its conception and working out as the Plymouth colony had been more than a decade before Maryland began. Basically, however, Maryland marked the coming to fruition of a trend in English thinking, dreaming, and planning which went back to more than half a century before the *Ark* and the *Dove* entered the Potomac and finally came to rest at St. Mary's, the site which was to mark the center of the colony, ambiguously dedicated both to Queen Henrietta Maria and to the Virgin. In concept it antedated the Plymouth settlement by many years, but in execution it was delayed until Plymouth had entered its fourteenth year.

Over the past generation, we have been taught, correctly, to think of Tudor England as a state in which the authority of the central government, represented by bureaucratic institutions, took command of the utmost extremities of English territorial limits, even if it did so in Ireland only in the dying

11

moments of Queen Elizabeth I.[1] Henry VIII destroyed not only the independent power of the church but also the autonomous powers of the great nobility along the borders of England, Wales, and, ultimately, Ireland. The notion of any individual or corporation being able to resist the orders of the crown and maintain rights of jurisdiction which were not common to the whole realm was anathema to the Tudor sovereigns, though perhaps less so to the Stuarts, whose compromises with feudal autonomy in Scotland had been less absolute in their result. Modern research has informed us also that, whatever the ultimate strength of state power as created by the Tudors, it was based less on absolutism than on a division of authority. Instead of the liberties and honors of medieval England, the county community, usually a collaboration of aristocratic magnates and nonaristocratic gentry, was left to its own devices in strictly local affairs. By limiting its demands and creating a traditional relationship, compounded of obedience and autonomy, the Elizabethan state operated with reasonable efficiency and continuity. It lasted into the Stuart period and remained the basis for local government, even if growingly subject to religious, economic, and political strains in the decades before the Civil War.

To an outsider it might appear that a unique balance had been struck between centralism and local autonomy. There were individuals who had vague glimpses of a much more open society (their slogan was "popularity and parity," the dread herald of democracy), but they were submerged until the Civil War gave them body and strength. There were larger groups who looked backward to a truly hierarchical society, to a utopia in which landowning might come again into its own as a symbol not only of wealth but of political and judicial power, to be wielded under the crown, it is true, but without interference, and with the capacity to expand indefinitely the power as well as the wealth of the landowner. And indeed, if the laws of England had steadily enhanced the authority of the crown at least from the accession of the Tudors, the defenders of reaction had put up an intermittent fight. The most recent of these struggles in England

12

was the aristocratic and Catholic northern rising of 1569 for the restoration of the former autonomy of its leaders. Although the insurgents were defeated, their concepts were not incapable of realization, since the legal traditions of the royal prerogative still enabled the monarch to grant such powers to a subject within legal frameworks almost identical with those used for the great feudal lordships of the Middle Ages.

Ireland was perhaps the breeding ground for the revival of such feudal utopias. The theory that the royal officials in Dublin controlled the whole island was, until 1603, a legal fiction. English power vacillated over the last half of the sixteenth century; from time to time backward-looking utopians might gain royal support for plans to restore feudal autonomy on ground conquered and settled from its Irish inhabitants or from invading island Scots. Thus between 1568 and 1576 feudal grants were discussed and, on some occasions, granted for parts of Ireland, foreshadowing the principal lines of planning that led toward American experiments and which were to culminate (in one form at least) in the Maryland of 1634. Sir Thomas Gerard of Bryn, Lancashire, several of whose family were to settle in Maryland, was a Catholic reactionary, envisaging a lordship in County Antrim which would act as an English Catholic bulwark against the Scots, but he asked for too much assistance from the queen to be permitted to go ahead.[2] Queen Elizabeth was more generous to her statesman-lawyer, Sir Thomas Smith, when in 1571 she permitted the granting to him of lands, mainly in modern County Down, which were to be held as an independent feudal principality under the queen herself, who was to be honored (as the queen in 1634 was honored in the name of Maryland) by calling the central town Elizabetha.[3] But the Smiths disturbed existing local relationships, and the presence of their settlers was soon regarded by the royal officials in Dublin as more of an impediment than an asset to English government in Ireland. The Smith venture was allowed to wither and die.

The grant to the earl of Essex in 1573 to bring over the body of English gentlemen to occupy County Antrim as a bul-

13

wark against Scottish intrusions was a more grandiose feudal
venture, though Essex was expected to obey the orders of the
queen's lord deputy in Dublin. In fact, his gentlemen followers took a brief look at these northern lands and mostly
returned to their less extensive but more fully developed English properties. Essex became, instead, the regional commander of a state-controlled English army. During these same
years as a young army captain, Humphrey Gilbert (knighted
for his services in the field in 1570) had a comparable if somewhat different vision. Ireland had land to spare; her inhabitants could be pushed aside or forced to forfeit their lands if
they resisted. Why should Englishmen not step in and take
over substantial estates and build up an immigrant tenantry?
At that time, from 1568 to 1574, Gilbert was not so much concerned about feudal powers as about landed revenues. The
younger sons of English gentry and aristocrats might have the
chance, denied to them in England through the laws of primogeniture, to make landowners of themselves, with great opportunities for enlarging their wealth. Nothing came of Gilbert's
plans in face of the Smith and Essex fiascos, but they were to
grow in his mind over the next decade and focus, not on Ireland, but on North America.

Over the years after his first Irish project, Sir Humphrey
Gilbert gradually built up, on the basis of his knowledge both
of feudal law and institutions and of the wide powers the
Spanish crown conferred on its conquistadores (even if it took
many of them back if they succeeded), a remarkably consistent
body of theory on the articulation of a renewed feudal society.
He knew what elements of authority should adhere to the lord
proprietor and how much autonomy he could, in turn, allow to
his tenants, ranging from poor, landless émigrés to lords of
immense areas of soil and their subtenants, in the elaborate
social pyramid which could be constructed. There is no doubt
that Gilbert, for all his failures, was the father not only of the
concept that the colonization of the whole of eastern North
America fell by rightful theory to England (despite realistic
and unrealistic Spanish, Portuguese, and French claims), but
also that this was the area in which could be constructed a

wholly feudal society (though not ignoring commerce for agriculture alone). The claims of the native American population to any rights in their own territories were irrelevant to him, and indeed Gilbert scarcely mentions their existence. It is also clear that Gilbert's utopian projects lie in a line of direct descent to those which Lord Baltimore attempted to implement in Maryland half a century later.[4]

Gilbert obtained from Queen Elizabeth an extraordinary blank check in the patent of June 1578, which allowed him to seize and govern, under the vaguest possible commitments to conform to her wishes, any lands not occupied by Christian people. This he took to apply to the whole of eastern North America and, by elimination of some northern areas, the coastline and hinterland between "the Cape of Florida and Cape Breton," ignoring wholly, for example, the settled Spanish territory in Florida. His first voyage of 1578–79 and its failure leave us with many questions, but it is clear that on this occasion his support came primarily from Protestant gentlemen, mainly land-hungry younger sons of gentlemen like himself, though we have no information on precisely how he intended to organize them if he ever got them to America. His planning came to light, fully developed, in 1582. By then he had convinced many court nobles, Protestant gentlemen, and even townsmen of ports such as Bristol and Southampton that his voyage could bring riches from land and minerals, but his new instrument—which was to be the moving force in his plans—was the Catholic gentry of England. They were men of old families who had withstood the reformation of 1559 and who looked back to a period when there was no state interference in their relations with either their religion or their dependents. In their minds religious, social, and political reaction formed a single attitude.

The result was that the Catholic gentry formed the core of Gilbert's conceptual scheme for an American landed empire. Sir Thomas Gerard and Sir George Peckham were among the Catholic gentry who were particularly sharply affected by the tightened regulations of 1581. These were designed to make nonconformity to the established church

15

much more expensive and painful for all but the very rich (since fines for nonattendance at church were high), unless they were willing to spend a considerable part of their lives in prison. Gilbert appealed to such men, promising not merely landed estates for themselves but millions of acres which they might exploit even in advance of their discovery by selling them to their friends and relations. We know that, besides Catholic gentlemen in Lancashire and southern England, many Protestant gentry were attracted by the scheme, so that a huge land speculation movement developed in the summer of 1582.

Gilbert sketched an overall scheme for an American dominion, with himself as lord paramount and with strong administrative, executive, and military powers. His own estates were to be enormous: seignories (using the medieval term) for himself, his wife, and his sons and daughters, ranging in size from 400 to 10,000 square miles. Peckham and Gerard, when in paper control of some 4 million acres of land, were prepared to be more modest about their own estates, a mere 30,000 acres being the largest unit they initially contemplated occupying for themselves, while their subtenants, in accordance with the size of their subscriptions, could obtain similar estates, as large or smaller, down to a mere 1,000 acres. A document recently acquired by the Public Archives of Canada shows them preparing a fleet in 1582 to define and limit land for themselves and their supporters.[5] Though Florida to Cape Breton was the limit of search, we know they were intending to occupy southern New England first of all. There each landowner would have rights of jurisdiction over his tenants and, in turn, pay service to the next landowner above him in the feudal pyramid, with all paying taxes and rents to the lord paramount at the apex of the structure. The details laid out in this document are of the greatest interest for later developments. There was one fatal flaw: not enough money could be found to get a fleet to sea in the time contemplated. This was to provide a limiting factor in all future Catholic emigration efforts, even adversely affecting the occupation of Maryland.

Gilbert himself was no more fortunate in putting vessels to sea in 1582, and when he set out in 1583 he turned from a south-north expedition along the American coast to a north-south one. He thus was able to switch his personal interests from land on the mainland to the annexation of Newfoundland and a seignory of 100 leagues in all directions from St. John's for himself and his family, a mere 90,000 square miles. He was going to leave Peckham, Gerard, and the rest to establish their own estates, but he considered that he must first reconnoiter the territory he had sold to them farther south, sight unseen. On his way there his flagship was wrecked and his remaining vessels forced to return, he himself being lost in mid-Atlantic. But his surviving captain, Edward Hayes, did his best to forward Peckham's plans on his return. Peckham's pamphlet, *A true reporte of the late discoveries,* which came out in London before the end of 1583, is the fullest statement of the conservative land acquisition plan, though it lays less stress on the feudal hierarchy than had Gilbert. A table of land to be acquired by investment under Peckham promised much for little. However, poverty, threats by the Spanish ambassador to English Catholics who went to America, and Gilbert's fate led to the failure of the scheme. In 1584 Peckham retired from it (to spend some time in prison thereafter), but his ideas and master plan lived on in documents and in the minds of men throughout the fallow period of the Spanish war between 1585 and 1604, to be revived and experimented with during the following generation.[6]

To us, the whole scheme seems most unrealistic. The plans showed no realization of what colonization in America involved in physical and economic terms, let alone in connection with the resident inhabitants, but the idea of territorial lordships in North America in one form or another was to last for well over a century.

From 1584 to 1603, Walter Ralegh (knighted in 1585) held rights to North American lands theoretically almost as wide as Gilbert's. But he was a much more sophisticated colonial projector. He never set out any theoretical program for colonization or any blueprint for the creation of a lordship headed by himself, even though in 1584 he had a seal made for himself as lord and governor of Virginia. The Roanoke voyages and colonies from 1584 to 1590 (with a possible residue down to 1607) consequently were conceived empirically. The first colony of 1585, following a close reconnaisance of the North Carolina-Virginia shore in 1584, was an experimental station, manned by men he employed to assess the possibilities of Roanoke Island and its surroundings as a location for military and naval bases and as footholds from which a thorough survey of natural and Indian resources could be made, as well as to test the healthiness of the climate. The result was an important collection of data, but no conclusive evidence of rich farming country or of exotic products.

Ralegh's eclectic approach was seen in 1587 in the leasing to a group of self-supporting families of the City of Ralegh territory, located near the southern shores of Chesapeake Bay, to exploit as self-sufficient farms in close association with the Indians and in proximity to a deep-water port on the bay. This plan miscarried. The settlers were left to make their way from Roanoke Island to the site of the intended city. They obliged the governor, John White, to sail home to assure supplies from England. His failure to return until 1590 led the party which awaited him on Roanoke Island to give up and depart for Croatoan, while the main body settled down to develop their own resources at a still unidentified site near modern Norfolk, Virginia. They lived peacefully with the Chesapeake Indians until wiped out in 1606 or 1607 by Powhatan. The naval base was never established, since the ships and personnel were taken over in 1588 to serve against the Spanish Armada. Thereafter Ralegh held on to his rights on the assumption that the Lost Colony was still in existence, but his probing expeditions established little more than that trade with coastal Indians was possible. He lost his title to American land and his powers in 1603, when they were confiscated by the crown.[7]

Gilbert's plans and Ralegh's experiments had produced information that colonization was an expensive and long-term project, but had left sufficient details to indicate that it might well be a profitable one. The Virginia Company (1606–24) appeared to be the correct type of solution, combining merchant expertise with the ability to accumulate capital to establish settlers over an extended probationary period. If that venture proved a "fiasco," as E. S. Morgan has called it, it nonetheless produced in the end a society of planters.[8] The group of big estates and their owners which dominated Virginia when it was taken over by the crown in 1624 was kept viable by the one major export crop which at that time suited Chesapeake production, tobacco. From 1624 on, Virginia was curbed by the crown in that the future extent of its territory was to be determined, not by earlier charters, but by the royal will and by the potential power to coerce the existing settlers. This left the northern fringes of the Chesapeake territory to be filled in by the Calvert grant of 1632, to the dismay and hostility of the Virginia planters and their London merchant associates, but the grant provided unique advantages for the Catholic colony to establish itself in a favorable environment, economic as well as physical, even though health problems were still far from being overcome.

Much had happened elsewhere in North America that was relevant to the eventual Maryland experiment. If James I was more sympathetic than Elizabeth to the surviving Catholic aristocracy, and welcomed a number of its members to his court, he was not without suspicions of their creed and resolutely opposed the political implications of papal claims. There was considerable doubt whether he would make some measure of toleration dependent on the formal renunciation by Catholics of papal authority in temporal matters. Consequently, Sir Thomas Arundell (soon created Lord Arundell of Wardour) in 1605 revived plans to create an aristocratic Catholic colony on the shores of Norumbega, not yet known to Englishmen as New England. This involved, at one stage, the bringing to America of Catholic English soliders who had fought for Spain and who, after James made peace in 1604, were unemployed. They would provide both the labor and protection which a handful of loyal Catholic gentlemen required if they were to make a success of such a venture.

Through the sea captain George Waymouth, Arundell made a loose liaison with a group of Plymouth fishing merchants, and the expedition which Waymouth made to Monhegan, the Georges Islands, and the St. George River in 1605 seemed to promise suitable land and fishing bases for both parties in the enterprise. Unfortunately, Arundell had deserted the scheme when official Catholic opposition to using disbanded soldiers in America had emerged and had agreed to become, instead, colonel of an English regiment to be hired from these discharged soldiers and others for the Spanish service. Waymouth found the Plymouth merchants enthusiastic about his reports of fishing bases, but he had some difficulty in selling the idea of an aristocratic shore-based venture to other gentlemen.

Finally Sir John Zouche, not himself a Catholic but with Catholic connections, agreed to get together an expedition to make the settlement, with himself as the lord paramount and James Rosier's pamphlet, *A true relation,* as his main propaganda instrument.[9] It is reasonably certain that this pamphlet appeared only after the Gunpowder Plot of 5 November 1605 had turned royal and public opinion against all Catholics for the time being, and so it made no mention of Zouche or of the possible participation of Catholic gentry and, indeed, exaggerated the range of Waymouth's exploration and evaluation of the St. George River and its adjoining shores. At the same time, throughout the latter part of 1605 and the early months of 1606, Zouche and his friends continued to plan and organize. The two ships they arranged to get to sea in April were not ready, the permit they sought to carry out their venture was held up by the earl of Nottingham, the lord high admiral, and it was not until August that Zouche was given permission to send the ships and attempt to establish the long-deferred New England aristocratic settlement.[10] Ironically, once again lack of money and the diversion of merchant interests to the Jamestown ventures led to the plan's being dropped, and it was never revived in this form. His close connections with the Arundells and his later enlistment of members of the Gerard family in his American ven-

20

tures indicate clearly, if circumstantially, that George Calvert was aware of the plans both of 1582–83 and of 1605–6, and that they played a part, perhaps a significant one, in his eventual schemes for new colonies headed by aristocratic Catholics in Newfoundland and in the Chesapeake.

Meantime, of course, the Virginia Company had been formed, and Sir John Popham had identified himself with the formation of its Plymouth division, which would develop the Norumbega fishery and also settle a company colony to defend the area against the French and act as a base for fur-trading and exploration of the interior. The Sagadahoc colony failed in 1607–8 because it did not succeed in establishing either an economic or a territorial base, the land of Maine being totally unsuited to rapid agricultural development. Monhegan alone remained as a fishing base and the progenitor of later mainland fishing stations.

The Arundell-Waymouth venture, especially by bringing back some Eastern Abenaki Indians who could extol the merits of Mawooshen (their name for the Maine coast from Casco Bay to the Penobscot), set one imagination on fire, that of Sir Ferdinando Gorges. From the time of the failure of the Sagadahoc colony until his death at a great age in 1647, he kept in mind the prospect of himself as a new Gilbert or Arundell, but with a following of Protestant gentlemen and in association with West of England fishing interests.[11] It was he, more than any other individual, who kept alive the concept of the backward-looking feudal colony over the period when George Calvert slowly became involved in a variety of colonial projects and finally in a revival of the Catholic venture. Like the Catholics, however, he was hampered by lack of funds. He could only plan and experiment and hope that some day he would emerge as the prince of his dreams, lord paramount of Maine.

In 1620–21, King James gave way to Gorges's pleading and that of other gentlemen and courtiers whom he had influenced and created the Council for New England, whose members were free to grant colonizing rights to groups of settlers of any persuasion and eventually to divide the whole area into

21

sections in which they might, under the guidance of a governor general, develop aristocratic properties for themselves. As is well known, while some of the council's subsidiary grants to associations of settlers were productive, none of its members seriously aspired to create proprietorial colonies except Gorges himself. His repeated attempts to establish settlers in southern Maine were not wholly unsuccessful, but the tiny pockets of fishermen-farmers made a pitiable caricature of the plans he continued to project. After he received full royal authority over his Province of Maine in 1639, he was planning a full-scale European city, Gorgeana, at the Accomenticus settlement which, as the letters written between 1640 and 1643 by his deputy governor, Thomas Gorges, show, was wholly unrealistic.[12] But Gorges and his Maine dominion were the standard-bearers of the proprietary system through the period when very different communities were being established successfully in southern New England.

By 1617 Sir George Calvert had climbed far enough in King James's service to have begun to accumulate capital to add to his landed income (he was soon to slip into the most lucrative post of all, that of secretary of state), and having married Anne Arundell, daughter of Lord Arundell of Wardour, he began to look across the Atlantic for a foothold where he might develop his father-in-law's short-lived passion for an American lordship. The Newfoundland Company had, in 1611, established a small successful fishing, fur-trading, and farming community of English people at Cupid's Cove on Conception Bay, but lack of capital, the narrow limitations of agricultural development possible for the settlers, the small scale of the fur trade and, especially, the growing objections of the summer cod fishermen to settler competition prevented its development into a multisettlement venture. From 1617 on, the company sold off its rights to much of the southern part of its territory to English and Welsh landowning speculators, from one of whom Calvert obtained land and began a settlement at Ferryland in 1621. This inspired him, in 1623, to obtain a direct royal patent for his lands (and indeed those of the adjacent proprietors, although he did not propose to displace them) under the name of the Province of Avalon. He was to be lord proprietor there on terms no less extensive in theory than Gilbert had sketched for himself in 1582–83.

Sir George had evidently put to good use his years in the service of the crown to establish what were the limits of royal concessions to medieval vassals. The Avalon patent was a masterpiece of legal research. The bishops of Durham, before Henry VIII trimmed their powers, had enjoyed palatine liberties wider than those of any other feudal noble, so the Calvert patent stated that the grantee should have powers as wide as ever the bishop of Durham had had. It went even further, since he was allowed to create titles of nobility, provided they did not duplicate those already current in England. Subinfeudation, the right to create dependent feudal dignatories and establish manors and lordships, had been denied to subjects of the crown by Edward I in the Statute of *Quia emptores.* The "bishop of Durham" clause, as it is known since it was used in later grants (including that for Maryland), gave the grantee exemption from the statute. In his territory he could also prosecute war; institute martial law in the face of rebellion, tumult, or sedition; proclaim ordinances; pass laws under certain limitations, establish courts; issue pardons; and appoint officials necessary to maintain peace and administer justice. He could regulate trade, impose taxes and customs duties, and incorporate cities.[13] Such power represented a formal delegation of sovereignty unparalleled for centuries, but perhaps necessary for the government of a dependency at such a distance from England.

Sir George was clearly well satisfied with the reports he had had from Newfoundland and expected much benefit from Ferryland and its now greatly enlarged surrounding territories. We cannot yet say that he envisaged the establishment of a Catholic community there, though in theory at least it was to be an aristocratic one. He had been granted lands in Ireland, and it is probable that he intended to send some of the displaced Irish laborers and farmers, and Catholic aristocrats too perhaps, out to Newfoundland to work for and with him there.

The report of his agent in Newfoundland, George Winne, had already been published in London in 1621 to interest possible supporters.[14] In 1623 he engaged in a parallel recruiting campaign in Ireland, in association with the lord deputy, Lord Falkland, who was also anxious to acquire a foothold in Newfoundland, and the first piece of printed propaganda in Ireland for North American settlement was published under their auspices, though anonymously, in the same year.[15] The result was that several additional small settlements were established over the next few years. They survived, though they are unlikely to have produced much profit.

After he lost his secretaryship and had declared his open adhesion to the Roman Catholic church, relinquishing his place on the privy council of the new king, Charles I, Calvert was created baron of Baltimore in the County of Longford in the peerage of Ireland. But his eyes were fixed on Newfoundland, not on Ireland. Southeastern Newfoundland can be an attractive place from May to perhaps November, but his informants had evidently made light of the long cold winters which apparently had deterred all settlement before 1611. In 1627 he paid a summer visit to Ferryland, approved the small manor house which had been built for him there, and returned home to prepare for a permanent settlement. With additional settlers, his wife, his children, and their household goods, he settled in Ferryland. Forty of the settlers were Catholics, many or all of them Irish. But if the summer passed actively and profitably, the winter was very different. The house was exposed to wintery blasts; snow and ice set in to bar all activity by sea or land.

The household shivered its way through winter to summer again, but this time Lord Baltimore called a halt. Leaving his more seasoned men behind, he sent his children and some of his men home to England; with his wife and the remaining settlers, he then sailed southward to seek a warmer clime. New England was not barred to him outside the settlements already made, but he would not find congenial associates there, and he may have received a hint that he could find a warmer place and a better welcome in the royal colony of Virginia. Consequently his ship put into the attractive waters of Chesapeake Bay and sailed up to Jamestown, but he found neither welcome nor even acceptance. The stoutly Anglican colonists would not even allow him to land unless he took the oaths of allegiance and supremacy, the latter of which, as a Catholic, he could not do. He did get water and wood, and so he sailed home.[16] But he had at last found the scene and the climate which he desired. A utopia of a backward-looking sort could indeed, he thought, be fashioned in such a setting. He determined to attempt to create it.

The times had changed in England. The entrenched Catholic gentry of the north, especially those of Lancashire and Cheshire, together with their devoted and disciplined Catholic tenantry, were not now willing to move en masse to North America, as they may possibly have been in 1582, since their local arrangements with the Protestant magistracy were adequate for at least their short-term security. The gentry from other parts of England, whom Calvert might indeed enlist, would have to take with them largely Protestant tenants and indentured servants, which were all that were available. On the other hand, the Society of Jesus was now in a position to render material as well as spiritual support for a venture which promised the Jesuits a missionary outlet in eastern North America. Even if the wealth of the Calvert family had been diminished by the Newfoundland venture, Jesuit help, and such enthusiasm as he expected to engender among Catholics with the offer of territorial power and riches, seemed to make such a venture as Calvert intended to make politically, socially, and economically viable. Moreover, Charles I was now willing to demonstrate his ideological commitment to the revival and development of reactionary forms of government. His encouragement to Sir Ferdinando Gorges and Lord Baltimore alike, so much warmer than his father's, reflected his policy of restoring aristocratic influence under the crown in both England and Scotland. This policy was to serve him well by postponing his defeat in the First Civil War. It is clear that he wished to see authoritarian and aristocratic regimes in North America which would be, in some sort, a counterpoise to the heretical "democracy" which he could see arising in New England and to the upstart planter class which was attempting to impose limitations on his royal governor in Virginia. The regime envisaged for Lord Baltimore's patrimony represented, perhaps, his idealized picture of a restored monarchical authority in England.

Lord Baltimore died before the charter was sealed on 20 June 1632, and the grant was in fact made to his son Cecilius, but the Maryland charter, modeled on that of Avalon, realized the hopes expressed by Gilbert, Peckham, and Gerard in 1582–83.[17] The carving out of the territory of Maryland, north of the Potomac River and across the Eastern Shore, from land which had long been regarded as part of Virginia was to cause lasting controversies, but it created a viable territory, large enough, even if its undefined western border is ignored, to satisfy the desires of the most medieval-minded feudalist.

As "the true and absolute lords, and Proprietaries of the Countrey aforesaid," Baltimore and his heirs were to have the benefit of the bishop of Durham clause, with the easier tenure of "free and common soccage" and the annual quit rent of two Indian arrows, to hold by his allegiance only from the crown. A limitation which had appeared in the Avalon charter, though it had no practical effect there, was that his laws, not being repugnant to the laws of England, should be made "with the advise, assent and approbation of the Freemen of the said Province." Gilbert had long before planned to have a council to advise him in war and other matters, while he appears to have promised Peckham (in a document which has not survived) that the greater proprietors should have some legislative authority, because Peckham speaks in one place of not being bound except by "act of parliament" (that is, an act of a local assembly) in certain matters. Such an obligation to involve the settlers in the lawmaking process did not (as Maryland assemblies were to argue) infringe the power of the lord paramount to have the last word in all matters concerning the colony, though a general and ambiguous clause granted to the settlers "all liberties, franchises and privileges of this our kingdom of England," though only after virtually all powers in such matters had been granted first of all to Baltimore. The king could also intervene if the laws were "not consonant to reason" or were repugnant or contrary to those of England. A clause which is usually ignored by Maryland historians empowered Lord Baltimore to appoint to all offices in the church and to erect ecclesiastical buildings, but only "according to the Ecclesiasticall Lawes of our Kingdome of England." If he was to use this power he would have to establish the Anglican church in Maryland; if he did not, he was virtually obliged to decree the separation of church and state which was to be a distinguishing mark of the colony. Otherwise, Cecilius Calvert, second Lord Baltimore, obtained what his father had sought, a viable charter in which a proprietary colony could be erected in an area which offered a considerable hope of success, and one in which Catholics might at last attain a degree of freedom and autonomy in worship which they could not hope for in England.

Under Leonard Calvert, Lord Baltimore's younger brother, some 130 persons left England in November 1633 and arrived in the Potomac River in March 1634. From the island they named St. Clement's Island, they dropped down the river and entered St. George's, soon to be renamed St. Mary's, River, where an Indian village had been vacated by agreement for their arrival. There, on 27 March, they landed and formally founded the town of St. Mary's as their capital to be. Would the handful of Catholic gentlemen, the Calvert household, the Jesuits, the mainly Protestant indentured laborers, and a few smaller investors make good in the new colony? Time and careful management alone could tell. But from their first settlement, Maryland began.

NOTES

1. G. R. Elton's works, notably his textbook, *England under the Tudors*, 2d ed. (New York, 1969), most clearly emphasize these aspects of English development, though Penry Williams, *The Tudor Regime* (Oxford, 1979) should also be consulted.

2. See D. B. Quinn, *England and the Discovery of America* (New York, 1974), pp. 368–70.

3. See D. B. Quinn, "Sir Thomas Smith (1513–1577) and the Beginnings of English Colonial Theory," *Proceedings of the American Philosophical Society* 89 (1945) :543–60. On the general Irish context, see Nicholas Canny, *The Elizabethan Conquest of Ireland, a Pattern Established* (New York, 1977), and R. Dudley Edwards, *Ireland in the Age of the Tudors* (London, 1977).

4. On the Gilbert enterprise, see D. B. Quinn, *The Voyages and Colonising Enterprises of Sir Humphrey Gilbert*, 2 vols. (London, 1940); D. B. Quinn and Neil M. Cheshire, *The New Found Land of Stephen Parmenius* (Toronto, 1974); see also the documents in D. B. Quinn, ed., *New American World*, 5 vols. (New York, 1979), vol. 3 passim.

5. Two documents summarized in Quinn, *New American World*, 3:217–39, are now in the collections of the Public Archives of Canada (unclassified). See Peter Bower et al., *What Strange New Radiance. Sir Humphrey Gilbert and the New World*, Exhibition Catalogue, Public Archives of Canada (Ottawa, 1979).

6. See Quinn, *England and the Discovery of America*, chap. 14. Peckham lived until 1608 and may have known of the revived Catholic plans; Gerard had died in 1601.

7. Ibid., chaps. 11, 17.

8. Edmund S. Morgan, *American Freedom—American Slavery* (New York, 1975), pp. 71–91. But see the limiting conditions assessed in Carville V. Earle, "Environment, Disease, and Mortality in Early Virginia," in Thad W. Tate and David L. Ammerman, eds., *The Chesapeake in the Seventeenth Century* (Chapel Hill, N.C., 1979), pp. 96–125.

9. *A true relation of the most prosperous voyage made in this present yeare 1605 by Captain George Waymouth in the discovery of the land of Virginia* (London, 1605). This appeared either very late in the calendar year 1605 or early in 1606 (before 25 March). Rosier claimed to have the support of a wide range of courtiers, privy councillors, lords, gentry, and merchants—mostly withdrawn, we may assume, when the Virginia charter was granted on 10 April 1606. Documentation will be found in Quinn, *New American World*, 3:363–90.

10. Quinn, *England and the Discovery of America*, p. 391; documents in Quinn, *New American World*, 3:390–95.

11. R. A. Preston, *Gorges of Plymouth Fort* (Toronto, 1953), is the best general biography; J. Phinney Baxter, *Sir Ferdinando Gorges and His Province of Maine*, 3 vols. (Boston, 1890), contains the documents. The best discussion of proprietary colonies in general is that in C. M. Andrews, *The Colonial Period in American History*, 4 vols. (New Haven, Conn., 1934–39), vol. 2.
12. Robert E. Moody, ed., *The Letters of Thomas Gorges, Deputy Governor of the Province of Maine, 1640–1643* (Portland, Maine, 1978), for the first time penetrates the actual working of the lordship.
13. On the Newfoundland settlements, see Gillian T. Cell, *English Enterprise in Newfoundland, 1577–1660* (Toronto, 1969). The Avalon charter is printed from Sloane MS 170, British Library, in J. Thomas Scharf, *History of Maryland*, 3 vols. (Baltimore, 1879), 1:33–40.
14. Published as Edward Winne, *A lettetr [sic] to Sir George Calvert from Feryland in Newfoundland* (London, 1621).
15. T. C., *A short discourse of the Newfoundland* (Dublin, 1623).
16. On Calvert's Newfoundland experiences and his Virginia rebuff, see Cell, *English Enterprise*, pp. 92–95; Lawrence C. Wroth, *Tobacco or Codfish: Lord Baltimore Makes His Choice* (New York, 1954); John D. Krugler, "Sir George Calvert's Resignation as Secretary of State and the Founding of Maryland," *Maryland Historical Magazine* 68 (1973) :239–54; Thomas M. Coakley, "George Calvert and Newfoundland: 'The Sad Face of Winter'," ibid. 71 (1976) :1–18; R. J. Lahey, "The Role of Religion in Lord Baltimore's Colonial Enterprise," ibid., 72 (1977): 492–511.
17. The most accessible text is in Clayton C. Hall, ed., *Narratives of Early Maryland, 1633–1684* (New York, 1910; reprt. 1967), pp. 101–12; the most authoritative is in William Hand Browne et al., eds., *Archives of Maryland*, 83 vols. (Baltimore, 1883–), 3:14. On the bishop of Durham clause and its appearance in the "Carolana" grant to Heath in 1629, see William S. Powell, "Carolana and the Incomparable Roanoke," *North Carolina Historical Review* 51 (1974):4–5.

THE WIDER WORLD

SHIPS AND THE SEA:
VOYAGING TO THE CHESAPEAKE

Melvin H. Jackson

Since it is my intention to talk about the navigation techniques of the seventeenth century and to touch upon Chesapeake maritime affairs, I suggest that we examine these matters in the context of a hypothetical voyage made in a very real ship—the *Fox* of Enkhuizen in Holland, a vessel of 160 tons burden. The *Fox* was chartered by William Wright et al. on 4 September 1646 from one Reinhard Cornelius Fox, ship's husband and master and undoubtedly one of the vessel's owners.[1] Master Fox of the good ship *Fox* contracted to deliver his vessel to the charterers at Enkhuizen in seaworthy condition—"tight and well caulked . . . fitted with all necessaries to her needs," on 9 September, ready to sail in twenty-one days with no further delays.

Some terms of the charter party are of interest for what they reveal of navigation and business arrangements of the period. The charterers engaged to pay a minimum guarantee for a seven-month voyage of 700 guilders per month, together with the assumption of pilotage and average costs, if any. The freight, that is, the charter cost, was to be payable upon the vessel's return to the Texel, after which the freighters could proceed to the cargo's port of delivery. Demurrage beyond the seven months was to be payable at the same monthly rate. Some minor provisions called for the master to live and subsist in the cabin at the freighter's expense, although his wage was to be paid by the vessel's owners. The master was also to have the privilege of "primage"—that is, "to laye into the shipp so much goodes as may produce fowre hogsheads of tobacco without paying Fraight for"—and, finally, the freighters were to supply "one Jack & Flagg" and pay for such powder as they shall "unnecessarily shoote away."

It would appear from the foregoing that the *Fox* was indeed of Dutch registry and her crew half Dutch and half English.

How do we explain an English syndicate chartering a Dutch vessel to participate in the English tobacco trade? In spite of the then generally accepted dictum of international law that no direct trade was to be allowed between a colony and a foreign country, the Virginia colony, due to a chronic lack of English shipping, had long depended on the Dutch to carry her tobacco to market, generally a Dutch market. Nieuw Amsterdam and her enterprising merchants lay only a few days sail to the north of the Chesapeake colonies. Even the Navigation Acts of 1650 and 1651, still several years in the future at the time of our voyage, failed to end the flourishing carriage trade by the Dutch of the Virginia staple, a trade which prompted the English attack on, and seizure of, Nieuw Amsterdam in 1664. It will be recalled that England had just come through a very disturbed period of internal strife at the time the charter was made. Charles I, at the end of the First Civil War, was in the hands of the parliamentary army, and prospects were still not bright for the resolution of political differences. In 1646 business and trade had not yet recovered and the shipping market was still severely dislocated. Another factor that may well have prompted the charter of a Dutch vessel was the rather general recognition of the superiority of Dutch-built vessels for the bulk trade in terms of lower running expenses per deadweight ton.

The *Fox*, although rather large for the European trade at 260 tons, was about average for the tobacco trade at this time. A "large" vessel for the trade would have run about 400 tons. A "small" vessel would have measured between 50 and 100 tons. The latter were not extensively employed. During the second half of the seventeenth century, the average size of the tobacco carrier declined to between 150 and 100 tons. This decline was largely due to developments in the packaging of the product. During the earliest period, tobacco leaf was rolled up in a comparatively loose bundle for shipment. This meant that a high-cube vessel would be required to make up any reasonable lading. As tobacco began to be packed into casks, barrels, and hogsheads, ever-increasing pressure (prizing or steving) was resorted to. Thus more and more weight could be stowed in a given container. (The container itself was not standardized until the eighteenth century.) By the end of the seventeenth century, the weight of a hogshead of tobacco was quite close to the weight of the same cubic content of water. Smaller vessels of proper design could handle much the same quantity of cargo as the larger vessel carrying rolled tobacco.

With the *Fox* delivered to the charterers, the work of preparing for sea went forward: a crew was signed on, cargo, stores, and water were taken in, and the thousand-and-one details attending an adventure of this nature seen to. Doubtless the twenty-one days were filled up and the vessel was finally ready for sea in the last week of September.

We do not know what the *Fox*'s outward cargo consisted of, but field and household needs certainly ranked high: spade and hoe irons, iron pots, nails, firearms, with arms, powder, and trinkets for the Indian trade. Another important item of cargo which helped defray the expenses of the outward voyage was the indentured servant. We have no evidence that the *Fox* carried servants to Virginia, for no manifest has survived, but we will ship a consignment of thirty-five servants—a reasonable number to assume—for the account of the charterers. Whether they were taken aboard in Holland or the *Fox* called in at an English port before finally sailing for Virginia will have to be left undecided.

With the lading we suggest, it is difficult to conceive that a vessel of 260 tons could be brought down to her sailing lines. Ballast would certainly be called for. The ideal ballast

35

was one that could be turned to account at the end of the voyage—that is, one consisting of flint, broken brick, cut-stone, old cannon, or even gravestones, which had a very ready sale in the fever-ridden colonies. However, most often masters resorted to gravel and even sand. These could prove dangerous, since gravel and sand very often were rubbed smooth by the tumbling action of wave and water, and hence tended to be unstable in the bottom of a ship liable to rolling deeply or subject to knock down. Great care had to be taken to make certain the ballast would not shift. There is reason to believe that during the actual voyage there had been some problems arising from the stowage of the ship, in addition to concern with the physical condition of the vessel and her equipment. However, once committed to an adventure men easily overlooked conditions that would ordinarily give them pause.

In the seventeenth century a sailing date at the end of September from a northern European port for the North Atlantic crossing would be dictated only by particularly urgent considerations. Shipowners were already beginning to think of winter lay-up. North Atlantic weather was unpredictable during the equinoctial season; even the possibility of an extra tropical hurricane was still strong. (The old jingle warns, "September remember.") In October the westerlies were already becoming boisterous, and by November the ugly North Atlantic winter had set in. The "urgent considerations" to start a voyage in the face of such prospects lay in the nature of the tobacco crop.

In the Chesapeake region, harvesting, curing, and packing went on over a period of several months. The first tobacco, that is, loose tobacco, became available in August. The first packed hogsheads were to be had in limited quantities by October, with the bulk of the product being ready for lading between November and January. So, in order to be on hand when the tobacco flow was at its height and the chance for a full lading at its best, a November arrival in Chesapeake Bay was considered strategically correct. The vessel could plan to winter in the relatively mild climate of the Chesa-

36

peake, and adequate time would be had for the amenities of the business of lining up cargo. But let us return to the *Fox*. If she sailed as early as 15 September, she would have had only eleven days from the time of the charter to take care of the manifold preparations for a long voyage, and if she made an eight-week passage from the Texel to the Virginia Capes, she would arrive in mid-November, a faster than average crossing. Five months of her charter remained. Allowing six weeks for her return to the Texel, that leaves four months to offload her outward cargo, make voyage repairs, book and load her homeward cargo, provision for the voyage, and clear out of the bay. The *Fox* would then be putting to sea again by February or March, months of very heavy Atlantic weather, albeit of fair westerlies.

This itinerary assumes very close planning. Everything would have to go off like clockwork: no adverse weather could be encountered; no extensive voyage repairs could be required. Her tobacco cargo had to be practically completed and ready for loading. If the charterers could carry it off, they would get their cargo to market when warehouses would be depleted of last year's crop and prices at their optimum. As can readily be appreciated, a first-rate vessel and highly favorable weather were the keys to such a success. As will be seen, neither was the *Fox* capable of filling the bill nor was the weather what was needed.

So, at some time between the middle and end of September, the *Fox* unmoored, put to sea, and dropped her pilot off the outer buoy of the Texel. Once free of the land, the *Fox*'s pilot normally would have shaped a course to the south, down the North Sea and into the English Channel. The chances are that she had a fair wind at that time of the year. Then as now, the channel could be a very nasty body of water, with fickle winds, strong tidal currents, dense fog, and sudden storms that piled up a short, vicious sea that brought despair to the masters of the contemporary bluff-bowed sailing vessels of poor windward working qualities. Such weather left no alternative to seeking a harbor or roadstead to wait out the adverse winds. This delay might last for weeks;

37

as long as a month was not unusual. In the meanwhile the crew, afterguard, and passengers would be eating their way through provisions at a great rate. With his eye on the balance sheet, only the rare master would take on additional provisions.

The navigator of 1646 was well prepared for emergencies. His trusty "Waggoner"—very possibly the 1626 Dutch edition of "The Mariner's Mirror"—would certainly be at hand.[2] This was a remarkably complete and sophisticated collection of fine charts, covering the English and continental coasts of the Narrow Seas and beyond, containing sailing directions, soundings, buoyage, lighthouses, sketches of coastal aspects with bearings, leading marks and ranges, and recommended anchorages, as well as tidal data, such as the establishments of the various ports. It would serve well for European voyages, but closing the American coast would be a far different affair, for no such navigational aid for American waters would be available for another century.

Once out of the English Channel, the ship's company still had to face the dreaded Bay of Biscay and its notorious storms, but once south of Cape Finisterre favorable winds and a mild climate could be expected, which along with the south-setting African current would help push the *Fox* southward. This was a well-traveled sea route, followed by the Portuguese more than two centuries before, and by the Greeks, Romans, and Arabs before them. At this point we might consider why the *Fox*'s master held on so long to the south. Why did he not turn west once clear of the channel? One important reason already adduced was the wintertime conditions on the North Atlantic and the prevalence of heavy westerly weather. Why fight these, when to the southward lay the region of the northeast trade winds? Somewhat roundabout, but so much easier on ship and man. The square-rigger was at its best sailing with the wind free rather than braced up sharply, butting her full bows into the heavy seas of the wintry western ocean. But there were also navigational considerations to urge the use of the more southerly passages.

The seventeenth-century navigator, by virtue of his instrumentation, was given to parallel or latitude sailing. It was his custom to take his departure from a latitude as close as possible to that of his desired landfall. On the ocean crossing he would do his best to cling to that latitude. If borne north or south of his rhumb line, or base course, he would alter course as soon as possible to intercept it and again proceed along his chosen parallel. To accomplish this he had available to him tables which dictated his best intercepting course; these were the traverse tables. It must be kept in mind that our navigator could only determine latitude by his observation of celestial bodies. Ascertaining longitude at sea was still a century in the future.

For a winter passage of the Atlantic Ocean bound for the Virginia Capes, two geographical points recommended themselves as departures: Funchal in the Madeiras and Las Palmas in the Canaries. Both would place the *Fox* well south of Cape Hatteras on the American coast, although the Funchal departure would place the vessel uncomfortably close to the lonely Somers Islands (Bermuda). In addition, experience dictated that, because of the seasonal southward dip of the northern limits of the trade winds belt, the Las Palmas departure might be the wiser of the two. A due-west course from that island would intersect the North American coast in the vicinity of St. Augustine, well above the Bahama Bank and below the Bermudas. There the Gulf Stream would provide a longitude seamark and give the vessel a strong push on her last northerly leg to the Virginia Capes.

So the *Fox* worked her way south as the weather became balmy. Within six to ten days from dropping Cape Finisterre, Las Palmas rose over the horizon. With the island abeam, the master would order the *Fox* on a due westerly course and take his departure from the Old World. With good luck he would soon pick up the northeast trade winds that carry moderate to fresh breezes, varying from the starboard beam to the quarter for almost the entire westward passage. The uneasiness of the landsmen with this strange new mode of life gave way to expanded spirits. The *Fox* swung along with bone in her teeth. Warm sparkling days of blue seas and rosy banks of trade winds clouds alternated with nights made brilliant by starry skies and the bubbling phosphorescent wake. Nautical routine was reduced to little more than slight alterations to brace and sheet, while standing and running rigging was overhauled in preparation for what lay ahead. Passengers dragged their damp clothing and bedding (if they had such) on deck, where they were festooned from the rigging, and through open hatches the fresh warm breeze scoured out the stinking 'tween decks and hold.

What of the navigation that brought the *Fox* and her consorts to this point of their voyage?

The compass, of course, was the most indispensable and ancient of the navigator's instruments. It had already evolved structurally in all its essential points into the ship's compass we know today, except that it lacked the liquid dampening system, which was not introduced until the latter part of the nineteenth century, and the degree markings, which were to appear in the eighteenth century. The compass was divided into thirty-two compass points (of 11° 15′ each); hence seamen traditionally thought in terms of points rather than degrees. Thus, a course might be ordered as "west by north half north." The same would hold true for bearings. The north-seeking component of the compass, the magnetic needles, were bunched in a vesicate shape, upon which was fixed the fly, and the assembly was mounted atop a brass pivot in the compass bowl. In a lively ship the compass card was apt to gyrate quite wildly and often flew off its pivot unless the compass bowl was ballasted and set in a pair of gimbal rings. By the mid-seventeenth century, however, compasses were so fitted. The compass was mounted in a small houselike structure convenient to the helmsman called the "bittacle" ("binnacle" is a later corruption), which was lighted at night by a candle.

It might be noted that at this period the helmsman did not necessarily steer by the compass. In many cases the officer of the watch kept his eye on the compass and directed the helmsman, who steered by a star or by the raise of the luff of the sail. On a vessel the size of the *Fox,* the steering station was probably under the roundhouse deck, and she would have been steered either by a tiller fitted with relieving tackles or by a vertical whipstaff, the operation of which brings to mind the control stick of a light sport plane. The whipstaff was economical of space, since it eliminated the wide sweep needed by the tiller, which was moved down into the lazaret or steerage.

By the mid-seventeenth century, navigators were aware of most of the vagaries of the compass. Ironwork in the hull of wooden vessels was negligible, and deviation caused by that element could be practically ignored. It is not known with any precision how long ago seamen were aware of the phenomenon of variation—that is, the deflection of the compass needle east and west because of the vertical deflection of the magnetic pole. Columbus seems to have been the first to have reported on the phenomenon, although it is probable that late medieval Mediterranean cartographers were aware of the effects of variation. The progressive deflection of the compass needle variation became quite apparent during the long Atlantic crossing, and on such a voyage it was essential to correct a ship's heading to maintain a true westerly (in distinction to the magnetic) course. Our navigator could determine the change in variation by observing the bearing or amplitude of the sun at rising and setting, or by comparing equally spaced azimuths of the sun with an instrument not too different from those developed in the eighteenth century for this purpose. Such a bearing, when compared with those tabulated in one of the navigation manuals of the era for the date of the month of observation and corrected for latitude, would show the divergence of the ship's compass from true east or west. The course correction could be applied accordingly.

The keeping of correct time was a constant concern on an east-west crossing. Pendulum clocks, needless to say, were quite useless at sea in a rolling, pitching vessel. The "running glass" provided the only feasible means, but even the finest Venetian glass filled with carefully graded marble dust was subject to unpredictable errors. An advertisement in a

London newspaper of 1682 gives an insight into the variety of glasses obtainable. John Seller offered "All sorts of running glasses: one two three and four hour glasses. One minute, half minute and quarter minute glasses." The glass that measured the length of time of a watch was calibrated to a half hour and was termed the "watch glass." In practice the glass was turned each half-hour and the ship's bell was tolled to keep account, once for the first half-hour of the watch and twice for the second and fourth, while eight bells would summon the new watch on deck.

With each degree of westing run, the time at the ship retarded fifteen minutes. Hence it was necessary to adjust the time at the ship daily. To find his latitude each day the navigator observed the sun when it bore north-south—that is, just at the instant when the sun on the ship's meridian seemed to hang motionless, neither rising nor falling, before it started its descent. At that instant the navigator would proclaim it noon, whereupon a fresh glass was turned, marking the beginning of a new day. Thus the sea day began at noon rather than at midnight, as was the case ashore. This custom was observed well into the nineteenth century. What if there were no sun visible? Four or five days of overcast weather could bring considerable embarrassment.

Time, of course, could be ascertained at twilight, dawn, or dusk with a clear sky with the nocturnal. This was an instrument of ancient lineage, probably predating the compass. It was usually made of fruitwood. It consisted of an outer circle indicating the month and day of the year; superimposed was a volvelle and a vane with a peephole in the center. The observer sighted on Polaris through the peephole, aligned the vane with the position of the two stars known as "the Guards," and read off the hour against the marking of month and date. By the mid-seventeenth century the nocturnal was equally important for helping the navigator calculate a reliable latitude.

This leads us to the consideration of the state of the art of celestial navigation by the epoch of the *Fox*'s passage, independent of accurate timekeeping. Latitude could be calculated with reasonable accuracy by a variety of instruments. Two of these were the quadrant and the astrolabe. Although John Smith in his *Sea Grammar* of 1626 called for their inclusion in the navigator's kit,[3] they were already considered obsolete by the succeeding generation of pilots. While both of these instruments seem to be delightfully simple to use, in practice employing them must have been a most trying exercise on a lively ship. For the most part their utility was confined to shore observation or to a vessel in a quiet anchorage.

By the beginning of the century Davis's quadrant, or back-staff, had vastly improved the accuracy of celestial observation. Even the older cross-staff (Jacob's staff or forestaff) in the hands of an able observer was superior to the astrolabe and quadrant and had the advantage of being the least expensive. The cross-staff, possibly derived from the Arabian *kamal*, consisted of a staff of hardwood, square in section of one-half to three-quarters of an inch, and between thirty and thirty-six inches long, graduated on each side to correspond to one of four cross-pieces or transoms of different lengths. Each transom was of a length to subtend a given angle when mounted at the extremity of the staff when held by the observer in position for observing. By moving the transom along the staff, the observer sought to subtend the angle between the center of the celestial body and the horizon. At that point the observer would add the angular value of the transom to that read off the appropriate scale of the staff. Thus, the greater the body's altitude, the longer the staff chosen. A rough approximation of the altitude can be obtained by extending a closed fist (about eight degrees) or an open hand (about twelve degrees) between the horizon and the body. One can imagine the blinding effect that this system had on the eye of the navigator until some anonymous seafarer thought of fixing a smoked-glass screen on his staff.

Although efforts were made to adapt the forestaff to a shadow and target arrangement which would enable the navigator to take an altitude with his back to the sun while sighting on a clear horizon, it remained for the celebrated English navigator John Davis to accomplish this in his rationalized

43

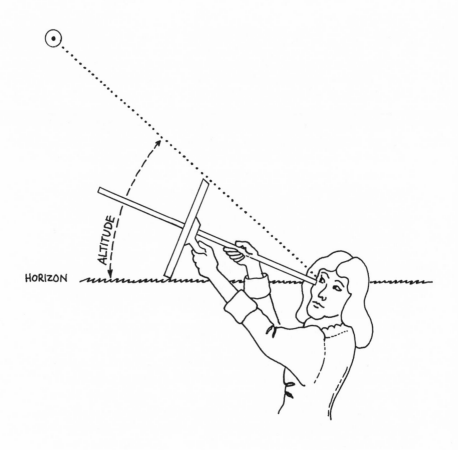

The Use of the Forestaff. Adapted from John Seller, *Practical navigation* (London, 1680).

version of the cross-staff bearing his name. On a central staff there were two quadrants, one at each end; one was on one side of the staff and the other on the opposite side. Each had its own moveable index arm. The smaller of the two filled the function of the multiple transoms of the cross-staff. The observer set the approximate altitude of the sun on the small quadrant by clamping the index to the approximate angle of the body. On this issue was fitted a pinhole aperture. The observer then turned his back to the sun. After locating the pinpoint of light on the horizon slit of the large index arm, he maneuvered the instrument up or down while adjusting the index arm until the horizon came into view through the slit, with the pinpoint of light centered in the horizon slit. The reading of the altitude of the body was the sum of the readings of the two quadrants. It is easy to appreciate the vast improvement of the back-staff over its predecessors. Indeed, it so suited the navigator by its simplicity that it was a consistent best-seller even after Hadley's optical quadrant had long proven its worth. It remained so until the end of the eighteenth century.

These then, were the principal instruments available to the navigator of the *Fox*. Once the technique of using them was mastered, how did her master go about finding his latitude? To accomplish this it was necessary to fulfill two simple requirements: first, that the sun be observed exactly at the ship's noon; and second, that he know the sun's declination for the time of the observation. We have already seen how precise noon was ascertained. As for solar declination tables, they were to be had since at least 1415. These were to be found in almost all the sailor's manuals, listed for every day of the year at noon and referred to some particular datum place. By interpolation and the application of a rough correction for longitude, a navigator could determine the declination at the place of the ship. By using the altitude and the declination in a simple formula, he could find the ship's latitude. Such refinements as parallax, refraction, the sun's semidiameter, and the height of eye above the sea were ignored.

An altitude of Polaris, corrected for the actual displacement from the pole (which was ascertainable by the use of some nocturnals or in published tables of correction), also provided the navigator with a reliable latitude at dawn and dusk in northern latitudes and for a few degrees south of the equator, given a sharply defined horizon. However, while tables existed giving the celestial position of fixed stars, it is doubtful to what extent they were used at sea. A combination of a star's transit of the ship's meridian with a sharp horizon would have been too fortuitous to make such an observation anything more than a rarity.

What with the limitations of the instruments, whether cross-staff or back-staff, an accuracy of thirty miles might be taken as average. Fifteen miles would have been considered excellent. With a modern optical sextant in the hands of an experienced observer, two miles could be considered average accuracy. Thus it can be appreciated that, on the largely north-south run from Cape Finisterre to Las Palmas, a reasonably accurate account of the ship's position could be kept by a combination of dead reckoning and observations for latitude—always providing that bright weather prevailed. Keeping account of 8° 30′ difference of longitude in the Cape Finisterre-Las Palmas leg was no great trial. At the very worst, if the longitude account proved to be a hopeless muddle the vessel could be put on an easterly course until the African coast was raised. Once the coast was identified, a new course could be set for Las Palmas.

It was the long stretch of the Atlantic Ocean, however, that presented the greatest challenge to the determination of one's longitude. The theory of determining longitude was quite well understood in the middle of the seventeenth century. Timing eclipses, observing the transit of Jupiter's moons and lunar intervals or culminations, and noting moon and planet conjunctions would yield longitude, but these systems required firmly fixed shore-based observatory equipment. They were not feasible for use at sea. The seventeenth-century attempt to utilize the phenomenon of magnetic variation to yield terrestrial longitude to the navigator—a harbinger of modern electronic navigation—was doomed to failure due to the unrealized fact that the isogons did not follow the meridians, but wandered about in an unpredictable manner.

Hadley's optical quadrant (1731) brought with it a degree of precise observation that made the system of lunar intervals, or distances, available to mariners, but the complexity of the calculations and the difficulties of lunar observation meant that it offered no real competition for determining longitude by time comparison. This system, suggested as early as 1522 by Gemma Frisius, was brought to practicality through the genius of a Yorkshire carpenter, John Harrison, who in 1735 brought the marine chronometer to a remarkable state of perfection.

So, lacking any astronomical means of determining a ship's longitude, there remained the process known as "dead reckoning." This consisted of the painstaking recording of the ship's course, corrected for the effect of magnetic variation, leeway, current, the scend of the sea and steering errors, and including an as accurate as possible estimate of the vessel's speed. With these elements in hand, by consulting the traverse tables the navigator could determine the difference of longitude, east or west, made good, and the difference in latitude made good, north or south.

The set and drift of ocean currents, beyond the most obvious ones, were largely unknown, and course corrections could only be guessed at. It is easy to appreciate that dead reckoning was the high art of piloting, combining keen observation, intuition, and a large dash of luck.

Masters and watch officers were particularly demanding of good helmsmanship. A trick at the helm might consist of one or two hours, depending on the size of vessel and crew. When not requiring constant physical effort to keep a vessel on course in heavy weather, steering tended to be a very monotonous affair. Very often the helmsman, hypnotized by the flickering of the dim binnacle light, dozed off; when awakening with a start, he chose the wrong compass point to steer by. Hence the watch officer kept a constant watch on the helmsman and an eye on the compass.

Keeping a careful account of the ship's speed and distance run was a very important element of dead reckoning. By the mid-seventeenth century, the chip log had replaced various primitive methods (such as the so-called Dutchman's log) of timing the vessel's way through the water. The log chip in its full development was a quadrant of wood six to eight inches in radius, ballasted along the arc so as to float low and vertically in the water. A three-part bridle was attached to the chip, one leg of which was secured to the apex by a removable peg, while the two lower legs were made fast to the chip at the extremities of the arc. Attached to the bridle was a length of some five hundred feet of hard-laid small line. Ten fathoms from the bridle, the stray, as it was called, was marked by a red rag. This marked the beginning of the log line proper, which was marked at every forty-three feet by a knot. Twelve of these knots were generally used. The whole was wound on a wood reel which revolved freely on a shaft terminating in two handles.

The important rite of heaving the log usually took place twice a watch at the taffrail. Under circumstances when distance run was of particular importance, it might take place hourly. The watch officer and two men were involved. One man held the reel aloft by its handles; another held a thirty-second glass. The watch officer secured the loose leg of the bridle in its hole and hove the chip overboard into the ship's wake. Acting as a drogue, it hauled the log line off the reel. As the red rag ran out over the taffrail, the glass was turned and the knots counted as they went out over the counter. When the last of the sand ran out the glassman called "mark," the log line was checked, and the number of knots and quarter intervals representing the ship's speed was recorded. At the checking of the log line the peg had pulled out of the chip. With the resistance reduced, the line could be overhauled, reeled up, and made ready for the next heaving.

The chip log gave a pretty fair indication of the ship's speed through the water. To reduce this to way over the bottom the navigator had to correct the reading by averaging out any variations in the speed of the previous hours of the watch, the effect of ocean currents, if known, as well as take into consideration sea conditions which might cause the log to over- or underrun. The log streaming astern also gave an opportunity for the watch officer to make a very fair estimate of the vessel's leeway. It might also be observed that the log gave the speed of the vessel through the water and not over the ground.

The ship's logbook of the era of our voyage, in which the vital information of course, speed, distance made good, course corrections for variation and leeway, and wind direction and force was entered, had achieved a rough standardization modified only by the master's individual preferences. These data were kept in columns on the left page of the logbook. On the right fold, usually divided into watches, was noted details of the voyage, such as sails carried and their changes, the state of the sea, ships sighted and spoken, meteorological and hydrographic information, crew employment about the vessel, provisions consumed, state of the sailors' health, injuries, punishment, deaths, and such vital data. Unlike today's navigating practice, the ship's track was not laid down on plotting sheets but was kept in tabular form. At the end of the sea day (noon) the navigator worked up his course and distance (in sea leagues), made good for the past day in terms of latitude and longitude. This would reflect the results of successful celestial observation that might have been made. He would convert this into a bearing and distance from the point of departure and then calculate a course and distance to landfall. This information would be recorded centrally across the left-hand page. The faithful recording of the essential elements of dead reckoning would not only afford the navigator the data to work out an estimated position after days or even weeks of adverse weather when celestial observations were impossible, but it also constituted the official record of the voyage in courts of maritime law.

So went the nautical routine aboard the *Fox* from day to day as she swung westward in the Trades. Her consorts spread over the circle of the horizon, now near, now far, but giving a sense of human company in the monotony of the immense sea. Day after day the *Fox* romped along, logging between five and six knots. Each noon, after working up his day's dead reckoning and applying his latitude by observation, Master Fox unrolled his sea chart on the cabin table—in this case William Blaeu's fine *West Indische Paeskaart,* published more than a dozen years before, in 1631—and with a leg of his dividers gently pricked the ship's position on it as the afterguard looked on.

Then, one day three weeks after Las Palmas was dropped astern, the *Fox* ran into the indigo waters of the Gulf Stream and the master began to shape his course to the north. Day after day the temperature fell. The glorious days of the Trades lay behind. The ship's motion became less easy and the sea less blue, more slaty, the spray that came over the bows more chilling. The almost indolent workday of the subtropics was replaced by more purposeful routine as the crew set up on the standing rigging and overhauled running gear. Lifelines were rigged fore and aft. Hatches once open to the soft balmy wind were boarded over; triple tarpaulins were spread, battened, and wedged down. The galley on deck during the fine weather was struck below.

The sea continued to mount, short, steep, and vicious, and the sky was covered by dark, fast-moving, ragged clouds. The *Fox,* close-hauled on a northeast wind of gale force, staggered along under close-reefed topsails, battered by squalls of rain and sleet that howled in the rigging. The ship pitched and rolled violently. Water poured into the hull from every seam, decks, sides, and underwater, threatening to ruin the vessel's cargo. The *Fox*'s pumps, once manned for a short while each watch, worked ceaselessly, requiring all hands and even some passengers to man the brakes. Below deck, where the passengers normally were sealed up under hatches, the awesome noise of the gale aloft assumed a new dimension. There the noise of the working of the ship, the grating timbers being wrenched by ponderous forces, was amplified. In the pitch dark—lights were forbidden—sick and exhausted passengers risked being dashed to leeward by the sudden and erratic motion of the vessel were they not lashed to stanchions and ringbolts. Boarding seas thundered on deck and poured intermittent torrents of icy water through every seam, seeking out and soaking the miserable human cargo. Bilge water crashed with every roll of the ship. The air, dank and fetid with the odor of vomit and excrement, was unspeakable. To those who suffered the nightmare, time stood still.

For three days and three nights the *Fox*, her consorts mostly scattered, fought gale after gale as the fabric of the ship deteriorated. So alarming had her condition become that one of the charterers, Owen Powell, had the ship's carpenter make a thorough investigation to determine her condition and suggest what might be done to stiffen her. The carpenter's report was ominous. In her bows the main knee, that great hooked timber that served to stiffen the stem, had given way. Water poured in from the wracked stern. In the hold the 'tween deck knees had sheared their bolts and trunnels. Beams that proved to be permeated with rot were crushed, allowing the vessel to work alarmingly. To make matters worse, the main mast cracked and was working to such an extent that it was feared that the mast would go by the board, undoubtedly carrying with it the fore and mizen masts. The only solution was to attempt to stiffen the mast by fishing it, that is, by splinting the mast with spare spars and passing lashings about the whole, much as one would splint a broken leg. Very discouraging was the fact that there was to be found "not one spare boult, nor Rope, nor block in the ship."

It was the carpenter's opinion that nothing could be done for the ship, whereupon the master ordered two lights hoisted as a signal of distress. This action brought up one of the consorts, under the command of Peter Smith, who agreed to stand by the stricken ship for the night. The next morning the *Fox* managed to hoist out a boat that took the master and two of the charterers to seek aid and supplies. Few supplies and less aid were received. For his own reasons, Powell stayed aboard Smith's vessel for two days and two nights where, as he deposed, he brooded about the fate of his adventure. Perhaps it was a break in the weather that prompted him to return to his vessel.

Once aboard, he found the *Fox* in even worse condition than when he left her. The vessel's sides and decks were parting company. The crew had apparently performed prodigies during his absence. In order to ease the ship, her guns had been struck down into the hold; these were followed by the heavy bower anchors and their cables, as well as the rest of the complement of anchors. It had been a most difficult piece of seamanship in a vessel that wallowed about in what was to prove to be a temporary lull in the storm. The *Fox*'s violent motion worked the fishing on the main mast loose and the work had to be repeated. In trying to set up the shrouds the deck beams were wrenched up, requiring shoring below decks. The situation was clearly hopeless. The vessel was making water heavily, well beyond the capacity of the pumps to keep her afloat.

At this juncture the ship's company believed that the ship should be abandoned. We can imagine the incredulity of the hands when they learned that Peter Smith, who was still standing by, would not or could not take them aboard. Nothing was left to do "but to commit themselves to the Mercy of God" and to undertake the last heroic measure of wolding the ship. This maneuver consisted of passing three hawsers under the keel in the way of the three masts, passing them through the gun ports, marrying the two ends of each, and heaving them taut with Spanish windlasses. Very probably the underbody was first fothered with spare sails passed under the hull to help stem the inflowing water. This was a work of complexity and exacting seamanship that required great physical exertion from cold and hungry men exhausted by days of fighting the sea under extremely trying conditions.

It is a wonder how the *Fox* survived this ordeal, but survive she did. The stormy siege was left behind, and with the return of fair weather and a moderate sea, thought was given to putting the ship in condition to pursue her way toward Virginia. Even if the navigator had been confident of his reckoning upon entering the Gulf Stream, the gales and the nightmare of saving the vessel had made the careful maintenance of the ship's log a secondary concern. Now the most experienced pilot would have been confused as to the ship's position. The vessel had been hove to, scudded before the storm under bare poles, or helplessly wallowed broadside in the trough of the sea. What progress she made and in what direction was a matter to be given careful consideration now that the ship was riding easier.

Starting with the last position in which he had confidence, the navigator carefully assessed the set and drift of the vessel during the storm, made an allowance for the Gulf Stream current, worked up a traverse, and came up with an estimated position from which he could project a new rhumb line to the Capes of the Chesapeake. The reemergence of the sun gave him the opportunity to establish his latitude, but how far off the American coast he lay was problematic. By extending his observed latitude to the coast, he could at least assure himself of his position with respect to Cape Hatteras as well as Bermuda, his two chief dangers. Once north of the former, he would have to rely on his dead reckoning as to whether or not the Bermudas lay to the east. Once reassured of this, he shaped course for his landfall.

Throughout that wreck of a ship a new feeling of anxiety took charge. A new and grotesque danger lay ahead. What if, after their miraculous escape from the horrors of foundering in the storm, one dark night their ship would stumble ashore on the terrible Hatteras coast and destroy herself and all her exhausted people?

Luckily the weather was fine and a light southerly breeze eased the vessel along. The galley, back in operation, offered what comfort it could, and the men at the pumps had a brief respite during the watches. At sundown the navigator took a bearing of the sun to check the accuracy of his compass and the ship's deep-sea lead was got out, overhauled, and made up in three separate coils. The line with the lead was secure in the lee forechains and the others in the main and mizen. During the night lookouts ceaselessly searched the horizon from beam to beam, and in the silence every ear was tuned for the low rumble of surf on a beach or reef.

At dawn the sea was empty. The master called for his leadsmen to take their stations. The foresail was backed and the way taken off the ship. The man in the fore chains, holding the coil in one hand, with the other paid out line until the lead was just clear of the sea. He then began to swing slowly the heavy lead, which might weigh as much as fifty pounds. Gaining the momentum he sought, he let go and the lead snaked through the air and into the sea. The leadsman watched the markings as they sped through his hand, crying out to the man in the main chains, seeing no check to the speeding line, in turn warned the man in the mizen chains. Down the lead continued to plummet, finally fetching up at the bitter end, which had been seized to one of the shrouds. "No bottom at 120 fathoms," sang out the leadsman, and the laborious task of hauling the heavy lead and its more than seven hundred feet of line was begun. With the foreyards braced up, the sails filled and the ship forged ahead.

Each watch the deep-sea lead was hove. At sunset the compass was again checked by an amplitude of the setting sun and an altitude of Polaris was successfully observed. The next morning the lead struck at eighty-five fathoms. It was a momentous event to the seaweary ship's company. When the lead was hoisted aboard and taken aft to the master, it was found to have a dark sticky mud adhering to the tallowed arming stuffed into its hollowed-out bottom. To the master this meant that they were somewhere in the outpourings of the great bay of the Chesapeake. This, combined with the sounding, led him to estimate a distance of eighty to ninety miles offshore.

Watch after watch the lead was hove. In the afternoon watch the lead read fifty fathoms, and thereafter the decrease was slow and uniform. The deep-sea lead was replaced by the lighter coasting lead. The uniform shoaling of the Virginia coast gave comfort and aid to the navigator approaching the entrance to the bay. Beyond the ten-fathom line, the depth of the water could roughly be equated with the distance off the coast. All sail was reduced for the night; a minimum of steerage way was kept on the ship. At dawn the *Fox* suddenly entered a low-hanging fog bank. Each masthead was manned by the sharpest-eyed seaman aboard. The wind dropped light and the leadsmen were placed in the main chains, larboard and starboard. They alternated in casting the lead and droning out the depths read from the line.

The ship's company spoke in hushed tones. The clatter of the pumps, the creaking of spars and blocks, the gurgling of the water running past the cutwater—all were magnified and echoed around the ship. Then, almost simultaneously with the leadsman's call of "By the deep, four fathoms," came a faint hail from the mainmast head. "Land ho! About a point off the larboard bow, bright and clear." A shout of jubilation rose from the deck.

By the end of the morning watch the fog had dissipated as suddenly as it was entered. There in the winter sun shone the land of Virginia, ninety-seven days out of the Texel.

AFTERWORD

The details of the storm damage suffered by the *Fox* narrated in the preceding paragraphs, as well as the terms of the charter and the events that took place aboard the ship are taken, with minor elaborations, from the fascinating documents cited in n. 1 below.

I have taken one major liberty in narrating the *Fox* voyage: I have transposed the dates when the storm occurred, moving it from the beginning of the voyage to the end. I did this not so much for dramatic effect as for sheer credibility, for when the depositions are analyzed, a disturbing element emerges. Owen Powell's deposition clearly states that the *Fox* ran into the storm that caused so much havoc to the vessel two hundred leagues from the Texel. While Powell does not date the storm, the crew's deposition does: "at Sea the seaven & twentieth of November 1646," presumably soon after the storm. Since we predicate that the *Fox* departed the Texel about 29 September, the storm occurred about thirty-three to thirty-eight days after her departure. It is certainly possible that detentions in the English Channel, a call at an English port, awaiting a convoy, or a combination of such events, in addition to actual sea time, could account for such a seemingly inordinate length of time to achieve the "about two hundred leagues out from the Tassell." This would place the *Fox* in the region of the Bay of Biscay, a most likely place to encounter a storm of such intensity that it could batter to pieces an already ill-found ship as is so vividly described in the depositions.

But how does one explain a vessel in such extremely decrepit and dangerous condition pursuing a voyage of some three thousand miles, a portion of which traversed the North Atlantic in wintertime? How much more reasonable and sea-manlike to make for the nearest continental or English port for such desperately needed repairs, or where the charterers could seek financial satisfaction at law. The depositions of Owen Powell and his associates and that of the seamen are dated 15 January 1646/47, the same day that the suit against the owners and master of the *Fox* came to trial. There is no indication as to when the *Fox* actually arrived in Virginia, but assuming that at least a month had elapsed between her arrival and the date of the trial, 15 December 1646, this would call for a sixty-eight-day voyage from the Texel to Virginia, or an elapsed sea time of forty-five days from the scene of the storm. Although a slow passage even by contemporary standards, averaging about two-and-a-half knots, it was not long enough to have allowed for a vessel to have had a shipyard overhaul, nor yet long enough for a vessel damaged to the extent described in the depositions. What reader with the slightest acquaintance with the sea and ships could swallow such a yarn?

So, in order to satisfy the reader's credulity, I shifted the storm to the last leg of the voyage, the one between the point where the *Fox* entered the Gulf Stream and her arrival at the Capes of the Chesapeake. How much more reasonable to have a badly crippled ship limp into port under such conditions. Or was it really the way the depositions have it?

NOTES

1. George Carrington Mason, "An Atlantic Crossing of the Seventeenth Century," *American Neptune* 10 (1950) :35–41. This article includes transcriptions of three depositions contained in the Lower Norfolk County Wills and Deeds, 1646–1651, Ms Book B, pp. 30–31, and the proceedings of the county court held on 15 February 1646–47. It is preceded by a brief explanatory introduction. See the Afterword at the end of this article for a further note on the documents and my use of them.
2. An English corruption of the surname of Lucas Jansson Wagenaer (or Waghenaer), the author of the Dutch pilot book, *Spieghel der Zeevaerdt* (1584 and later eds.); the English translation by A. Ashley was called *The mariners mirrour* (London, 1598; Amsterdam, 1605).
3. John Smith, *An accidence or the pathway to experience. Necessary for all young sea-men* (London, 1626); revised as *A sea grammar . . . with Smiths Accidence for young sea-men, enlarged* (London, 1627). The first edition was reprinted in E. Arber and A. G. Bradley, eds., *The Travels and Works of John Smith*, 2 vols. (London, 1910), 2:785–804, and the second in John Smith, *The Generall Historie of Virginia. . . . The True Travels . . . and a Sea Grammar*, 2 vols. (Glasgow, 1907), 2:211–99. The second edition was also edited separately by Kermit Goell (John Smith, *A Sea Grammar* [London, 1970]).

SPAIN AND ITS EMPIRE IN THE SIXTEENTH AND SEVENTEENTH CENTURIES

J. H. Elliott

One of the greatest empires in world history is known to us as the "Spanish empire," but this is not the name by which it was known to the Spaniards themselves.[1] In the sixteenth and seventeenth centuries there was only one true empire in the western world—the Holy Roman Empire— even if other western monarchies were beginning to appropriate the title of empire for their own special purposes. With Charles I of Spain securing in 1519 the title of Holy Roman Emperor as Charles V, there was no possibility at that moment of the Spaniards formally accepting the existence of two distinctive empires, the Holy Roman and the Spanish; and even the imperial title passed in 1556 to Charles's brother Ferdinand rather than to his son, Philip II, "the empire" continued to denote for Spaniards the Holy Roman Empire, the German lands. Their monarch was not an emperor but a king, ruling over an agglomerate of territories known as the *monarquía española* ("the Spanish monarchy") and consisting of Spain itself, the possessions of the king in Italy and northern Europe, and his American territories, known to Spaniards as *las Indias*.

But this does not mean to say that Spaniards lacked the

capacity to think in imperial terms about the widespread dominions of their king. Already in 1520 Hernán Cortés was
writing, in his second letter to Charles V from Mexico, that
"one might call oneself the emperor of this kingdom with no
less glory than of Germany."[2] Almost at the start of the discovery, conquest, and colonization of the American mainland
there existed in some quarters, then, the idea that the king of
Spain was in the process of acquiring an empire. Philip II
would later be urged to style himself "Emperor of the Indies," a title which was sometimes applied to him and his
successors; and "empire of the Indies" was a phrase that
acquired a certain currency in the seventeenth century. But
the Indies tended to be set into the context of a wider and
more nebulous imperialism that was at once ideological and
geographical in conception.

The humanist circle around Charles V embraced the imperial theme with enthusiasm and represented him as being
on the way to achieving universal empire—an empire in
which, in the words of Saint John's Gospel as used by Ariosto
in the *Orlando Furioso*, "there shall be one flock and one
shepherd."[3] Here, ready to hand, was the theme of a providential mission, of the union of all mankind beneath the government of a single ruler, foreshadowing the return of universal harmony.

Along with this rather vague messianic universalism
there went a more specific sense of geographical expansion
of a kind appropriate to the great European age of discovery.
The traditional limits of Europe were the Pillars of Hercules,
"beyond which," as Dante wrote, "one does not go." That
"beyond which" (*piu oltre*, rendered into Latin as *Plus Ultra*)
became the imperial device of Charles V, twisting in scrolls
around the twin pillars. *Plus Ultra*, symbolizing first the endless expansion of the dominions and power of Charles V,
came to incorporate the more specific idea of the exploration
and conquest of the New World.[4] In mentally and physically
breaking out beyond the confines of the Pillars of Hercules
into a wider world, the Spaniards were conscious of achieving something that surpassed even the feats of the Romans.

59

They were on their way to a universal empire which was genuinely universal, in the sense of being global. This global advance can be simply plotted by a series of dates: the 1490s and early 1500s, the conquest of the Caribbean; the 1520s, the conquest of Mexico; the 1530s, the conquest of Peru; the 1560s, the Philippines; 1580, the annexation of Portugal and the consequent acquisition of Portuguese Africa, the Far East, and Brazil. From this moment the empire of the king of Spain was indeed one on which the sun never set.

As such it surpassed in extension, and in the number of its inhabitants, the greatest empire in the history of Europe, that of Rome. This is a fact of great importance for understanding the Spanish—or, more exactly, the Castilian—mentality of the sixteenth and seventeenth centuries. The Roman empire became a model and a point of reference for the sixteenth-century Castilians, who looked upon themselves as the heirs and successors of the Romans, conquering an even more extended empire, governing it with justice, and laying down laws which were obeyed to the farthest ends of the earth. It was a potent myth, and it had important psychological consequences for those who believed in it. The sixteenth-century Castilians saw themselves as a chosen, and therefore a superior, people, entrusted with a divine mission which looked towards universal empire as its goal. This mission was seen as a higher one than that of the Romans because it was set into the context of Catholic Christianity. The highest and most responsible duty of Castile was to uphold and extend the faith, bringing to a civilized and Christian way of life (and the two were regarded as synonymous) all those benighted peoples who, for mysterious reasons, had never until now heard the Gospel message.

It seems that every empire needs its ideology, that the empire-builders have to justify to themselves in terms of a higher mission their government of dependent peoples. The Spanish crown and the Spanish ruling class found this sense of justifying mission in their obligations to their faith. Whatever services this or any other imperial mission may perform for the conquered, its impact on the conquerors does not generally

60

seem to have been very healthy. Empire-builders, seeing themselves as entrusted with a providential mission, are all too prone to arrogance. This was one of the principal charges leveled against the Castilians, and it was essentially they who conquered and governed Spain's overseas empire. The psychological effect of their successes was betrayed in their attitude to the king's non-Castilian subjects, both in Spain itself and in other parts of Europe. For instance, a comment scribbled on a letter sent to Philip II by the governor of Milan in 1570 reads: "These Italians, although they are not Indians, have to be treated as such, so that they will understand that we are in charge of them and not they in charge of us."[5] This is the characteristic comment of a member of a master race, and it is not surprising to find a Catalan writing in the 1550s that the Castilians "want to be so absolute, and put so high a value on their own achievements and so low a value on everybody else's, that they give the impression that they alone are descended from heaven, and the rest of mankind are mud."[6] If we are to look, then, as I wish to do here, at the implications of empire not so much for the peoples of that empire as for the imperialists themselves, it seems important not to ignore one of the most intangible but also one of the most far-reaching implications of empire—the psychological. It is in this context of a conscious sense of imperial mission, imperial functions, and imperial duties that I want to examine some of the consequences for sixteenth- and seventeenth-century Castile of its conquest and possession of a global empire, and more especially of an empire in America.

These Castilians, consciously following in the steps of the Romans, first had to conquer, then to colonize, and then to organize, govern, and exploit their conquests. A great deal of research has been done into the impact of their imperial activities on the subject populations of America. We know, for instance, about the devastating demographic impact of their presence: the decline of the indigenous population of Mexico from 25 million to 2.5 million between 1520 and 1600 as a result of war, subjugation, enforced labor services, and contact with European diseases. We know a good deal about

61

the attempts to Christianize this population and to bring it within the confines of a European polity. We know too about some of the ecological, technical, social, and economic changes brought to the life of the inhabitants of the Indies by Spanish rule. These are fascinating and important subjects, which have received a considerable amount of attention. What has received much less attention—and this is equally true of the history of other empires, such as the British—is the way in which the possession of overseas empire affects the mother country.

What did its great overseas extension, its heroic conquering and colonizing effort, its attempt to rule over and defend its far-flung possessions, mean for the history of Habsburg Spain? The acquisition and retention of overseas empire necessarily represent a vast national investment of people, energies, and resources. Investments yield benefits, at least in theory, but they also imply costs. No serious attempt has been made to measure the costs and benefits of empire to Habsburg Spain, and indeed such an undertaking is not really feasible. There are, after all, intangible consequences, like the development among Castilians of messianic nationalism, which is obviously unquantifiable in terms of benefits or costs. It may be counted as a benefit that the morale and determination of Cortés and his colleagues were no doubt immensely fortified by their identification of their cause with that of God, Charles V, and Castile. But equally it may be counted as a cost that this confidence in their cause was rated by others as arrogance, that the Castilians earned for themselves the hatred of their fellow Europeans, and that their barbarous exploits in the New World added a whole new dimension to that vision of Spain and the Spaniards which has come to be known as the Black Legend. By the late sixteenth century, Spain stood condemned in the European dock for its atrocities against innocent peoples. The effect of this European consensus on the innate barbarism and cruelty of the Spaniard was to fortify the resolution of Spain's numerous enemies to prevent the Continent from falling beneath its bloody domination.

So there are, and must always be, strict limits to any attempt to balance the gains and losses arising to metropolitan Spain from the possession of its "empire of the Indies." But something can be done to suggest profitable areas of inquiry for an investigation into the ways in which investment in empire influenced the history of the imperial power itself.

If we ask ourselves what the acquisition of an American empire entailed for sixteenth-century Spain, it clearly entailed first of all the export of people. It is difficult to say with precision how many people were involved, but the most recent estimates suggest that about 240,000 men and women emigrated from Spain to the New World during the course of the sixteenth century, and perhaps some 450,000 in the seventeenth. An emigration of some 700,000 over the course of two centuries would average out at just under 4,000 passengers a year, as compared with a suggested emigration rate from the British Isles in the seventeenth century of 7,000 a year. If the total population of the Iberian peninsula was around 7 to 8 million, this implies a yearly emigration rate of 0.5 to 0.7 for every 1,000 Spaniards, which would not in itself appear a very high figure. But it is a misleading one in the sense that emigration was not evenly spread over the peninsula as a whole, and some parts of Spain produced far more emigrants than others. This is especially true of the southern areas of Andalusia and Extremadura, where the emigration rate was something like 1.4 per 1,000. But to make sense of this figure, and of the kind of demographic impact which it represents, much more information is required about the character and quality of these emigrants. In the later sixteenth century, for example, about a third of the emigrants from Spain were women. If this rate of female emigration was maintained, the loss of potential population to the Iberian peninsula must have been considerable.[7]

In the circumstances of sixteenth-century Europe, where an expanding population was pressing more and more heavily on limited food resources, this loss of population or potential population may have been beneficial. America represented a safety value for the excess population of the Iberian peninsula, and contemporaries thought that this had important political and social consequences for Spain. During the period of the French religious wars, some Frenchmen believed that the lack of colonies in which to dump France's surplus inhabitants was one of the causes of their country's domestic troubles, and they contrasted their own situation with the extraordinary political stability of the Spain of Philip II. "It is an established fact," wrote La Popelinière in 1582, "that if the Spaniard had not sent to the Indies discovered by Columbus all the rogues in the realm . . . these would have stirred up the country."[8] In other words, the export of riffraff and desperadoes was the best way to avoid a civil war.

But were they the riffraff? Emigrants emigrate because they think they can do better overseas than at home. This means that disadvantaged groups will be particularly liable to emigrate if they can. One of the major disadvantaged groups in sixteenth-century Spain consisted of the *conversos*—those who, because of their Jewish ancestry, were penalized by the statutes of purity of blood and excluded from important opportunities and positions in Castilian society. It would seem a plausible guess that the emigrants included a significant proportion of Spaniards of Jewish blood, many of whom were likely to be of above-average ability. Is it, for instance, a coincidence that the seven brothers of Saint Teresa of Avila, now known to have been of Jewish ancestry, all emigrated to the Indies? It is worth remembering, however, that the emigration of these people did not necessarily mean a permanent loss to the mother country. One at least of Saint Teresa's brothers came home to Avila, having made his fortune in America.[9]

In general, though, even those emigrants who intended to stay in the Indies only long enough to get rich were liable to end their lives on the far side of the Atlantic. The lure of the Indies was very powerful, and those who had successfully emigrated would write home to their relatives begging them to join them. "Don't hesitate. God will help us. This land is as good as ours, for God has given us more here than

64

there, and we shall be better off."[10] It seems a fair assumption that the emigrants were drawn from the abler and more dynamic sections of the Castilian and Andalusian population, and if some of these were misfits at home, and their departure for America was therefore a source of relief to the authorities, it also deprived Spain of people who possessed certain talent, like entrepreneurial capacity, which it could ill afford to lose. One also could argue that, in the circumstances of sixteenth-century Spain, even the export of missionaries had its disadvantages. By 1559 there were 802 members of the religious orders in Mexico,[11] and one would assume that some of the ablest and most intelligent members were drawn to an overseas mission. But there was missionary work to be done at home, too, among the Moorish population of Andalusia and Valencia; the failure of the sixteenth-century Spanish church to tackle the problem of really Christianizing the Moriscos may have been the price of devoting its best men and energies to the task of Christianizing the Indians of America.

To create its American empire, Spain had to export people—people to convert the Indians to Christianity, to found cities, and to settle the land. But these new territories, once conquered and settled, had also to be governed. By its nature, the acquisition of empire poses an enormous challenge for the metropolitan authorities. In studying the history of Habsburg Spain, it is too easy to ignore the unprecedented problems and the heroic effort involved in providing effective government for a global empire. No European sociey until this moment had been faced with an administrative task of such magnitude and such complexity. First of all, the Spaniards had to resolve a problem for which again they had few precedents to guide them, that of determining the juridical status of the large indigenous populations which had now become subjects of the crown of Castile. Were the Indians, for instance, to be treated as slaves, or were they free men? And, if free men, what tributes and services could be demanded of them as vassals of the crown? These were not easy problems to solve. For Europeans these Indians were a new kind of people, and there was great uncertainty and confusion about their origins and capacities. Were they men, in the full sense of the word, or sub-men, whose inferior capacities demanded that they be placed under some kind of tutelage? This was the type of problem with which the Spaniards found themselves confronted as soon as they arrived in the Antilles, and it became even more complex when they came face-to-face with the peoples of the settled empires of the Aztecs and the Incas. The problem led to a passionate debate during the first half of the sixteenth century in governmental circles, in the universities, and among the clergy and members of the religious orders—a debate with which the names of Las Casas and Sepúlveda will forever be associated. The effective outcome of this fifty-year debate was that the Indians were not slaves and were not to be treated as such; that, lacking Christianity and true civility, they had to be instructed in the faith and in the ways of Christian men; that this required close spiritual and temporal supervision, which placed the Indians in a special but subordinate status where they must be given the protection of the crown; and that it was right that they should perform certain services in return for this protection.

A prime object of imperial government, then, was the protection of the Indians, and this meant especially protecting them from exploitation by the colonists. Consequently, one of the great problems facing the Spanish crown was how to prevent rebellions and breakaway movements by the settler community, and it was a problem which it successfully solved. Apart from the struggle between the crown and the followers of Pizarro in the aftermath of the conquest of Peru and the abortive conspiracy by Martín Cortés in Mexico in 1566, there was no major open challenge to the crown from the settler community in the New World in the nearly three hundred years of Spanish rule before it was overthrown by the independence movements of the early nineteenth century. Considering that it might take as much as two years for a message to travel from Madrid to Lima and the reply to come home, this is an extraordinary achievement. The Spanish crown managed to overcome the unprecedented problems of time and space to the extent of preventing the centrifugal forces inherent in a worldwide empire from triumphing over the forces of control emanating from Madrid.

How did the crown succeed in achieving this degree of control? The very challenge of empire—of having to govern such distant territories—acted as a major stimulus to the development in Habsburg Spain of a strong bureaucratic structure and an administrative class to staff it. In terms of well-developed and professionally run bureaucratic organization, the Spain of Philip II was the most advanced state in sixteenth-century Europe. In reality it could not afford to be otherwise, since in the absence of a large and formalized bureaucracy it could never have held its empire together. We all know the defects of this bureaucracy, that it was cumbersome, corrupt, and appallingly slow, and we may well recall the despairing comment of one viceroy patiently waiting for his orders: "If death came from Madrid, we should all live to a very old age." But perhaps more significant than these glaring defects is that Spain did succeed in building a global bureaucracy, that the bureaucracy did function with greater or lesser efficiency, and that it did manage to hold the king's many disparate territories together.

The challenge of empire therefore produced a bureaucratic response, in the form of government by paper, on a scale previously unknown in European history. We have hardly yet begun to grasp the sheer quantity of paper used for the government of the Spanish monarchy and empire in the sixteenth and seventeenth centuries. For example, when a viceroy or any major official left office, a formal investigation, known as a *residencia* or *visita*, was conducted into his tenure of office, with sworn statements being taken from those in a position to speak. In 1590 one such *visita* was begun on the retirement of the count of Villar as viceroy of Peru. By 1603 the judge conducting this *visita* had used 49,555 sheets of paper and was not yet finished. The ex-viceroy himself was long since dead.[12] What a different world this was from the world of seventy or eighty years before, when the emperor Charles V had allegedly asked for pen and ink and none was to be found in the palace![13] Although royal administration was not really as casual in the early years of Charles V as this story would suggest, the avalanche of paper in the later sixteenth century (not to mention the plethora of pens and the torrents of ink) suggests that, between the early years of Charles and the later years of Philip, there had intervened a revolution in the operations of government.

The essence of this revolution was the creation of an administrative structure designed to link the center of the Spanish monarchy with its periphery. The method used was to elaborate and build upon a system already in existence in the Spain of Ferdinand and Isabella, which owed much to the practice of government in the Catalan-Aragonese empire of the later Middle Ages. In accordance with this system, the king was represented in his distant territories by a viceroy, while the territories were represented in the presence of the king by a council composed of spokesmen for those territories. This was the conciliar system developed in the Spanish monarchy during the first half of the sixteenth century: a system of councils meeting at the court, and receiving information from—and sending orders to—viceroys at the periphery. It was accompanied by a judicial system which acted as a check on the viceroys, whereby each of the territories had its tribunal of judges, known as the *audiencia,* which was responsible for the administration of justice and could when necessary curb and control the viceroy's administrative powers. For example, the government of Mexico (New Spain) depended first of all, in Spain itself, on the Council of the Indies, sitting at court and advising the king on all major questions relating to Mexican affairs. Its recommendations, if approved by the king, were then transmitted to Mexico, where the viceroy might or might not put them into effect; his activities were watched by the *audiencia* sitting in Mexico City, which advised, warned, or defied him according to the situation and the personalities involved.

This system, which functioned reasonably well, inevitably led to a proliferation of paper and a proliferation of officials. The government needed secretaries to draft the regulations, scribes to write them out, and a whole host of lesser officials to ensure their enforcement, along with another tier of officials to ensure that the first tier of officials had indeed ensured it. All this required a massive bureaucracy, which had to be recruited and trained. This in turn meant an expansion of Spain's educational system. At the beginning of the sixteenth century there were eleven universities in Spain. A hundred years later there were thirty-three. Much of this growth is explained by the state's growing need for officials to man the higher echelons of the bureaucracy, and especially officials trained in the law. It has been estimated that under Philip II Castile supported an annual university population of 20,000–25,000 students, representing perhaps 5.43 percent of its eighteen-year-old male population—a figure that seems to have been very high by contemporary European standards.[14] Those students who studied the law and survived their course emerged as *letrados*, law graduates who formed the recruiting pool for the bureaucracy. Since supply was outrunning demand by the end of the century, many of these graduates would then find themselves without jobs. But the best of them—or, perhaps more accurately, the best-connected—might with luck secure a foothold on the lowest rung of the bureaucratic ladder, which they would be painfully climbing for the rest of their lives.

It was these *letrados* in government service who really held the Spanish monarchy and empire together. Their whole career was spent in the service of the crown, and they would be moved around the world in accordance with the king's orders. One such official was Antonio de Morga, born in Seville in 1559, the son of a banker.[15] He was sent to Salamanca University, where he graduated in canon and then in civil law. In 1580 he entered government service as a lawyer. Thirteen years later, aged thirty-five, he was appointed (being a man with good connections) to a legal post in the Philippines, where in due course he became the senior judge of the *audiencia*. In 1603, at forty-five, he was transferred to the *audiencia* of Mexico. Here he was enough of a success to secure promotion ten years later to the presidency of the *audiencia* of Quito, Ecuador. This could have been the last stop before a post at the very top of the bureaucratic hierarchy, a seat in the Council of the Indies back in Spain. Morga petitioned for this in 1623, but unfortunately by this time his addiction to women and gambling had got the better of him. His conduct became a source of grave scandal, bad enough to prompt an official inquiry into his activities. He was sentenced to be relieved of his office, but before the news reached him he died in Quito, aged seventy-six, after a not very distinguished twenty-one-year presidency.

Assuming that Morga had achieved his ambition of a seat in the Council of the Indies, the council would have been reinforced by a man of enormous practical experience in the problems of overseas administration. But he would have been over sixty-five by the time he took up his appointment in Madrid, and it seems improbable that he would have been a dynamic or innovating councillor. On the whole, the government of the Spanish empire was a gerontocracy because it took such a long time for officials to pass through the various stages of their administrative careers. One therefore finds, as one would expect to find, that the councils were staffed by elderly, status-conscious officials, tenacious of tradition and legalistically inclined, who were above all determined to enjoy in comfort the prestige and rich pickings of the high office which they had worked for so long to secure. They were not a dynamic crowd, but they were nothing if not tenacious. They kept the empire in being, but they also kept it static.

Throughout their careers these men looked to the king, for both their orders and their promotion. They had a very exalted sense of the royal authority of which they were the representatives and official upholders, whether in the Philippines, Ecuador, or Mexico. This sense of the royal authority, reinforced by firsthand awareness of the vast extent of the king of Spain's dominions, created a kind of mentality which deserves to be taken into account in any history of Habsburg Spain. It was difficult to get away from the sense of the overwhelming and universal authority of the king, and while this sense helped to bind the bureaucrats of the empire together in a kind of fraternity of loyal adherents of the crown, it may also have led the government in Madrid to exaggerate the resources of power at the king's command. Madrid for these men was the center of the universe, the bureaucratic capital of a worldwide empire. A judge who returned from Lima to serve on the Council of the Indies or a returning viceroy—a Castilian grandee like the marquis of Montesclaros, who served as viceroy of Mexico and Peru and was then appointed a member of Philip IV's council of state—saw the world from a peculiar angle, which was not the angle of other men. From Madrid it must have seemed that one could rule the whole world. But unfortunately this did not always happen to be true.

The acquisition of empire, then, entailed the creation of a vast bureaucratic structure whose central point was Madrid. The creation of Madrid itself was in reality a response to the problems of empire. In the early sixteenth century Spain had no capital city, and the court moved around the peninsula with the king. Madrid itself was little more than an overgrown village, with some 5,000 inhabitants. But from 1561, when Philip II settled his court there, it began to grow very fast indeed, and had reached over 100,000 inhabitants by the 1620s. This mushroom growth of Madrid as the capital of a worldwide empire was enormously significant for the future history of Spain. Here was a city at the very center of the barren tableland of Castile: an artificial city of courtiers and bureaucrats, deriving its rather febrile prosperity from the profits of empire which flowed into it from all over the world; a distorting element in the economic life of the Castilian *meseta* in its role as a center of conspicuous consumption for luxury goods brought from other parts of Europe and paid for with the silver of the Indies.

If we can regard the rather unhealthy growth of Madrid as a direct consequence of the bureaucratic demands created by the growth of empire, we can regard the equally remarkable growth of Seville as a direct consequence of the economic demands of empire. Just as Madrid was the bureaucratic capital of Spain's global monarchy, so Seville was its

71

commercial capital. Early seventeenth-century Seville was one of the largest cities of the western world—a city of some 150,000 inhabitants, against 70,000 a hundred years before. Thanks to its monopolistic position as the sole Iberian port for the Indies trade, it had become the center of the so-called Spanish Atlantic system. Its extraordinary prosperity, and the prosperity of its hinterland in southern Andalusia, was directly related to the sixteenth-century prosperity of that trading system. As the system began to break down, from the second decade of the seventeenth century, so Seville's prosperity began to crumble.

This system was so crucial for the European as well as the Spanish economy in the sixteenth century that its actual working is a matter of some importance. The Indies were prized, developed, and exploited primarily as a source of commodities which were highly valued and in short supply in Europe itself: pearls, obtained from the waters round the coasts of Venezuela; dye-stuffs; emeralds; and, most important of all, gold and silver. Between 1500 and 1650 something like 181 tons of gold and 16,000 tons of silver reached Europe from America officially, which means that further very large quantities must have arrived by contraband. At first more gold arrived than silver, but the proportion began to change as a result of the great silver discoveries of the 1540s: the Potosí mines of Peru in 1545 and the Mexican mines of Zacatecas in 1546. But it took both time and the introduction of new refining processes by means of an amalgam of mercury to get a large-scale and regular output from these mines. Silver remittances to Spain were already substantial in the 1550s and 1560s, but it was only from the 1570s—after the discovery of mercury mines in Peru and the introduction of the new refining process there in 1571—that the remittances became very large indeed, with Peru producing two-thirds of the silver to Mexico's one-third.

Spain and Europe needed this silver. The king of Spain needed it to meet his expenses (especially the expenses incurred in war), and Europe's mercantile community needed it to lubricate its transactions and to provide a means of paying for luxuries from India and the East. Therefore the organization of the silver mines and the silver trade became a major preoccupation of the Spanish crown, and the whole Spanish system—and to some extent the European international system—came to depend very heavily on the regular flow of precious metals from America to Europe. But all the silver had to be paid for, apart from the *quinto,* or one-fifth of the mines' production, which belonged to the Spanish crown of right. Payment came from the export to America of Spanish and European commodities to meet the needs of the growing settler community, which hankered for luxury objects and articles of consumption unobtainable in the newly settled lands. From the start, therefore, Seville's commerce with America was a two-way trade, designed on the one hand to satisfy the needs of a growing American market, and on the other to satisfy Europe's insatiable demand for precious metals.

The receiving point at the European end of the transatlantic network was Seville, with its port of San Lúcar enjoying a monopoly of the American trade. By the system of the treasure fleets, which was finally regularized in the 1560s, two fleets left San Lúcar each year, both in convoy with armed protection. The first of these fleets, the *flota,* left in May, destined for Vera Cruz in Mexico. The second, the *galeones,* left in August, and took a slightly more southerly course, making for Nombre de Dios (Portobello) on the isthmus of Panama; and then, after unloading its cargos for the colonists—wine, oil, grain, swords, books, clothes, and luxury objects—it would retire to the more sheltered harbor of Cartagena for the winter.

The outward journey took five to six weeks, and the size of the fleets varied a good deal, but the average was around sixty to seventy ships. Once they had unloaded their cargos, both the fleets would winter in the Indies. The trickiest problem was to arrange the timing of the return journey to Seville. The pattern was for both fleets to rendezvous at Havana and start back with their precious silver cargos in the early summer, before the hurricane season arrived. To do this, the Mexican *flota* had to leave Vera Cruz in February,

73

laden with silver and cochineal and other goods from Mexico, to make its three- to four-week voyage against the trade winds to Havana. The isthmus fleet, the *galeones*, had a much more tricky assignment, because it had to pick up, while en route for Havana, the silver coming from the Peruvian mines. Its voyage therefore had to be synchronized with the transport of silver all the way from the Potosí mines to Panama.[16] This in turn depended, in the final analysis, on the rainfall in Bolivia. If the rains came late, there was insufficient waterpower for the mills to prepare the ore and turn the silver into bars. From the point of view of the return journey of the fleets, the Peruvian silver should have been in Panama by March in order to get to Havana before the hurricane season started. But usually the rain was so delayed in the Bolivian altiplano that the silver only reached Panama in May. Once the rains had fallen and the silver had been minted, a great llama train carried it down from the mountains on the fifteen-day journey from Potosí to Arica. At the port of Arica the silver was transferred to ships, which took eight days to reach Callao, the port of Lima. Here it was transferred into three or four special treasure ships, which took twenty days to reach Panama. At Panama it was taken out of the ships and placed on the backs of mules, and the mule train took four days to cross the isthmus, where the *galeones* were waiting at Nombre de Dios to load the silver. They then sailed for Havana and joined up with the Mexican *flota;* with luck, the combined fleets were back in Seville by the late summer or early autumn.

This, very briefly, was the mechanism of the Seville trade—a cumbersome and expensive, but on the whole efficient, mechanism, which, with only two or three exceptions, got the fleets safely across the Atlantic and back for over two centuries. This itself was a remarkable feat of organization, considering how dependent it was on careful synchronization all the way along the line. It demanded, in the first place, reasonably accessible deposits of silver, a regular supply of Indian labor to work them, and a regular supply of mercury to refine the metal. It demanded rains at the right time in

Bolivia, llama trains and mules in abundance, and large fleets whose sailings had to be carefully arranged according to the winds and the seasons. When we talk, therefore, about the Spanish empire, we must think not just in terms of vast and widely scattered territories, nor even simply in terms of a complex bureaucratic structure, but also in terms of an intricate economic mechanism which required the most careful regulation.

What did the existence of this mechanism mean for the Spanish economy and Spanish society in the sixteenth century? Obviously the gold and silver of the Indies meant a windfall for Spain, although it could be argued that much of this windfall was unprofitably squandered. Riches were flowing into Seville in large and growing quantities, and those which did not almost immediately flow out again to pay debts to foreign bankers were transmuted into benefits for a wide variety of individuals. Aristocratic families fallen on hard times would hope to recoup their fortunes with revenues from the Indies; hence the competition among the Castilian grandees for the American viceroyalties, since a viceroy of Mexico or Peru could reasonably expect to reline his coffers during a normal tenure of office. We should therefore regard the overseas empire as a means of providing outdoor relief for at least a section of the high Castilian aristocracy. Government officials and clerics, and the relatives of settlers who had done well in the Indies and chose to remit money home to their families, would also acquire their silver nest eggs, and then use them as they would: to pay off debts, acquire property, send a favorite nephew to Salamanca University, or construct a family chapel in the local parish church. The merchants of Seville, who were the recipients of large quantities of silver, would use it for their own transactions, and especially for purchasing cargos for the next Indies fleet. Apparently half the silver that arrived in the fleets of 1568 and 1569 was used to fit out and freight the next two fleets.[17] This meant that the system was, as it were, self-generating. Something like half the annual revenues of the Indies were needed for shipping commodities back there in

75

order to yield more revenues in the future. But all this activity in the dockyards of Seville itself generated employment and new skills; it encouraged artisans to develop products for the Indies trade and Andalusian farmers to produce more wheat or wine or oil for shipment to America. If Castile experienced a minor economic boom during the opening and middle decades of the sixteenth century, part of the explanation for this lies in the opening of the new American market, with the new demands that it created.

The influx of all this silver into the Spanish, and then the European, economy has notoriously been held responsible for the "price revolution" of the sixteenth century. Much debate has been generated around the thesis of Earl J. Hamilton's *American Treasure and the Price Revolution in Spain* (1934), which attempted to illustrate statistically the existence of an extremely close correlation between the increase in sixteenth-century Spanish prices and the quantities of American silver arriving in Seville. There would seem, however, to be many other besides purely monetary reasons for the sixteenth-century price rise, although American silver played its part in pushing up prices and still more in keeping them at a high general level. Hamilton's thesis tends to assume that all the silver which arrived in Seville found its way into the Spanish economy, and this clearly did not happen. Large quantities were in fact shipped abroad again, for one purpose or another, immediately after registration. It is very difficult to secure exact figures, but in the later years of the sixteenth century it is probable that, in an annual consignment of 10 million ducats from America, 6 million at once left Spain.[18]

There are various explanations of this rapid exit of silver almost before entry. A certain amount went to pay for European rather than Spanish commodities, which were then shipped to the Indies. But much of it was sent abroad, largely through bankers, to keep Spain's various European armies in pay and to sustain the expensive foreign policy of the Spanish crown. For one of the greatest of all the implications of overseas empire for sixteenth-century Spain was that it helped provide the crown with the resources to launch military ventures which were quite beyond the scope of its European rivals.

Sixteenth- and seventeenth-century Europeans saw America, with some justice, as the true source of the Spanish monarch's power. Sir Benjamin Rudyard told the House of Commons in 1624: "They are not his great territories which make him so powerful . . . for it is very well known that Spain itself is but weak in men, and barren of natural commodities. . . . No, sir, they are his mines in the West Indies, which minister fuel to feed his vast ambitious desire of universal monarchy."[19] Rudyard was probably correct, in so far as the possession of the Indies made the thought of universal monarchy thinkable and encouraged the rulers of Spain to assume that grandiose schemes could in fact be realized. But in terms of the actual figures, America's contribution to the king's coffers was not quite as impressive as Rudyard's remarks might lead one to believe. It is true that, in the second half of the reign of Charles V, the emperor became increasingly dependent for his revenues on Spain, at the receiving end of the American silver supply, and less and less on his traditional sources of income, Italy and the Netherlands. But even as late as 1554 the American contribution amounted to only 11 percent of the crown's total income.

Things were rather different under Philip II, but even when the silver of the Indies was flowing into Seville in enormous quantities, it still hardly reached 25 percent of Philip's total revenues. But to speak simply in terms of proportional contributions is unsatisfactory. Silver was a highly desirable international commodity; it was because the king of Spain had at his disposal large and regular supplies of silver that the great international bankers of the sixteenth century, the Fuggers and the Genoese, were prepared to serve as royal bankers and perform the necessary bridging loan operations between the arrival of one fleet and the next. The imperialism of Charles V, and then of Philip II, was financed by borrowing, and neither of these monarchs would have been able to borrow for so long, or on such a massive scale, if they had not been able to attract the international financial community with the lure of New World silver.

It would be fair, then, to say that the possession of America helped to sustain Europe's first great imperial venture of the sixteenth century, that of Charles V, even if it did not originally launch it. But Charles's empire was and remained obstinately European; it was only in the second half of the century that the political organization of Europe adjusted to the new economic realities, and that Habsburg imperialism reconstituted itself round the Spanish Atlantic of the age of Philip II. Madrid, Seville, Lisbon, and Genoa—not Augsburg or Antwerp—were the effective centers of this new imperial system, and it was because the resources of those centers were accessible to him that Philip II could attempt with some success over half a century to check and throw back the forces of heresy and disorder which threatened to engulf the orderly, hierarchical world that was the only world he understood. The effort was an enormous one, as witnessed by the three million ducats a year (the equivalent of the crown's total annual revenues from the Indies) required to sustain the famous army of Flanders in its desperate struggle to crush the revolt in the Netherlands. In the end, it is hardly surprising that the strain began to break the system. Sooner or later the moment was bound to come when the costs of empire began to outweigh its presumed or real benefits. It is not easy to pinpoint this moment, and perhaps it is a mistake even to make the attempt. But between the 1590s and the 1620s there seems to have been a significant shift in the relationship of Spanish America to the metropolis—a shift which began to raise doubts in certain quarters about the value to Spain of having an empire at all.

There was, for example, the question of emigration. In the sixteenth century the Indies may have represented a useful outlet for an excess population which Castile could neither feed nor employ. But Castile was struck by a devastating plague in 1599–1600 and increasingly began to be perceived as an underpopulated country. The rapid rise in Castilian wages in the reign of Philip III suggests that Castile

78

could no longer afford the loss of able-bodied men. Yet it was at this moment that the deepening misery of Castile led to a massive increase in illegal emigration, and the consequent drain of people to the Indies became a cause for profound concern.

About the same time, it also began to look as though Castile could no longer take for granted the benefits of empire which it had for so long regarded as a matter of course. During the sixteenth century both the Spanish crown and the Castilian economy had become dangerously dependent on the Seville trade and on the regular arrival of silver from the Indies. In moments of crisis they had looked to the New World and had not looked in vain. But now, in the early seventeenth century, circumstances had changed. The American market was beginning to dry up, at least as far as Spanish commodities were concerned. The colonists no longer wanted traditional Spanish goods in the same quantity as before; the Seville trade itself began to run into difficulties after 1610; and the silver remittances started to decline. This, for a variety of reasons, is especially true of remittances for the Spanish crown, which slumped from 2 million ducats a year at the beginning of Philip III's reign in 1598 to around 1 million in 1615 and 1616, and to a mere 800,000 in 1620, before rising again to around 1.5 million a year in the following decade.[20]

So the tangible benefits of America to Spain were dwindling, and they were dwindling at a moment when the costs of empire were climbing sharply. English attacks on Spain's American possessions in the reign of Elizabeth had already forced the crown to embark on a costly program for building fortifications in the Indies. Under Philip III, money had to be scraped up year after year for the war in Chile against the Araucanian Indians, and the issue of naval defense in the Atlantic and the Pacific grew increasingly urgent as the threat from the Dutch increased. This problem of imperial defense began to overshadow everything else in the final years of Philip III because of the enormous burden that it was now imposing on the Castilian taxpayer and the Castilian economy.

It compelled ministers to reconsider the general distribution
of taxation within the Spanish monarchy and to reassess the
various ways of defending an empire consisting of widely scattered territories. The solution devised in the 1620s by the
count-duke of Olivares was an ambitious scheme for a Union
of Arms—a pooling of the monarchy's resources for military
and naval defense—which placed such an intolerable strain
on the fragile constitutional structure of the Spanish monarchy
that by the 1640s it seemed on the verge of total collapse.

This growing realization of the burdens of empire was
sharpened by the intense awareness of the misery of Castile.
The Castile of Philip III and Philip IV went through a period
of deep soul-searching, accompanied by many anxious attempts to identify and analyze the causes of distress. It
seemed an extraordinary paradox that Castile, the head of a
great empire, should be poverty-stricken, that it should be so
rich and yet so poor. González de Cellorigo, analyzing in
1600 the troubles of Castile, traced at least some of them
back to the psychological effects of the discovery of the Indies.[21] In his view, the effect of an apparently endless flow of
American silver into Seville had been to create a false sense
of wealth as consisting of gold and silver, whereas true
wealth lay in productive investment and the development of
industry, agriculture, and trade. If this was so, the discovery
of America could even be considered as prejudicial to Spain,
because it had diverted the country's attention from the real
sources of prosperity and dazzled it with the mirage of false
riches. The Castilian, as a result, had abandoned work for
dreams. The Flemish scholar Justus Lipsius wrote to a Spanish friend in 1603: "Conquered by you, the New World has
conquered you in turn, and has weakened and exhausted
your ancient vigor."[22]

Once the overseas empire was beginning to be seen as a
liability rather than a benefit, as a source of misfortune rather
than prosperity, there was an inevitable revulsion against it.
The count-duke of Olivares himself said at a meeting of the
council of state in 1631: "If its great conquests have reduced
this monarchy to such a miserable condition, one can reason-

ably say that it would have been more powerful without that New World."[23] This was an extraordinary statement, coming from the principal minister of the Spanish crown. Here was the antiimperialist thesis finding expression in the very highest governmental circles of the Spanish monarchy—the rejection, as it were, of a hundred years of Spanish history. Although this was the despairing remark of an exhausted minister and should not be taken too seriously, it does seem to indicate a striking change of mood from the heady days of Charles V. In the early sixteenth century the Castilians had seen themselves as a people divinely favored with the gift (or the trust) of a global empire. Now, a century later, they had lost their confidence. The gift of empire had proved a poisoned chalice, which had sapped their vigor and aggravated their ills. This change of attitude appears to correspond to a change in the objective situation. The liabilities of empire *had* increased, and its immediate benefits had diminished. The difficulty came in adjusting to this changed situation.

Sixteenth-century America had made it possible for Castile to sustain itself as the dominant world power, but at an economic, administrative, and psychological cost which only slowly became apparent. When the cost did begin to appear, and the bills came in for payment, it was very difficult for a ruling class accustomed to thinking in imperial terms to change its policies and its ways. The possession of empire had created expectations and assumptions which it was difficult to jettison, and by the midseventeenth century the commitments of Madrid had so far outstripped its capacity to meet them that the jettisoning of expectations had become essential for the monarchy's survival. In fact, empire had become a psychological burden which made it almost impossible to think in realistic terms about the changing international situation. The sad history of the Spain of the middle and later seventeenth century is the history of a people and a ruling class which failed to rid themselves in time of imperial delusions.

The fate of Spain, and of other imperial powers which followed in its steps, prompts a final reflection as to whether the adverse psychological consequences of empire for the

81

imperialists do not, in the long run, outweigh all the more tangible assets that empire is supposed to bring in its train. And as we look at the course of Spanish history since the days of Charles V, and consider the remarkable achievements of a uniquely gifted people, we can still hear the mocking echo of those words of Justus Lipsius: "Conquered by you, the New World has conquered you in turn."

NOTES

1. Since this essay was intended as a general exposition rather than as a presentation of new research, only a few references will be given. Interested readers can find a more detailed discussion of many of the themes touched upon here in some of the standard works on Habsburg Spain and Spanish America. Expecially recommended are John Lynch, *Spain under the Habsburgs*, 2 vols. (Oxford, 1964, 1969); J. H. Parry, *The Spanish Seaborne Empire* (London, 1966); Charles Gibson, *Spain in America* (New York, 1966); see also J. H. Elliott, *Imperial Spain* (London, 1963), and *The Old World and the New* (Cambridge, 1970).

2. Hernán Cortés, *Letters from Mexico*, trans. and ed. A. R. Pagden (Oxford and New York, 1971), p. 48.

3. See Frances A. Yates, *Astraea* (London, 1975), p. 26.

4. See Earl Rosenthal, *"Plus Ultra, Non Plus Ultra,* and the Columnar Device of Emperor Charles V," *Journal of the Warburg and the Courtauld Institutes* 34 (1971) :204–28.

5. Quoted in H. G. Koenigsberger, *The Government of Sicily under Philip II of Spain* (London, 1951; emended ed. *The Practice of Empire*, Ithaca, N.Y., 1969), p. 48.

6. Christòfol Despuig, quoted in J. H. Elliott, *The Revolt of the Catalans* (Cambridge, 1963), p. 13.

7. The figures and arguments in this paragraph are drawn from two important essays: Woodrow Borah, "The Mixing of Populations," and Magnus Mörner, "Spanish Migration to the New World prior to 1800," in Fredi Chiappelli, ed., *First Images of America*, 2 vols. (Berkeley and Los Angeles, 1976), 2:707–22 and 2:737–82. The fundamental work on emigration statistics has been done by Peter Boyd-Bowman, whose publications are cited in these essays.

8. Henri de la Popelinière, *Les Trois Mondes* (Paris, 1582), introduction.

9. Valentín de Pedro, *América en las letras españolas del siglo de oro* (Buenos Aires, 1954), pp. 262–68.

10. Cited in Elliott, *Old World and the New*, p. 76. For a fascinating anthology of letters from emigrants, see James Lockhart and Enrique Otte, eds., *Letters and People of the Spanish Indies* (Cambridge, 1976).

11. Robert Ricard, *La "conquête spirituelle" du Mexique* (Paris, 1933), p. 35.

12. See Lewis Hanke, "El visitador licenciado Alonso Fernández de Bonilla y el virrey del Perú, el conde del Villar," *Memoria del II Congreso Venezolano de Historia*, 2, (1974), pp. 13–127.

13. The story is told by the count of Gondomar in a letter of 28 March 1619 (*Correspondencia Oficial de Don Diego Sarmiento de Acuña, Conde de Gondomar*, in *Documentos Inéditos para la Historia de España*, 10 vols. (Madrid, 1936–55), 2:143.

14. See Richard L. Kagan, *Students and Society in Early Modern Spain* (Baltimore, 1974), esp. pp. 199–200.

15. Morga's career is related in John Leddy Phelan, *The Kingdom of Quito in the Seventeenth Century* (Madison, Wis., 1967).

16. For a good account of this process, see Carmen Báncora Cañero, "Las remesas de metales preciosas desde el Callao a España en la primera mitad del siglo XVII," *Revista de Indias*, no. 75 (1959), pp. 35–88. The Seville trade has been exhaustively studied by Huguette and Pierre Chaunu, *Séville et l'Atlantique, 1504–1650*, 8 vols. (Paris, 1955–59), which is the starting point of all later work.

17. José Gentil da Silva, *En Espagne. Développement économique, subsistance, déclin* (Paris, 1965), p. 65.

18. F. Ruiz Martín, *Lettres marchandes échangées entre Florence et Medina del Campo* (Paris, 1965), p. xlix.

19. Quoted in Elliott, *Old World and the New*, pp. 90–91.

20. Elliott, *Revolt of the Catalans*, p. 189.

21. *Memorial de la política necesaria y útil restauración a la república de España* (Valladolid, 1600), p. 15v.

22. Alejandro Ramírez, *Epistolario de Justo Lipsio y los españoles* (Madrid, 1966), p. 374.

23. Archivo General de Simancas, Estado, legajo 2332, *consulta* of 7 September 1631.

THE SPANIARDS IN
EASTERN NORTH AMERICA

J. H. Parry

"It would seem to have been especially ordered by Providence that the discovery of the two great divisions of the American hemisphere should fall to the two races best fitted to conquer and colonize them. Thus, the northern section was consigned to the Anglo-Saxon race, whose orderly, industrious habits found an ample field for development under its colder skies and on its more rugged soil; while the southern portion, with its rich products and treasures of material wealth, held out the most attractive bait to invite the enterprise of the Spaniard." These rotund sentences and the confident—one might almost say smug—sentiments they contain are from Prescott's *Conquest of Peru*. Historians nowadays are much less willing to risk confident generalizations of this kind than they were a hundred years ago. In some way, perhaps, this is a pity. To a modern historian, trained within the Ph.D. industry and taught to value detailed research, the questions which Prescott raised might indeed seem too vast and too vague for useful discussion and the manner in which he phrased them too naive to command serious attention, and yet, if we discount old-fashioned phrasing, they are important questions, and certainly within the province of serious historians. To what extent are the considerable differences between the European empires in America, in social composition, economic productivity, and administrative style, attributable to differences in time, place, and circumstance? To what extent are they attributable to differences in the character and purposes of the colonizing peoples? In no part of the New World are these questions more apposite than on the long stretch of the North American coast, from the mouth of the Mississippi to the head of Chesapeake Bay.

The Spanish crown, as is well known, claimed a general lordship over the whole of the Americas, except where it had itself admitted exceptions. This immense claim, though unenforceable in its extreme form, and though only brought into the open when major Spanish interests seemed to be threatened, remained a basic principle of Spanish foreign policy for more than three centuries. In regard to the mainland viceroyalties, major sources of revenue and main areas of Spanish occupation, Spanish control was rigorously and consistently enforced and never seriously challenged. Elsewhere in the Americas, however, the list of admitted exceptions, tacit or explicit, came to be a fairly long one over three centuries. The largest explicit exception was also the earliest: a great area in eastern South America was reserved to Portugal by the Treaty of Tordesillas in 1494, and enlarged in 1751 by a secondary treaty which legitimized a century of *Paulista* encroachment. A number of smaller but still significant exceptions were made in the course of the seventeenth century, when Spain was constrained by military weakness to accept minor losses of Caribbean territory—Curaçao to the Dutch, Jamaica to the English, St. Domingue to the French—all taken by conquest and all subsequently ceded in formal treaties. Tacit exceptions to the general policy were equally extensive. Spaniards, though concerned to preserve fishing rights on the Newfoundland Banks and in Labrador, never showed any serious interest in Newfoundland itself (which, indeed, they regarded as juridically Portuguese), nor in the long coastline now occupied by Nova Scotia, New England, New York, New Jersey, and Delaware. Nor did they raise any serious objections when, in the seventeenth century, English, French, and

Dutch established new settlements scattered all along this coast. The coastline from Chesapeake Bay south, around Florida and west to the Mississippi, was a different matter. There is today very little of Spanish interest and very little evidence of Spanish influence or occupation except in a few areas. And yet it was initially explored by Spanish expeditions: attempts at settlement by other Europeans were always resented, and often, in the sixteenth century at least, effectively resisted. In the seventeenth century the Spanish government retreated, perforce, from its extreme position of the sixteenth; foreign settlements were many and Spanish attempts to prevent them largely ineffectual. But Spain made no explicit acknowledgment of retreat, no formal cession of territory, and in the early eighteenth century there was a marked revival of Spanish belligerence, at least on some sections of the coast. Spanish policy, in fact, fluctuated widely, and it is natural to inquire to what extent the fluctuations were due to *force majeure,* to what extent to recurrent doubts about the value of the territories concerned, and to what extent to short-term changes of extraneous circumstance.

Geographers were slow to recognize the continuous continental character of North America. Most surviving maps of the New World drawn in the first twenty years of the sixteenth century show big stretches of open water north of the Antilles. The most conspicuous exceptions are the 1500 map of Juan de la Cosa and the 1507 world map of Martin Waldseemüller, but la Cosa in 1500 (if the date on the map is correct) can hardly have been able to do more than guess, and Waldseemüller changed his mind later.[1] Open sea stretching from western Europe to eastern Asia was, of course, what most Europeans—almost all except the Portuguese—hoped to find, and probably many cartographers drew what they thought their patrons wanted to see. It was not until the 1520s, with the ineluctable evidence reported by expeditions, that the continent of North America, vast and unwelcome, became an established feature of accepted maps. Long before that, however, maps and reports had shown *some* land to the north of the islands. The Cantino map of

1502—perhaps significantly a Portuguese compilation—has a tongue of land, whether island or peninsula, northwest of Cuba which may be intended to represent Florida and is certainly too circumstantial to be a mere invention. It is probable, therefore, that there was at least one and possibly several sightings of the Florida coast before the first of which we have surviving record: that of Juan Ponce de León in 1513.

Ponce was a seasoned, favored, and well-connected entrepreneur of discovery, who had done well with gold washing in his government of Puerto Rico. He had the confidence of Juan Rodríguez de Fonseca, who was in effect the minister for the Indies in Spain at that time. He was a hard-bitten conquistador; the story of his searching for a fountain of youth was probably a chronicler's invention. Las Casas, who in his way was equally hardheaded, said that Ponce's main purpose was to capture slaves, and this seems much more probable. It may explain the frequent fighting with the local Indians, who were formidable archers with the long bow and who on several occasions succeeded in repelling Spanish landing parties. Ponce sighted the coast of Florida near the site where San Agustín was later founded, and coasted south, around Cape Sable, and north up the west coast as far as San Carlos Bay. He found nothing he considered of value, returned to Puerto Rico, and for some years lost interest in the area. The most important discovery made by this expedition, apart from the configuration of the Florida coast, was a navigational one; the navigator Antonio de Alaminos noted the broad and powerful current of the Gulf Stream sweeping eastward at sixty miles a day through the Florida Channel and grasped the use that could be made of it by ships returning to Spain.[2] This discovery, more than any other single factor, determined the future development of Spanish Florida.

Ponce's first expedition to Florida coincided almost exactly with Balboa's discovery of a route across the Isthmus of Panama to the South Sea. Reports of this famous exploit stimulated not only exploration, and subsequently devastation, in Central America, but also the search in other parts of the Americas either for open-sea passages to the South Sea and the Spicery or for other narrow necks of land which could be surmounted. Similarly, a few years later, reports of the voyages of Hernández, Grijalva, and Cortés to Yucatán and Mexico stimulated fresh interest in western Florida and exploration of the north coast of the Gulf of Mexico by people who hoped either to establish themselves profitably on the route from Mexico to Spain or to find a back door into Mexico itself. First among the latter was another island magnate, Francisco de Garay, governor of Jamaica, who in 1521 procured a title to discover and settle from the boundary of Florida west to the Pánuco river in eastern Mexico. As a preliminary, Garay sent a small fleet commanded by Alonso de Pineda to explore the coast. The chief result of this voyage was a negative one: Pineda closed the circuit of the Gulf of Mexico and showed that there was no strait to the South Sea in that area; the coast was continuous. As for Garay, he began his settlement on the Pánuco in 1523, but he was outmaneuvered by Cortés, as Narváez had been three years earlier. His men went over to Cortés, and he himself was captured, dying in custody shortly afterwards. Ponce's title to Florida was still in force, and in 1521 he made another attempt, this time to settle with two hundred men on the southwest coast. Strategically this was a good idea, for reasons which will appear, but the attempt failed, and Ponce was killed fighting the local Indians.

The last of the rich island magnates to make a bid for power on the mainland was one of the conquerors of Cuba, that same Pánfilo de Narváez whom Cortés had driven from Mexico in 1520. After Ponce's death, Narváez in turn attempted, in 1528, to settle western Florida. The expedition was a big one, too big for the local food supplies, and included four or five hundred men and a hundred and eighty horses. They landed in Tampa Bay and went north from there. Narváez was a habitual bungler. The whole expedition was mismanaged and ended disastrously in shipwreck and starvation. Its only significant sequel was the journey of a survivor, Alvar Núñez Cabeza de Vaca, with three companions, from Florida to Mexico, at first in makeshift boats and subsequently on foot. Núñez Cabeza de Vaca acquired on the way a reputation as a *curandero* (we might perhaps say "itinerant medicine man" in English), and so established a claim on the hospitality and protection of the Indians through whose territory he passed. His account of his adventures is one of the classics of Spanish discovery.[3]

The death of Narváez left all prior grants of Florida vacant, and so they remained until Hernando de Soto petitioned for the vacant title and in 1537 received it. Soto was a dashing but not particularly intelligent conquistador, already famous for his part in the conquest of Peru. He had acquired a great fortune there, but subsequently, like other leading captains, had incurred the jealousy of the Pizarro faction.[4] Seeing no prospect of an independent governorship in Peru, he had returned to Spain, looking for new worlds to conquer. He had no knowledge of North America and no long-range plans for his new government. His contract with the Spanish crown makes clear that plunder was his principal object. He had made his fortune in Peru partly by extorting treasure from living Indians, partly by robbing the graves of dead ones—an occupation which can still today yield profits in Peru—and he proposed, optimistically as it turned out, to do the same in Florida. It is significant, perhaps, that the austere and experienced Núñez Cabeza de Vaca, though invited, refused to take part. The expedition, which was by far the biggest and best-equipped to enter North America up to that time, consisting of more than six hundred men, about half of them mounted, left Spain in the spring of 1538. It wintered and victualed at Havana and landed the following spring at Tampa Bay, from where it began a march north, driving along with it a great herd of pigs to supply food on the march. These Spanish pigs—long of snout and leg, accustomed to foraging and to being driven in herds—had been introduced into the islands some thirty years earlier. When in the 1560s the French established their first colony in Florida, they encountered what they called "wild swine," which must have been the descendants of escapees from Soto's herd, Florida being far outside the range of native peccaries. The agile razorback hog of the south today is much more akin to Spanish range hogs than to the heavy, short-legged breeds later brought in by Dutch and English colonists. Their presence may well represent the only lasting result of Soto's endeavors.[5] His expedition has received far more detailed historical attention than its achievements warranted, attention ranging from the romanticized narrative of Garcilaso in the *Florida del Inca* to the careful and voluminous *Report of the United States De Soto Commission,* published to mark the quartercentenary in 1939. The army wandered aimlessly through parts of what are now Florida, Georgia, Tennessee, Alabama, Mississippi, Arkansas, and Louisiana, endlessly foraging and skirmishing with the inhabitants. Soto died beside the Mississippi. The survivors, about a quarter of those who set out from Tampa Bay, empty-handed and in rags, eventually made their way in makeshift boats to Mexico. The comment of contemporary chroniclers was severe. According to Gómara, Soto "went about five years hunting mines, thinking it would be like Peru. He made no settlement, and thus he died and destroyed those who went with him."[6]

While Soto and his predecessors were busy west of Florida, seekers after a strait or an isthmus had been active on the Atlantic coast. In the middle 1520s two expeditions explored the long coast between Florida and Nova Scotia, one commanded by Estavão Gomes and the other by Giovanni da Verrazzano. Both expeditions probably (Verrazzano's certainly) sailed from south to north. Verrazzano was a Florentine in French service: Gomes was a Portuguese in Spanish service. Gomes had been with Magellan, as master of one of Magellan's ships, and had deserted him to go back to Spain. Verrazzano's investigation was the more thorough and the better reported. He established beyond doubt the continuous continental character of the North American coast. Oddly, however, though he failed to find a strait, he thought he had found an isthmus; apparently he mistook Pamlico Sound for the Pacific, and several maps drawn shortly afterwards show, so to speak, a wasp waist in the middle of North America.[7] Gomes started his explorations from Santiago in Cuba and passed rapidly and perfunctorily up the east coast, much of which was already known to Spaniards, until he reached approximately Point Judith in Rhode Island. From there northeast he explored the New England coast in careful detail. He was the first to place Cape Cod upon a chart and the first to explore the estuary of the Penobscot, which initially offered hopes but soon disappointed them. Gomes returned directly to Spain from Cape Race, carrying with him a shipload of Indians from that area.[8]

A third expedition at about the same time sailed from Hispaniola, not to look for the strait but to plant a colony in the country which the Spaniards knew by the Indian name of Guale, part of what is now South Carolina and Georgia. The promoter and leader was Lucas Vázquez de Ayllón, who was a judge of the court of appeal in Santo Domingo and who also owned a sugar mill in Puerto Rico. Ayllón got his information about Guale from a captive Indian boy, to whom he took a fancy and whom he took with him to Spain when he went there to negotiate the contract for his expedition. This youth, Francisco, developed a talent for tall stories about the riches and the curiosities of Guale. Peter Martyr, not normally credulous, was taken in by him, though Oviedo was not.[9] The expedition duly sailed from Puerto Plata in 1526, and after some initial mishaps picked on a site surrounded by swamps at the mouth of the Savannah River. Settlements founded by people who arrived by sea and depended on the sea for supply and reinforcement naturally were close to the shore. Early sixteenth-century criteria for selecting healthy sites and fertile soil were no doubt largely guesswork. Nevertheless, the persistence with which Spanish settlers established themselves in febrile swamps seems at times almost perverse, and is certainly hard to explain. Ayllón had the best of intentions with regard to a serious colony and also with regard to the treatment of the local Indians; he even took with him the Dominican Antonio de Montesinos, who had started the campaign for Indian rights in Hispaniola in 1511. But even with all these virtuous ideas, he was no leader. The whole enterprise was a fiasco. Ayllón died shortly after arri-

91

val, and so did about two-thirds of the settlers, many of them killed—not without provocation—by Indians. The survivors, sick and starving, eventually straggled back to Hispaniola. And so, by the 1540s Spaniards had lost interest in eastern North America. Their record of attempted settlement was a record of almost total failure, and clearly the area had little to offer to men who could, if they wished, go to Mexico or Peru. Even the islands were becoming depopulated; there were no colonists to spare for Guale.

The sharp revival of Spanish interest which occurred in the 1550s and 1560s was due neither to a reappraisal of the value of the territory itself nor to private investment; it arose from extraneous circumstances and was directed by the government of New Spain, Mexico. The late 1540s and 1550s were the period of the great silver strikes, both in New Spain and in Peru. The prospective shipment of immense quantities of silver to Spain became, almost overnight, a major governmental preoccupation. The ships carrying this silver, whether from Mexico or from Peru via the Isthmus of Panama, would have to leave the Caribbean by way of the Florida Channel. Only by that route could ships, borne along on the broad and powerful current of the Gulf Stream, overcome the contrary pressure of prevailing east and northeast winds. It was a dangerous route, flanked by the reefs and banks of the Florida keys and by the shoals of east Florida, and prone in summer and early autumn to hurricanes. In 1550 and again in 1553, whole fleets, homeward bound to Spain, freighted largely with silver, were caught by hurricanes in the channel, and many ships were wrecked. A settlement in Florida was needed, not as a source of profit in itself, but as a port of refuge, rescue, and salvage. It would have to be fortified and garrisoned securely. Spain and France were constantly at war between 1551 and 1559: French raiders were active in the Caribbean, and French attempts at settlement had to be anticipated and if possible prevented. The proposed colony, as the Council of the Indies realistically accepted, would yield no revenue, so the treasury of New Spain would have to pay for it. In 1557 the governorship of Florida, left vacant by

Soto's death, was placed under the viceroyalty of New Spain. To avoid the long and circuitous communication route by sea around Florida, two settlements were planned, one on Pensacola Bay in west Florida, and the other at Santa Elena (modern Helena Sound and island) in the Sea Islands of South Carolina. They were to be connected by a land route of about 240 miles, passing through a fertile and relatively productive country capable of feeding both establishments. The plan was a good one, strategically sound and in accord with geographical realities. It was devised by Luis de Velasco, the ablest of all the sixteenth-century viceroys of New Spain; it was to be executed by Tristán de Luna, a competent and experienced officer who had been in New Mexico with Coronado. He was to have eleven ships, 1,500 men, and provisions to feed them for a year. This was to be no plundering incursion of the Soto kind. It was expected that the colony would produce its own food within a year.

Most European organizers of settlement in the New World underestimated the length of time that must elapse before a new colony became self-sufficient in food production. Commonly it was ten years or more, yet the myth that within a year colonists could feed themselves persisted well into the seventeenth century. Velasco, however, at least recognized that the proclivities of Spanish settlers were pastoral rather than agricultural, and he arranged for some hundreds of Tlaxcalan Indians from Mexico, free men, Christian and hispanicized, to be recruited with their families as agricultural settlers. Surely nothing could go wrong—but it did. Luna's ships were caught at anchor in Pensacola Bay, and most of them were destroyed by a hurricane. There was no arguing with hurricanes. Most of the food was lost at the bottom of the bay, and those settlers who got ashore were driven to begging from the local Indians or commandeering food from them. The Indians could not spare enough for so large a party, and the familiar sequence of sickness and starvation and ill will followed. Velasco, the viceroy, tried repeatedly to send help, but his resources had been strained to provide the initial outlay and were inadequate to replace it.

The project was finally abandoned in 1561, and with it was abandoned Velasco's plan for a Spanish frontier that was to stretch from Zacatecas to the Sea Islands. In the following year came the French invasion which Santa Elena was to have forestalled.

The Treaty of Câteau-Cambrésis in 1559 was an impressive triumph of Counter-Reformation diplomacy. It ended the war between Catholic Spain and Catholic France, advantageously for Spain. In one respect, however, it was unrealistic: it left out of account the semiindependent power of the French Huguenots and of their leader, Gaspard de Coligny, the admiral of France. It inaugurated a long period of intermittent religious war within France itself, and a rather shorter period of French Huguenot aggression in the Americas, a period in which Florida was a principal (though not the only) target. The Huguenots had special and urgent reasons for an interest in Florida. The country seemed, by all accounts, to be suitable for European settlement. If they could establish a successful colony, it would not only yield profit in itself but also provide a nucleus of Protestant population in a predominantly Catholic New World. Moreover, it might serve as a refuge if worse should come to worst and they should be driven, because of their religion, into exile. It would be available as a base from which privateers could make profitable and damaging raids against Spanish shipping. All ships homeward bound from the Caribbean had to sail for several hundred miles close to the Florida coast, and though the organized convoys were well protected, stragglers would always be vulnerable to raids.

The settlements established by Ribault and Laudonnière on the coast of Florida in 1562–64 represented the most serious challenge to Spanish power in America up to that time.[10] French ships had often visited the coast before then, on their return from raiding or smuggling in the Caribbean, to careen their ships and take in wood and water. The Spanish authorities had resented such visits but had been unable to prevent them. Now they were confronted by the much greater threat of permanent armed settlements on the convoy route, manned by hostile religious enthusiasts and backed by men of wealth and power in France. The Spanish reaction was correspondingly swift and merciless. Pedro Menéndez de Avilés, who was appointed *adelantado* of Florida in 1565, and in 1567 governor of Cuba also, was able, ruthless, loyal, and ferocious in his detestation of "Lutheran" heresy. He had been a highly effective captain-general of several transatlantic fleets, and he was the principal author of the general plan by which the movements of the convoys were governed from the 1560s onward. He knew the coast; in 1561 he had made a personal survey in small vessels, including a reconnaissance of Chesapeake Bay. His capacity as a naval tactician is hard to judge, since he never commanded a fleet in action against another battle fleet, but in his grasp of the strategic realities of the Atlantic he was equaled by few, whether Spaniards or Englishmen, in the sixteenth century. As a former captain-general, he knew perfectly well where Spain's priorities lay. The fleets and the treasure they carried were the first consideration; all lesser interests—the interests of the Antillean settlers, for instance—had to be sacrificed to it. Menéndez's consistent adherence to this principle explains why he was so hated in Cuba and Santo Domingo and why his services were so highly valued in Spain. He was able to raise an adequate force for his task, and in 1565 he destroyed the French settlements, massacred the settlers, and set about establishing a chain of forts and blockhouses to prevent further foreign encroachments. Of these, the fort of San Agustín was the most important.

Menéndez's actions in 1565 and subsequently served notice that the Spaniards intended to hold the coast of Florida by force, and that they would resent and might resist the intrusion of other Europeans anywhere along the Atlantic coast. They gave the first clear intimation that the Spanish claim to a monopoly of New World settlement—whether based on papal donation, prior discovery, conquest, or sheer force—was to be interpreted as including the whole of North America, save only those parts which might lie east of the Line of Demarcation. Spain appeared, at the time, to possess both the will and the resources to enforce this vast claim. In the face of Spanish hostility, attempts by other Europeans to settle in or anywhere near Florida were made to appear prohibitively dangerous. French attempts to avenge the Florida massacre amounted to little more than raids, though that of Dominique de Gourgues in 1568 achieved a bloodthirsty and destructive, if temporary, success. When, some twenty years later, Englishmen endeavored to settle as the French had done, but further north, on Roanoke Island off the North Carolina coast, fear of Spanish resentment governed their every move. Roanoke proved inhospitable and unsuitable, but the settlers refused to move to more promising surroundings on Chesapeake Bay, as the promoters wished, because they thought that at Roanoke they were less likely to be discovered by Spanish forces. The Spaniards indeed searched diligently for their settlement, and had they found it, they would probably have served it as they had done the French. In the event, starvation, Indian hostility, and English neglect saved them the trouble, though the English neglect could be laid indirectly at Spain's door, since it was the Armada crisis that prevented the promoters from sending reinforcements and supplies.

By scaring off possible foreign settlers from Florida and the coasts further north, Menéndez and his immediate successors (most of whom were also his relatives) achieved their primary object: that of rendering the exit from the Caribbean safe for the passage of the homeward-bound silver fleets. For the next half-century or so, apart from the hazards of the sea itself, the convoys had little to fear so long as they kept together, except on those rare occasions when Spain's enemies sent major naval armaments to the Caribbean. Even then, until Piet Heyn's exploit in 1628, the convoys suffered no major damage by human agency. The peak years in the whole history of the convoys, measured in terms of numbers of ships and quantities of silver delivered, fell in the last decade of the sixteenth century and the first decade of the seventeenth, the decades immediately following the disappearance of the Roanoke colony.

The Spanish control which Menéndez established on the coast of Florida lasted, with only one brief interval, for more than two hundred years. Throughout that period, however, it was a tenuous control, remotely exercised. Menéndez had an unerring eye for the sites of forts and outposts, but no clear idea of economic activities which could make his settlement self-supporting; in fact, it never supported itself. There were a few cattle ranches, a few missions—Jesuit initially, subsequently Franciscan—but no towns. Menéndez did his best. He repeatedly urged the crown to encourage Spaniards to settle in Florida.[11] He brought over, at his own expense, several hundred peasants from his native Asturias, who were given grants of land but did not have much idea of what to grow on it. He wrote glowing accounts of the prosperity and potential wealth of the province. No one believed him. It may be doubted whether he believed himself, or whether he was merely uttering the ritual incantations of any colonial promoter seeking governmental support. The Council of the Indies saw no reason to subsidize activities which would profit only the *adelantado*. For the council, the one essential factor in the Spanish presence was the garrison. Sometimes (at the turn of the century in particular) there was talk in high quarters of withdrawing even that, and of abandoning the province altogether.[12] It was difficult to maintain a garrison without a supporting civilian population. The local Indians were unhelpful and often hostile. The subsidies from New Spain, by which the garrison was supposed to be supported, came tardily and grudgingly. The fear of English or French encroachment prevailed, and the garrison remained, but crown policy, despite all that Menéndez's successors could urge, remained strictly defensive, and Florida remained a thinly held outpost of New Spain.

Gómara, in his comment on the egregious Soto, part of which has already been quoted, went on to say: "Never will conquerors do well unless they settle before they attempt anything else, especially here where the Indians are valiant bowmen and strong."[13] Why did the Spaniards fail so signally to establish vigorous settlements in Florida and the neigh-

boring territories? They might have done so if they had arrived in Florida earlier. They would in fact have arrived earlier if Columbus had pursued his original course due west
across the Atlantic, but on 5 October 1492, Columbus, notic-
ing flocks of migratory birds flying west-southwest, altered
course to follow them, and so made his first landfall in the
Bahamas instead of on the North American mainland. By the
time Ponce de León landed in Florida more than twenty
years later, European settlement was already spreading from
the Antilles to Central America; by the time of Ponce's second attempt, the move to Mexico had begun. Florida offered
no obvious attractions that could compete with the pull of
Mexico. It had, as far as could be seen, no precious metals. It
had no cities, no impressive public works, no sophisticated
arts and crafts. Its people, to be sure, grew crops and lived in
orderly communities, but they had relatively little surplus of
food or of anything else, and they lacked the powerful organ-
izations for mobilizing labor and collecting tribute in kind
which were so characteristic of Mexico and Peru, and which
in those places proved so convenient to the European invaders in supporting their early settlements. The Spaniards,
seeking to establish in the New World a ranching and mining
economy reminiscent of the economy of the parts of Spain
that most of them came from, needed a peasantry to supply
their bread. The Indians of eastern North America neither
would nor could fulfill the need.

Not only were the Indians relatively primitive and little
amenable to European discipline, but they were formidable
fighters. One of the most striking features of the European
conquest of America was the ineffectiveness of the large organized armies which Mexican and Peruvian rulers fielded
against the invaders. Densely ranked warriors armed with
spears, slings, and clubs were hopelessly outmatched by ar-
mored men, many of them mounted, armed with steel
swords, steel-tipped lances, crossbows, and firearms. Once
the formal armies had been defeated and the principal towns
occupied, organized resistance collapsed. In the eastern
woodlands of North America, in contrast, there were no for-

98

mal armies, but, instead, scattered bands of individual warriors. Horses, which gave the European invaders a decisive advantage in open country, were much less effective in woodland fighting. The advantages of steel weapons over wood and stone could be exploited only if the enemy could be made to stand and fight; against an elusive adversary skilled in hunting and in making use of forest cover, swords were rarely effective, and light, hand-carried missile weapons came into their own.

The Spaniards might appear, at first sight, to possess a decisive superiority in missile weapons. Their forts mounted light artillery—mostly small *pedreros*—and they used as hand arms both arquebuses and crossbows, whereas the Florida Indians relied upon longbows. The European superiority in this respect, however, was more apparent than real. Crossbow and arquebus alike were heavy, awkward weapons. The arquebus had the advantage of being slightly easier to carry; its mechanism was simpler and less prone to damage; it could, at a pinch, be used as a club at close quarters; and its noise, flash, and smoke had a psychological effect in frightening horses or savages. These were probably the principal reasons why arquebuses, and later muskets, steadily replaced crossbows in European armies and navies in the course of the sixteenth century. Both weapons had formidable stopping and penetrating power at close range; both had an extreme range of four hundred yards or so; but because of their inaccuracy, their effective range was much less. Neither arbalestier nor arquebusier could expect to hit an individual target at a range greater than eighty or a hundred yards. Both weapons had extremely slow rates of fire. The military effectiveness of a missile weapon depends not only on its accuracy and killing power, but also on the relation between its range and the distance a charging enemy can cover in the time taken to reload. Arbalestiers and arquebusiers in the open, having discharged their initial bolt or ball, were hopelessly vulnerable unless they had the support of a "hedge" of pikemen behind which they could reload.

The real advantages of crossbow and arquebus alike

99

were two. Neither weapon required a very high degree of skill, so that a recruit could be trained to use either with reasonable efficiency in a relatively short time. Both weapons could be aimed and discharged from a kneeling or lying position, and so could be used from behind the merlons of a rampart or the gunwales of a ship. These, rather than any technical superiority, were the initial reasons why the crossbow, the arquebus, and subsequently the musket replaced the longbow in the armies and navies of Europe. The longbow, in skilled hands, was no less deadly. Its extreme range was comparable with that of the crossbow and arquebus. It was (again, in skilled hands) far more accurate than either, and since the penetrating power of its flighted arrow was not much less than that of ball or quarrel, its effective range was considerably greater. Its rate of discharge was at least six times greater. It had two major disadvantages. For one thing, the archer had to stand erect to loose his shaft. The bow was unsuitable, therefore, for shooting through loopholes or from any kind of shelter. In forest warfare, however, this was unimportant. The more serious disadvantage was that the bow was effective only in highly skilled hands. Raw recruits could not be turned into archers by routine training. The eye, the skilled control, and the specialized muscular development of the good archer came only from constant, lifelong practice. The natural and obvious way of practicing was by hunting. Among the Amerindian peoples, only those accustomed to hunting used the bow. The massed armies of central Mexico were manned by peasants; there were no archers among them because in the thickly settled, intensively cultivated lands in which they lived there was little or no wild game. Those Amerindian peoples who posed a long and successful resistance to Spanish invasion—the Araucanians of Chile, the Chichimecas of northern Mexico, and the forest dwellers of the Andean *montaña*—were all hunters and all had the reputation of being formidable archers.

All this helps to explain the relative ineffectiveness of Spanish settlement in Florida. The small groups of Spanish settlers tended to stay in the neighborhood of the forts,

100

where they were usually, but not always, reasonably safe. Except in actual war, the Indians tended to withdraw from the areas near the forts and to establish their villages out of range of Spanish foraging raids. Most of them remained either indifferent or hostile, and when English or French raiders visited the coast they could usually count on finding Indian guides and allies. The Florida Indians were never hispanicized. Spaniard and Indian—in marked contrast with the situation in, say, Mexico—remained separate, foreign one to another, except for the few converts and hangers-on about the missions. Even the missions needed *presidios* to protect them, to the end of the sixteenth century and beyond.

Throughout the seventeenth century, the Spanish presence in eastern North America stagnated. The missions in Florida gained in strength and effectiveness as more missionaries mastered native languages and also learned to offer material inducements to their converts. On the other hand, in Spanish diplomatic claims there were signs of tacit retreat. The English settlements in Virginia, Maryland, and the Carolinas established themselves with no more than a formal rumble of Spanish diplomatic protest. In the early eighteenth century, English advances into Georgia and the French movement down the Mississippi provoked a more vigorous response from a new and more active government; San Antonio in Texas and Pensacola in western Florida were deliberate retorts to French New Orleans, but Florida itself remained, as always, a precarious outpost. The Florida annexed by England in 1763 did not differ greatly from the Florida of Menéndez. There were not many more settlers; there were still a few cattle ranches, still the garrison, still no towns. The English, during their twenty years of occupation, found little of interest in the place, and after the recognition of American independence it became for them a source more of embarrassment than of prospective value. The Treaty of Versailles (which ended the only major eighteenth-century war in which England had been soundly defeated) restored Florida to Spain. The retrocession was made in partial payment for the abandonment of Spanish claims to Gibraltar, an agree-

101

ment which some modern Spanish governments have found it convenient to forget. At the time, those in authority in England congratulated themselves on their bargain, and many would have echoed Rodney's comment that Spain had added another desert to her empire.

NOTES

1. J. H. Parry, "Asia-in-the-West," *Terrae Incognitae* 8 (1976):67.
2. J. H. Parry, "The Navigators of the Conquista," ibid., 10 (1979): 61–70.
3. Alvar Nuñez Cabeza de Vaca, *Relación*, ed. Manuel Serrano y Sanz, 2 vols. (Madrid, 1906).
4. James Lockhart, *The Men of Cajamarca* (Austin, Tex., 1972), p. 193.
5. Carl O. Sauer, *Sixteenth Century North America* (Berkeley, 1971), p. 184.
6. Ibid., p. 178.
7. Lawrence C. Wroth, *Giovanni da Verrazzano* (New Haven, Conn., 1970), pp. 164–66 and plate 19.
8. Louis-André Vigneras, "El viaje de Esteban Gómez a Norte América," *Revista de Indias* 17 (1957):1–19.
9. Peter Martyr, *Decades*, trans. F. A. McNutt, 2 vols. (New York, 1912), 1:254–68. Gonzalo Fernández de Oviedo y Valdés, *Historia general y natural de las Indias*, 5 vols. (Madrid, 1959), 4:325.
10. Suzanne Lussagnet, ed., *Les Français en Amérique pendant la deuxième moitié du XVIe siècle. Les Français en Florida* (Paris, 1958).
11. Luis Cabrero Blanco, ed., *Colección de diarios y relaciones para la historia de los viages y descubrimientos*, 5 vols. (Madrid, 1943–47), 2:47–90.
12. D. B. Quinn, ed., *The Roanoke Voyages*, 2 vols. (Cambridge, 1955), 2:777.
13. Sauer, *Sixteenth Century North America*, p. 178.

CONTENTMENT AND DISCONTENT
ON THE EVE OF COLONIZATION

G. R. Elton

My purpose is to set out the background to early English colonization in the North American continent, to the way in which the English moved into the continent and began to settle it. I therefore propose to say a little about the society from which these settlers came and the impulses which drove them forth. In all history there are many open questions, and this sad truth certainly applies to the problems considered here. Though much has been written about these issues, much still remains obscure; in addition, much of what has been written arises from certain convictions that I must regard as doubtful, especially the conviction that among the early English settlers those who mattered were fleeing from oppression and were seeking liberty to live and worship according to their preferences. While I do not pretend that I can really close any of these open questions, I hope at least to indicate what they might be.

Why, in fact, did a part of a small nation on the edge of Europe decide to go out into the unknown and start new lives in new and strange worlds? As I have already said, it is a widely accepted view that the colonizing activity of the En-

---

Abbreviated and modified text of a lecture delivered and tape-recorded at St. Mary's College of Maryland, 16 November 1977.

glish in the sixteenth and seventeenth centuries owed most to discontent, to a profound dissatisfaction with the manner in which things were arranged in the home country. These emigrants were sick and tired of the way in which they were being treated and in particular were driven forth by religious intolerance, which compelled them to seek a way of managing their relationships with God in a country that was new, empty, and free of government. There is of course some truth in this—it applies to a small section of the colonists concerned to set up intolerant regimes of their own—but I should like to suggest to you now that it is nothing like the whole truth, or indeed anything like the important part of the truth.

Let me begin by asking what life was really like in Elizabethan and early Stuart England. What moved people? What were their ultimate ambitions? What, in the life they led, contented or discontented them? Well, in the first place, we need to grasp how miserable and indeed horrible by our standards (the standards of a generation determined to regard itself as the most ill-used ever) life then really was. You may at times have come to wonder—and if you haven't, I wish you would—how it was that human beings of a not unfamiliar kind, people like ourselves, could tolerate, for instance, the manner in which their law dealt with its victims. Have you considered the true meaning of that sentence of execution for treason: hanging, drawing, and quartering? I will not spell it out in detail here, merely remarking that those three words by no means describe everything that was done to such a traitor, because I like sparing finer feelings. Have you ever considered what the death sentence for heresy really meant: burning alive at the stake? What it meant when, as the books so calmly and smugly tell us, Thomas Cranmer, archbishop of Canterbury, pitifully and painfully degraded from that status, was led out and tied to the stake and, because he had signed recantations which now he wished to withdraw, put his hand into the flames until—to cite those books—it was consumed?

What sort of people are we dealing with, who can do such things and do them in public? You could not help supposing them to have been inhuman, inhumane and insuffer-

106

able, unless you grasped that in the conditions of the time what man could do to man was as nothing compared to what God was forever doing to man. Men's lives were governed (beyond our experience, perhaps beyond our comprehension) by pain, by physical pain and the proximity of death. Ever since painkillers and anesthetics came to our aid, we have lost a ready means towards an understanding of the past, but just contemplate what it was like to live in an age in which you could not reduce the pain inflicted upon the human body by the things that naturally happen to it. If you can make that effort, you should begin to understand how these people could do those things to one another and could suffer them, as well as what sort of lives they were really leading. If you survived the first year after birth, average expectation of life in Elizabethan England was in the neighborhood of thirty-five years. That is a rough average: many people died much younger, but if you reached sixty or so your expectation of life became approximately what it is now. But most people lived short and suddenly terminated lives. The killer diseases with which we are familiar did not much trouble them, because those are the diseases of old age and not commonplace before thirty-five. People died of injuries, many of them minor, and of the many infectious diseases that were running around, most of them painful. Try to think (but not for too long) what cutting for the stone really meant, and then try to think (even more briefly) what people suffered when the stone was not so treated. We are speaking of an age when pain was ever present and nasty forms of death encompassed all, quite unassisted by human agents except those well-meaning practitioners who pretended to be able to cure the one and stave off the other. Doctors caused a lot of agony.

Yet people of course lived, and often lived happily, but if they were to be able to face the miseries of life created by the frailty of the human body, they had to observe the two conditions which make contentment possible in such circumstances. In the first place, they accepted the promise of better things to come after death: religion was required to carry a man through his troubles in order to achieve the potential

107

ultimate bliss which was promised to him and which faith alone could guarantee. Secondly, they developed a degree of stoicism and resistance to the effects of pain and misery which we in our present state find hard to imagine, but which in fact accounts for much about the age, including its casual cruelty. Let me make myself plain. I am not saying that theirs was a good life and ours is bad; I am not saying that I wish to go back to the days before aspirin, anesthetics, painkillers, and so forth. But I wish to emphasize that in that very different age, despite all the miseries that we would regard as intolerable, people still managed to live perfectly contented lives. Much of what to you may seem strange and alien about the sixteenth and seventeenth centuries comes out of those basic human experiences, fundamentally different from ours and yet experienced by people in many ways recognizably like ourselves. There is something of a problem here. To treat the past as real is not as common a practice, even among historians, as you might think. Even those professionally concerned with it do not as fully and regularly open themselves to the reality of the past as they should, and for that reason so much history is dead as you read it. Do, when you think about the past, remember that you may now be alive, but so were they; that you may now be suffering, but so were they; that you may now be rejoicing, but so were they.

Therefore: those real people in that somewhat remote society underwent those debilitating experiences and coped with them, in part because they felt sure that they could, if only they did things right, achieve bliss in another world, and in part because they had schooled themselves to face the inescapable adversities decreed by God. It is out of this matrix, with its cure for helpless discontent, that the men and women came who transferred their existence to a new world. It is, of course, quite difficult to establish exactly why people started colonizing. It is even quite difficult to establish when people started colonizing, especially as the tally must not include voyages of exploration or of trade and plunder. Settlement in the North American continent is what concerns

108

us. Let us, however, take the years from the first Virginia foundation of 1585, temporary though this was, as defining our era. It so happens that in this era the English people experienced the return of several difficulties and problems that had been temporarily absent. After a relatively prolonged peace they found themselves at war; plague returned to England;[1] and economic depression came in the wake of both. One of the problems to make itself felt was overpopulation, or so at least contemporaries thought. There were supposed to be too many people in late Elizabethan and early Stuart England, and though historians have by and large concluded that the supposition was mistaken—the country could readily accommodate the extra numbers—what matters is that such views were current at the time and did have some support from what was happening.

The reign of Elizabeth had opened in a very peculiar fashion. Population had been growing in England from the middle of the fifteenth century or even earlier. When a total population runs at about two and a half million, it takes some time for increases to produce large absolute figures, but the rate of increase was considerable—probably something like 50 percent over the whole of the sixteenth century—which means that the impact was strongly felt. That increase had been effectively uninterrupted down to the 1550s, raising notable problems of unemployment and food supply much discussed at the time. But 1557 and 1558, the last two years of Mary's reign, witnessed really major epidemics: plague struck, as did the famous sweating sickness, a virus disease which remains unidentified. (John Shrewsbury, the historian of plagues, thought it was the same as the trench fever of the First World War, but that does not help because nobody knows what caused trench fever.) In addition, England was visited in those years by a devastating influenza epidemic. In consequence, I would suggest, the reign of Elizabeth started with the population suddenly reduced by probably something like one-fifth, which meant a marked reduction in the hitherto prominent problems of employment, food supply, and poor relief. Thus one reason why that reign started in a cloud of glory lay in the deaths of the superfluous. I don't think that those who lived through the experience were particularly pleased by it, but from the point of view of the great queen, who after all had a quite superb skill at exploiting the benefits that God scattered about here and there, it was a very interesting start.

Divine favor freed the realm from plague for thirty years, so that by the 1580s the population was again outgrowing the country's resources, with the result that some began entertaining thoughts of finding overseas outlets for excess people. On the other hand, in the nineties plague, war and economic depression combined to create the second most serious crisis in the whole of the century, so that suddenly life became very unpleasant indeed for a large number of people. Despite the peace of 1604, adverse conditions (combining alleged overpopulation and chronic economic difficulties) continued into the reign of James I. Thus the first age of colonization was one in which the conflicting pressures of general distress and apprehensions touching overpopulation created a patchy but widespread discontent. People had become unhappy about their condition in ways which previously had not been prominent, and the empty New World stood beckoning.

In addition, we can find in the years between 1590 and 1620 (or 1640) another form of discontent—political disaffection. Here I am in some difficulty. The accepted interpretation of the prehistory of the English Civil War, with its alleged constitutional conflicts between Parliament and the crown and its emphasis on the problems associated with the supposed rise of puritanism, seems to me to be totally at variance with the facts. Until 1642 there was no struggle between Parliament and the king. All those familiar earlier occasions of conflict turn out (as the closer inspection of recent years is beginning to show) to be struggles between various court factions of politicians using Parliament for their own purposes. There is no battle over sovereignty, no rise to power of the House of Commons. I apologize for striking all these things into the discard in a few sentences, but on this occasion I have no time to elaborate: I must ask you for the present to accept

110

this revision of hoary error on trust. Nor can I believe in puritanism as a revolutionary movement. All that had been genuinely revolutionary in puritanism had gone by 1590, and in the early seventeenth century puritanism simply describes the attitude of convincedly Calvinist members of the Church of England, content to live within it, ambitious to reform it, but in no way anxious to seek some other region in which to develop possibly disruptive forms of religion. Such discontent, in other words, as appeared in politics and religion in late Elizabethan and Jacobean England did not make for colonization, did not make for emigration, did not advance the spread of the English people over the western world; these are facts despite the attempts of a few very small groups of true dissidents who did set up some settlements of minimal survival value. The heart of English colonization at this time lay not in New England but in Virginia, where settlement owed nothing to any flight from those political or religious discontents.

What, then, of contentment, of which there was certainly a good deal around, despite the miseries of life? One of the things that you have to grasp about the English of the sixteenth century is that they were a confident nation. It would be an error to suppose that they were uncertain of themselves. Of course, they had no reason to be overconfident in the face of God, but I think I have said enough about this. Though quite sure that life was short and miserable and dangerous, by and large they faced those dangers and those miseries often with pessimism, but rarely with despair. I will not say that despair did not exist—some aspects of Tudor religious life were markedly morbid—but I will say that a more universal reaction was to accept man's fate and to confront it firmly. This made for confidence. In fact, the reign of Elizabeth was notable for chauvinistic arrogance, a fact which by itself must cast some doubt on the notion that what happened in the colonizing activities of the sixteenth and seventeenth centuries was a flight from England, a flight from home, a flight from familiar and no longer tolerable circumstances. You will, I think, have heard of Milton's famous remark about God's Englishman—that creature to whom God always first

111

reveals his will. You may not have heard of John Aylmer, who in 1559 wrote a treatise exalting the English, who, possessed of the best system of government, could triumph over all adversities. A marginal note says why: "God is English."[2]

Something like this conviction was widely held throughout the century. God was English, though—since God was not always kind—this did not mean that everything was always going well. But ill fortune did not affect the national conviction of the superiority of the English, a visible hallmark of the century. It is found, for instance, in Richard Morison's writings in the 1530s, perhaps the first sign of this kind of thing; it is fully ripe in John Foxe and in similar writers of the Elizabethan era. God has singled out the English for his own, as the true elect nation. Morison, for instance, pointed out that the English ate beef while the French lived on broth and vegetables, a plain proof of English superiority. And this was the view of a man who, I ought to emphasize, had lived many years abroad. We are not talking about ignorant men; we are talking about men who, having seen both sides, were (and I do not know that they were necessarily wrong) content to believe that the country they had been born into was especially blessed. That conviction is very marked among the Elizabethans and Jacobeans. It needs stressing because attention to the deeper and finer spirits of the age—to a Walter Ralegh or John Donne—will miss it. Deeper and finer spirits are always pessimists and rarely chauvinists. The convictions I speak of are found widely diffused in popular consciousness, among the aristocracy, the gentry, and the people at large, whether travelers or stay-at-homes. They might dislike one another, trouble one another, and be discontented with one another, but relative to the foreigner, relative to the poor and depressed subjects of supposedly despotic powers, they knew themselves specially favored. The objective truth of the situation is here irrelevant. What matters is not whether life and conditions in this demiparadise really surpassed anything to be found elsewhere, but only what it felt like to live in England in that age, on the eve of colonization. The English thought England was good and elsewhere was inferior. Thus, if they went forth from home it was not because they despaired of life there or dreaded it; with a very few exceptions, it was not even because they were driven thence. Let me repeat that emigration for causes religious was, before the age of Laud, the 1630s, a most uncommon event. The tiny sects that left England for the Netherlands and from there took ship for the New World kept moving on because they could not coexist with anyone. They could not even live together among themselves. As colonizers they were the freaks, not a main force.

Discontent existed, but it did not drive people overseas. Contentment, more widespread and prominent, positively operated against emigration. Why then did the English begin to found more and more colonies in the century after about 1580? This sort of venturing forth to settle in unknown lands is not, after all, an unremarkable thing to do. It requires a special sort of courage, or perhaps of recklessness. You will remember the moon capsule, now to be seen in the Air and Space Museum in Washington. A truly ramshackle construction it appears to be, of no particular shape (because apparently out in space there is no need for proper shapes), all stuck over with bits of foil, like a roasting chicken whose wrapping has come unstuck. And yet men could be found to enter this peculiar container and have themselves shot to the moon. So men boarded their cockleshells to cross the wild Atlantic. The conditions are not very alike: for one thing, we knew more about the surface of the moon when we sent men there than the Elizabethans knew about the hinterland of Chesapeake Bay when they set sail for it. Our moon-men also had a good chance of remaining in touch with base, unlike those voyagers, who were quite on their own once England had disappeared over the horizon. Yet the comparison may help a little to make us understand how those early settlers felt. Admittedly, they thought they knew something about the lands they meant to colonize, for over the years a good many ships had explored those regions and had returned with reports—always graphic and very often highly imaginative ones. Exploring, however, is one thing and settling

113

another; we still have not colonized the moon. Very special inducements, stronger than mere discontent and more lasting than a passion for adventure, were surely needed before people would transfer themselves for good to barely known territories, inhabited by possibly hostile natives and equipped with a certainly hostile environment. (The prospectuses of the day tried to disguise these facts.) Of course, emigrants had before them the example of Spanish success in settling the Indies, but they also had the example of the French who had already failed to settle in Florida. A cool assessment probably would have determined that the risks clearly outweighed the advantages. I therefore think it matters greatly that before ever the Elizabethans thought of America they had already had experience of colonization. They had been trying their hand in Ireland.

Ireland was not an unknown country, and it was not very far away. Perhaps symbolically, one of the earliest English attempts to take part in the great voyaging movement, John Rastell's expedition of 1517, ended up at Waterford and never got further. Really it was Ireland that the English were about to colonize, not the North American continent. So what drove them to settle colonies in Ireland—those plantations of Leix and Offaly in the reign of Queen Mary, of the Desmond lands in Munster in the reign of Queen Elizabeth, of Ulster in the reign of King James? Did those moves represent a great urge to expand, an intention to enlarge the realm of English power and to conquer the world for one small nation? Or were they produced by discontent and persecution at home? Not either of these, I fear: they demonstrated a drive for land and for fortune. What stirred people into these extraordinary activities were the common and acceptable human emotions of greed and the search for greater wealth. Ireland, I may say, as regularly disappointed such hopes as did later colonies.

Insofar as a desire to better oneself represents dissatisfaction with one's present lot, we might conclude that discontent rather than contentment lay behind the colonizing activity. But the term is much too strong and just possibly too noble. The colonists were attracted—deliberately so, in the advertising of the organizers—by promises of riches, not by visions of liberty. And here the expansion of population does play its part, even if contemporaries overestimated its effect, because it reduced a man's chances to improve his lot at home.

Let us remember one essential characteristic in the structure of this society. Where did its economic center of gravity lie? It was a landed society, a society which regarded only land and landed wealth as ultimately acceptable in creating status. True, there was wealth of other kinds. Mercantile and banking fortunes are found in Elizabethan England. Lawyers' incomes—a fact familiar to twentieth-century America—were considerable. There were—another familiar fact—far too many lawyers, busy creating a great deal of law upon which they could live. Money was being made and wealth created in other ways than by landed possessions, but the only form of wealth which could gain you social recognition was land, possession of land. However, the land law of England operated on the principle of primogeniture. By and large, unless you were the eldest son of a landowner, you inherited little or nothing in the way of that status-breeding wealth. You had to seek your own; you had to find land elsewhere. It so happened that down to the 1560s there was an available resource of landed property in England. The confiscation of church lands, from the dissolution of the monasteries onward, and their redistribution because of the crown's need for ready cash had created a very active land market in which many younger sons, cadet branches of gentle and aristocratic families who would normally have been driven out of landed ownership, found it possible to reestablish themselves in that society into which they had been born and whose acceptance they sought. But in the 1560s that supply was cut off as the crown resolved to stop selling. Free gifts in particular ceased totally. It is true that crown lands, though no longer sold, were readily being leased for terms of years, but that (while helping the queen's coffers) could not create the new estates which landless men wanted. You could not found status upon leaseholds, though you could add to your wealth by acquiring them; you needed freehold property before you could gain the position of a landed gentleman, or even of a man of weight in your county. Only freehold, for instance, qualified you for the parliamentary franchise.

Thus, from about the sixties onward, this preferred way of improving yourself was no longer open at home, but there were other lands to which the English crown extended its sway and where so far the possibilities of acquiring real property had not been exhausted. Ireland here quite evidently formed an experimental ground. Compared with the North American continent, Ireland was not empty, though it was rendered a good deal more empty than it should have been by internal strife and the warfare involved in the English reconquest of the semiindependent Irish. Ireland also posed legal problems because it was not "new land," but the lawyers soon developed some ingenious ways of eradicating the native arrangements and acclimatizing landholding in Ireland to English laws and social requirements. These were valuable experiments which could readily be extended into emptier and more extensive lands. In many ways, the expansion overseas, the colonizing activity of this society, can really best be understood by studying what was going on in Ireland from the 1570s to the 1600s. The prehistory of exploration, and of those intrepid voyagers seeking trade or piracy, is by comparison almost irrelevant, except inasmuch as it familiarized people with the notion of oceans and America. Settlement is something quite different; it is not expatriation but an extension of the *patria*, of that region in which the normal existence of the English landed gentleman and the yeoman farmer could be satisfactorily recreated. Here Ireland led the way and set the example; Virginia (in particular) and Maryland soon followed. What confronts us here is not a truly popular movement, a great rush of individuals all somehow taking off for the New World and settling down there; rather we are dealing with organized, controlled, and licensed transfers of the English existence to the American

116

continent. When the organizing agents settled the North American continent, they were not cutting loose or turning their backs on Europe; they were simply finding new areas for the exercise of their entrepreneurial qualities of which they had given sufficient evidence in England and Ireland for years before that. The colonizing activity of the English in the early seventeenth century resulted predominantly from an expansion of that sort of commercial (in this case, land-buying) enterprise for which the northern part of the North American seaboard has become more famous than the southern, but it started in the south. I may add that even those Puritan dissidents who settled Massachusetts and Rhode Island remained firmly in touch with the mother country. Colonization never meant separation, and thus it really testified to an energetic contentment with things English rather than to discontent.

The dominant theme of English colonization in the seventeenth century was that it was English, by license, enterprise, and continued connection, and not American, by conquest and the cutting of ties. If I am right about this, a rather important consequence follows. This conclusion must cast doubt on the conventional view that the ultimate disruption of this first British empire in the War of Independence and the Revolution of 1776 sprang as a natural outcome from the fact that the colonists were essentially freedom-seeking separatists, a bunch of especially inspired (and justly discontented) idealists who wished to be free of the ancient system and its constraints. Those who have seen it that way have, I think, committed the fundamental error of casting back later history upon the earlier. This history of the American Revolution continues to be written (on both sides of the Atlantic) by those who are on its side, as indeed the history of the English Civil War continues to be written by those who are very glad it happened. The historians of the English Civil War forget how very nearly there never was a war. Similarly, historians of the American Revolution tend to forget how large the number of loyalists was who, had they won as they so very nearly did, would certainly have put the black spot

117

on all those rebels who have ever since been sainted founding fathers.

That entrenched explanation of 1776 therefore owes a good deal to a certain notion about the years between 1580 and 1640 or 1650: that colonies were founded by dissent and discontent. Actually, they were founded by enterprise directed from above; by good and solid greed, and by the quite normal expansion of generally accepted attitudes and purposes prevalent in the governing order in the realm of England. That period of activity witnessed an expansion of the English crown, not a separation from it. If later there came, as indeed there did come, a breakdown in relationships, we must not seek its cause in their origins. We must remember that throughout the seventeenth and early eighteenth centuries contact between mother country and colonists was current, constant, and straightforward. There was no question of disruption, none of rebellion. Those colonists, leaders or followers, wanted one main thing from their enterprise: to better themselves by adding to the wealth they had and the wealth they could create for others. Such constraints as they escaped from were the mere accidents of home—shortage of land, too many people, economic distress, some details of the law—and not the essence of England, with which they were well content and which they endeavored to recreate across the ocean. They were seventeenth-century Englishmen, most of whom went to the colonies because a sense of adventure, a willingness to take risks, and hopes of profit made them ready material for those enterprising companies and individuals who were organizing the spread of English settlement throughout the western continent.

NOTES

1. See J. F. D. Shrewsbury, *A History of Bubonic Plague in the British Isles* (Cambridge, 1970), passim.
2. John Aylmer, *A harborowe for faithfull and trewe subiects* ([London,] 1559), Sig. D4v.

WHY THEY CAME

David B. Quinn

There is no easy way in which the question of why individuals and groups came to settle in North America as the earliest European invaders can be answered. For the sixteenth and most of the seventeenth century, it is a matter of looking at individual and collective incentives and propelling forces. Settlement may be understood best in a developmental context: the initial arousing of expectations in Europe (or in the case of Spain, perhaps in Mexico and the Caribbean) led, through various stages of planning, to summer visits for mainly trading purposes, to small-scale experiments in colonization, and finally, through many interim stages, to the creation of new European social and economic groupings across the Atlantic by the exploitation of natural resources in different regions, mainly in eastern North America.

The Americas were already well populated in 1492, and the population of North America is now known to have been appreciably higher than was believed until very recently. It can be said at the beginning that the existence of an aboriginal population and its prior rights to North American land played a surprisingly limited role in the planning of permanent settlement by Europeans. Spanish monarchs, like English and French rulers and many of their subjects, cut and carved North America on paper many times, without more

119

than a passing glance at the existence of an established population. Colonies such as Maryland were to come into existence as the result of private schemes aimed at aggrandizing
individuals or small groups. They induced the ruler to sanc-
tion their plans on the assumption that land could be appro-
priated freely in indefinitely large quantities from those who
had lived there for millennia.

It is true that, in certain circumstances, the existence of
native peoples played a considerable part from the first. While
the offshore and onshore fisheries were carried on for the most
part with little contact with the Indians, fur-trading involved
direct contact, and it grew to be the main channel by which
European products entered North America. In the end the fur
trade greatly influenced Indian society, creating an almost
symbiotic relationship between natives and intruders.[1] In
their settlement plans, Spaniards always assumed that natives,
if they would not work for the settlers, could be pushed out or
killed off unless they could be gradually pacified by missionaries, settled in villages, and made liable for taxation in kind
or in limited labor services. This was the pattern of established Spanish colonies in Florida and New Mexico. But Hernando de Soto had been concerned with Indians only as
beasts of burden and suppliers of foodstuffs, without any regard to their rights, and he was typical of the conquistadores
who entered North America. France assumed that exploration
by Verrazzano gave her rights to settle anywhere along the
eastern North American coast, irrespective of the wishes of the
Indians. The English felt the same, very often without even
invoking "rights" of discovery by John or Sebastian Cabot.
Nonetheless, in early English plans there was usually the expectation that the occupants would cooperate with the intruders by engaging in trade with them, forming a market for
European goods and producing the still largely unknown products of their soil in exchange. Richard Hakluyt was the most
optimistic of the planners as far as trade was concerned. There
were often injunctions in English plans that the natives
should be treated kindly and sometimes that they should be
Christianized and Europeanized, but it was always assumed

that they would not object to great portions of their land being taken from them or that they would be placated by nominal payments for the right to settle in particular tribal areas. These assumptions often rested on theories about the superiority of Europeans over supposedly savage people[2] and on the belief that much of North America was either uninhabited or so sparsely occupied that European settlements would scarcely impinge on existing inhabitants.

The reality, of course, was different. Indians would be swept off the land only by the fortuitous passage to them of epidemic European diseases or by long and savage military campaigns. In practice, early settlers depended on them for instruction on how to grow native food crops and on surpluses of corn and other foodstuffs to help out deficiencies in their own supplies. The Indians in turn came to depend on Europeans for metal goods (which rapidly transformed their cultural status) and for many articles of clothing and equipment. In many areas settlement involved a process of mingling between the two cultures, the extent of which has only recently come to be fully realized. But, except in the fur trade and to a very limited extent in other superficial contacts, this mutual learning process could not be forecast or provided for unless settlement had actually begun, and even then it was imperfectly understood by both native and invader.

This is, of course, only one aspect of a complex development. The main reasons why Europeans thought of settling in North America and did so arose out of problems in their own European societies. In the case of Spain, of course, North America was just another of the vast areas in the west which Spain could invade and settle as and when she chose: the incentives which led Spaniards to North America were marginal to those which led them to the Islands, to Mexico and Peru. For other Europeans, English, French, and Dutch, it was largely social and economic uncertainties in their particular polities which turned their attention to American lands and preoccupied them as they planned to go or even went there. If Indian lands and rights impinged on them in

121

the end, it was secondarily only, and at a comparatively later stage in the process of deciding why they went.

We may remember that when we think of early America, we are dealing with two very different periods. From the discovery (or rediscovery) of America by Columbus down to the early seventeenth century, a substantial number of Europeans thought of going to live in North America, but only a few actually went, and most of these either returned home or died where they had tried to settle. Only a handful of Spaniards remained to live in North America before 1607. Thus the sixteenth century was a period of discussion and experiment only, one in which North America slowly came within the consciousness of English, French, Spanish, and Portugese and which led to exploration, to experiments in settlement and to failures to establish, except in Florida, permanent European colonies. Yet it is an interesting and exciting period, when North America emerged physically, was talked about as a possible outlet for non-Iberian people, and when individuals and groups gradually began to think of going to settle and attempted to do so. The early seventeenth century is different: people came and stayed. We take the existence of North America for granted, but the people who lived in the sixteenth century could not do so; they had to learn gradually (the relatively small number who even heard of it) what it might be like and what possible reasons there might be for moving from the England or France they knew to pioneer a new life for themselves overseas.

One incentive we must face up to at the very beginning: imitation of what was happening elsewhere in the Americas. Europeans became interested in North America because they thought it was or might be like places where Spaniards and Portuguese were settling and becoming rich. Throughout the sixteenth century, thousands were going each year from Spain—officially only from the part of Spain known as Castile, but unofficially from other parts and from Portugal. Small handfuls also went from almost every country in western Europe; we can trace Italians, French, English, Irish, Greeks, and many others who had evaded the Spanish restrictions in some way or another and had joined what was in effect a gold and silver rush to Mexico and Peru. Altogether about 200,000 Europeans, predominantly Castilians, are thought to have settled in Spanish America in the sixteenth century;[3] how many other Spaniards and Portuguese there were is not known, and there were only a few indeed of all the rest. Portuguese, too, went to settle in some numbers in their own colony in Brazil. The whole process contrasts quite sharply with the position in North America.

From the time of Columbus's first letter in 1493, stories and rumors about America had been seeping into Europe. Once Cortés discovered and conquered Mexico, these stories took on many romantic colorings, and the gold and silver which followed in a growing stream as Peru was also found and conquered built up a simple-minded picture among Europeans of a New World full of easily obtained riches, an Eldorado which the Spaniards reserved for their own people, and which they would not allow other Europeans (especially Protestants) to share.[4] This picture was indelibly imprinted as Spanish gold (in reality mainly Spanish silver)[5] became a controversial issue in Europe, as the rivalries of France and Spain and of England and Spain developed into wars on land and at sea. The incentive to non-Spaniards to go to America sprang from this simplified view of the Spanish empire, though it was overlaid by more sophisticated concepts which produced added incentives to go, not just to the Americas, but specifically to North America.

It was only very slowly that any firsthand information about North America became readily available in Europe. Giovanni da Verrazzano, exploring the North American coast for France in 1524, and Jacques Cartier, exploring the St. Lawrence also for France between 1534 and 1536, were the first to give some clear and enthusiastic pictures of both the coastlands and a small part of the interior. Verrazzano was charmed by the trees and flowers and by the apparent fertility of the land as he worked his way from the Carolinas to Maine. Cartier thought the woods and animals of the St. Lawrence area would make it possible for Europeans to prosper there, though he had his doubts after he and a small exploring party stayed at Quebec through the cold Canadian winter in 1535–36. Their accounts only became widely accessible to Europeans when they were published in Italian in Venice by Ramusio in the 1550s.[6] It is surprising how often these accounts were used over the rest of the sixteenth century to describe what North America was like. It was only after another generation (in 1588) that the first directly observed description of part of North America, Thomas Harriot's little book on an area of modern North Carolina and Virginia, appeared to provide something like a true picture of the resources of part of the continent by an Englishman who lived there.[7]

As soon as there was any concrete information, a few men in France and England began to build on it, to turn their eyes toward the part of the America where there were no Spaniards and where they, too, might make their fortunes overseas. The men who advised them at home had to turn to Spanish America for analogies to fill out the very limited materials at their disposal by applying things that were known about the West Indies and Mexico to North America.[8] They were bound, for example, to ask why, if gold and silver were to be found in quantity in Mexico and Peru, they should not also be found in North America? If sugar could be profitably transplanted from southern Europe and the Atlantic islands to the Caribbean and to Brazil, why not to North America also? If Spanish cattle, pigs, and sheep, not to mention horses, could multiply in Hispaniola and Mexico, why not on the mainland to the north?[9] These were only the simplest questions which could and did arise. They were certainly present in the minds of the French who between 1562 and 1565 tried to settle in what are now South Carolina and Florida. The discovery of a certain amount of both gold and silver in native Indian hands seemed to suggest these suppositions were correct. Only the more sophisticated of the colonists discerned that the bullion came from the wrecks of Spainsh ships on those hurricane-infested coasts.[10]

The first real gold rush in North American history took

place on the unlikely shores of Baffin Island in 1577 and 1578, when an attempt to find a route around North America to Asia under Martin Frobisher led to the belief, fostered by inefficient or corrupt mineral experts, that stone brought from Baffin Island was auriferous. A fleet in 1577 and another in 1578 brought some thousands of tons of ore to England to be smelted before it was found that no metal could be extracted from it.[11] After that there was some caution exercised in claiming that North America must inevitably be rich in gold and silver. Yet mineral wealth remained one great incentive of exploring and colonizing expeditions, even though copper, lead, and iron came in as humbler alternatives to gold. Ralph Lane, after a year on Roanoke Island in 1585–86, said that unless a good mine or a passage to the South Sea were found, he could see little hope of an English colony succeeding.[12] John Smith thought he would find gold in the Potomac valley (and indeed there was a little alluvial gold, though he did not discover it).[13] The Calverts hoped there would be mineral riches in Maryland; so did the settlers in New England. The first settlers in Newfoundland in the early seventeenth century found excellent iron ore, but they did not exploit it to any extent;[14] no one successfully worked iron on a commercial scale before the Massachusetts men in the 1640s.

The incentive most often talked about in the sixteenth century, however, was timber, the most widely used natural product in European society, especially among the seagoing peoples of western Europe. They were using up their best oak and other hardwoods and did not have much good coniferous timber at their disposal. For planking and masts they depended very largely on the Baltic countries, which could also supply such products as pitch, tar, resin, hemp, and flax.[15] All observers noted that North America had unlimited timber. Communities that could build houses of wood and make ships and boats were, it was thought, off to a good start; other timber products might profitably be exported. In fact, the first and only product of the short-lived English settlement of 1607–8 on the Kennebec River (Fort St. George) was a stout pinnace of thirty tons burden, the *Virginia*, which was later employed between England and Chesapeake Bay.[16] New England was to get some of its early and much of its later prosperity from building vessels of all sorts. But what had to be learned by hard, backbreaking experience was how much of a problem trees created. Most land suitable for settlement (if it was not on Indian-cleared sites) had to be cut over. Eventually the roots had to come out as well. Slash-and-burn techniques with crops grown between the stumps was a temporary expedient. The labor and cost of transporting timber across the ocean to England proved prohibitive in most cases; Baltic timber remained cheaper. Exceptions were masts (sent from the Kennebec in 1608, from Virginia in 1611) and fine woods like cedar (brought from Roanoke Island in 1585, from New England in 1602, and from Virginia continuously from 1607). Other woods, such as cypress and walnut, followed cedar. Timber, processed for barrel staves or clapboard, could also be marginally profitable; timber in bulk could not.[17]

The idea of using American lumber to stoke furnaces for making iron arose early. This was tried in Virginia from 1608 on, but the bog iron available there was hardly suitable for mass production, while the large-scale ironworks planned in 1620 was aborted by the Indian rising of 1622; samples only appear to have found their way back to England.[18] The same was true of glass, though some glass was made in 1608–9 and in the 1620s.[19] Potash was made successfully, though it never became a major export in the early days; neither did resin nor tar. In the end the greatest value of timber was as a building material, essential for the development of any settlement, and so primarily an internal resource rather than an export crop.

A much wider appeal was made by that most basic of commodities, land. To Europeans in early modern times, land was not only what they lived on but what they lived off, since agriculture was the only major industry. But land was also the only major object of investment. Renting or purchasing land was the equivalent of investing in a business enterprise today, even though colonial trading and settlement companies were also among the first to issue shares publicly for cash. But many of them, notably the Virginia Company between 1606 and 1624, offered as dividends on the shares not money but land, and it was as dividends on cash invested or other consideration given that many of the Virginia settlers after 1617 and until the company expired in 1624 got their land.[20]

Land seemed almost like an abstraction to some of the people who were interested in North America. Sir Humphrey Gilbert began dealing in real estate (or maybe "unreal estate" would be more accurate) in quantity in 1582, when he handed out estates of 30,000 acres or larger to any of his supporters who put up more than one hundred pounds in cash. He got rid of 20 million acres in what we know as New England in this way. He never saw the land himself, and none of the men to whom he sold ever saw any of it either. Gilbert was only the first of many land speculators in North America who have raised money from insufficiently suspicious buyers down to our own day.[21] Landed estates were the dream of the gentry when they did not have land or enough land in England. We know that it was large estates that attracted the shrewder London businessmen to Virginia once land became freely available, and that the shrewdest and hardiest of them laid the foundations of the great plantations there. Maryland, above all, was a land speculation by a section of the English aristocracy and gentry, as the manors that were envisaged and to some extent created there under the paramountcy of the Calverts testify. Even in Massachusetts, where land holdings were to be so much smaller in general than in the south, it is clear that the families who came from England with capital, the means to exploit land, or were able and ambitious, took up sizable holdings for themselves, and that substantial estates in Massachusetts increased as the colony took hold.[22] In the 1630s, when Maryland was being divided, the first attempts to do the same thing were begun on the St. Lawrence. Extensive seigneuries were offered to French settlers who would bring men and women with them to work their holdings (though there the progress of the seigneurial system was to be very slow indeed until after 1663).[23]

Land in North America attracted only a few people who were already great landowners in England (or later, in France), though estates across the Atlantic which could be managed for them in absentia could be added to their European holdings. But the ocean was still too wide for such investment in land to be important in the early seventeenth century. Many of the richest subscribers to the Virginia Company did not take up their landed dividends. Nevertheless, the younger sons of lords and lesser landowners were especially attracted by North American land. Under the legal system by which the eldest son inherited all the landlord's land, the younger sons had to make their way in a profession, in commerce, at court, or by marriage if they were to acquire estates of their own. Many coveted and some obtained land in North America; certainly the attraction of North America for younger sons was widely advertised from the 1580s to the 1620s and even later.[24]

There were many other reasons, too, why persons sprung from the owning and ruling groups in Europe would be enticed to America by hopes of building up holdings there: pressures on them for religious reasons, because they were in debt, or because they had committed some offense for which it was desirable that they should leave their own country. Always such people expected that they would get land, but land where other people would do the work for them or pay them rents and services. They would move from the ruling upper class in the Old World to assume the same status in the New. The Spanish Indies, especially Mexico and Peru, had provided Spanish aristocrats or would-be aristocrats with just this translation. Even where the original inhabitants had been killed off, black slaves could be brought in to produce plantation crops on the new estates. This generally was not the case in North America. North American Indians were not willing to turn themselves into a laboring or even a tenant class for intruding white landlords, though they did so occasionally under coercion.[25] The problem was not obvious so long as the aspiring landlord looked at his potential estate from Europe. It could become critical when he came to

America; thousands of acres were of little value if they remained both virgin and unprofitable.

There were ways of getting round the problem. A few settlers brought their family servants and estate tenants with them to Virginia and Maryland. More usually, indentured laborers were hired, normally through agents who made a business of it; individuals bound themselves into a steady occupation with some hope of land and an independent existence at the end of the period.[26] Later, criminals too might be sent to serve the remainder of their sentence as servile laborers on American land. Finally, blacks could be brought in expensively, first as indentured servants and later as slaves from Africa.[27] By such means, sometimes even including the extreme of the landowner and his family doing some work themselves (which they would never condescend to do in Europe), some great plantation estates were built up in the south, but there were still very few of them by the midseventeenth century. Many of the farms in Virginia and Maryland were small. There were no great plantations farther north; the big farms of Massachusetts were working farms, not estates for gentlemen. Sir Ferdinando Gorges and his friends in Devonshire spent a whole generation trying to evolve some form of manorial estate for themselves and their followers in Maine, but they never succeeded on any substantial scale.[28] In Canada the early seigneurs found it difficult to hold their tenants once they had got them to Canada; there were too many opportunities for a freer and potentially profitable life on the frontier.

Apart from bullion and jewels, Spaniards might make fortunes from Old World crops like sugar or New World products like cochineal; they might learn to produce and export large quantities of hides (leather was, after wood, the most important raw material for the equipment of early modern societies), but English colonies made heavy and unsuccessful weather of trying to find a novel American staple. Oranges and lemons, like sugar, were not suitable crops for Virginia or Maryland. Silkworms, tried repeatedly, did not flourish; they died from insufficient care, or they did not like the mulberry as found in America, or ultimately their culture failed because a pioneer society was not really suited for the specialized task of assembling and spinning the delicate filaments into usable thread.[29]

Tobacco—Trinidad tobacco, *Nicotiana tabacum*—was the savior.[30] When John Rolfe successfully raised a crop at Jamestown in 1612, the Virginia colony had a reason for keeping going. Tobacco was far from being Virginia's only export for some years, but it became the only really profitable one, and the infant colony, after the Virginia Company expired, drew itself by its aid to some degree of prosperity between 1624 and 1640. Maryland might have been founded even without tobacco; it was not intended that it should be grown and certainly not that it should become dominant as it did. But the colony would have found much more difficulty in taking root without it. Monoculture in an export crop always had its dangers—the tobacco market was always vulnerable to merchant pressures, as well as to the vagaries of the seasons and of markets (and in England to governmental interference)—but it made the southern colonies viable exporting communities. For many years one of the main objectives Englishmen had for crossing the ocean was to grow tobacco, even though for a substantial number their actual occupations in America were different. If they had any useful skills or trades at their command, they often carried on with them in their new environment, while learning and developing other skills as planters. This trend arose largely from the dispersed patterns of settlement associated with tobacco cultivation and commerce, which did not encourage the development of towns and certainly not of cities. Farther north, urban life began much earlier; because of the carrying to the New World, most specifically to New England, of patterns of nucleated settlement analogous to those in Europe. Northern craftsmen often did better by continuing their trades in a town rather than becoming farmers, especially if they were specialized ones, like those of jewelers, printers, and booksellers. This fact was early true of Boston, for example, but in smaller townships the basic craftsmen, such as smiths, car-

130

penters, and shoemakers, usually held and worked land as well.

One basic obstacle to all early attempts to plan settlements in North America was the obstinate convictions of Europeans that climate in North America could be equated precisely with climate in western Europe. Since eastern North America has a continental climate dominated by the great land mass that lies behind it, extremes of heat and cold as compared with western maritime Europe were unexpectedly great. The Gulf Stream so moderates the climate of western Europe that the British Isles, for example, have a much more equable climate than eastern North America, equivalent to that of latitudes five or more degrees to the south. It is also now realized there was a little Ice Age in the sixteenth and seventeenth centuries, and that cold winters, bad harvests, and floods in western Europe provided an incentive to leave home, but the first settlers found comparable conditions in North America, whose natural differences were exaggerated by this phenomenon. The decade 1600–1610 saw especially cold winters, as Champlain and the settlers at Jamestown and on the Kennebec were to find to their cost. The double defect in knowledge, difference in climatic zones, and the carry-over of specially severe weather from Europe to America meant that most planning of settlements, when only summer voyages had previously been made to American shores, was very faulty, and that consequently incentives offered to potential colonists were grossly misleading. It was only gradually in the early seventeenth century that this came to be fully understood and fully appreciated, so that the necessary social and economic adjustments made empirically to meet it could be incorporated in the social pattern of a particular area.[31]

So far we have ranged widely and slightly over the more obvious attractions North America had or might have had for Europeans. The incentives, and we might say the impulsion, that affected particular groups ranged over a wide spectrum of possibilities. The Roanoke settlers of 1585 were employees of a syndicate headed by Sir Walter Ralegh; they had

131

little choice about what lay ahead of them. This fact did not prevent many of them from complaining at the indignities of pioneer life, at no soft beds or servants and no gold to spice their future if they stayed. The little group who came in 1587 and were lost were different again. We think that in the main they were craftsmen who wanted to turn themselves into independent farmers and may well have succeeded in doing so, but we do not really know. A handful of radical English Puritans took a look at the Magdalen Islands in the Gulf of St. Lawrence in 1597 with the idea of escaping religious persecution and establishing their little "gathered church" on the basis of a walrus and cod fishery, but they decided in the end that Amsterdam was better.[32] A band of French convicts, placed on Sable Island in 1598 to catch seal and walrus, were supplied annually for several years; when supplies did not come they turned on and killed their jailers and then one another.[33] Only a few desperate men survived and were eventually pardoned. A small party of Frenchmen at Tadoussac on the St. Lawrence lost most of their men from scurvy in 1600–1601, and did not persevere. Cartier's pioneers in 1535–36 were merely on a reconnaissance, but his colonists of 1541–42 wanted to stay, though one winter was too much for them. Roberval's settlers of 1542–43 hoped for farms and furs and a richer life than they had had in Europe, but they, too, were driven off after one Canadian winter. Laudonnière's men in Florida in 1564–65 were mainly an anti-Spanish garrison but hoped to lay foundations for a settlement based on agriculture and gold. Jean Ribault had women and children with him when be brought reinforcements in 1565; they were overrun by the Spaniards and had no opportunity to experiment. Champlain's men in 1604–5 on St. Croix Island also were almost driven out by the extreme cold, but found at Port Royal a place where they could winter fairly safely and carry on a useful but not too profitable fur trade with the Micmac Indians from 1605 to 1607.[34]

It is hard to find a common denominator for these settlers of the pre-1607 period. Some were men who were prepared to go anywhere for pay; a few were sent by force; a few thought of coming to obtain religious freedom. (The Florida colony could have become a refuge for the French Huguenots if it had been allowed to survive.) Many must have thought that land was the one really desirable item and that it could be had easily. Spanish civilian settlers in Florida in the 1560s and 1570s had hopes of becoming free farmers, but all lost their land and stock. The *adelantado*, Pedro Menéndez de Avilés, never realized his plans for a great slave-worked plantation. Soldiers assigned for duty there, their wives and families, a few officials, and a few craftsmen to serve their needs, together with a scattering of missionary friars, made up the population of Spanish Florida after 1576.

Many sixteenth-century immigrants who returned to Europe as failed colonists were henceforth hostile to colonization.[35] Because North America, for one reason or another, did not give them a living, they considered it unhabitable by Europeans. Hundreds of Spaniards, French, and English formed that opinion. The drive to colonize came rather from a few enthusiasts, some of whom had good reasons for their optimism; others had very little except a desire to take part in marginal speculations. These attitudes did not change in the earlier years of the seventeenth century. There were a number of groups of failed colonists who came back to speak against Virginia or Maine or the Maritimes or Canada. But by then the pressure of propaganda and the existence of more mobile capital which rich men were willing to invest in America (after the peace treaties made with Spain, by France in 1598 and England in 1604) made a difference. Rising costs of living and declining resources at home made movement more attractive. The state was taking a greater part in stimulating commerce and so gave more encouragement, if little cash, to overseas developers. North America, like the West Indies and the Spice Islands, became a better field for speculative investment in a variety of new export crops and, later, in tobacco, and so propaganda for colonization became both greater and more effective.

The one area little affected by this change was Florida, a frontier garrison of the Spanish empire. By limiting their aims to maintaining two or three small garrisons, Spain had succeeded in establishing the first permanent roots for Europeans in North America.[36] This early assertion of a military presence was not to be without influence in later colonial experiments.

It was from 1607 on that incentives began to pile up for Englishmen, but it was a long time before North America provided either a good living or cozy subsistence. The colonial theorists kept harping on three advantages.[37] First, North America could supply products to vary and expand English imports; the products that formerly had come from the Iberian peninsula and from Mediterranean Europe (olive oil, wine, and dried fruit, for example) could be produced abundantly in North America, and such exports would profit colonizing companies, replacing the need for European imports and giving settlers a good living. As we saw, all these experiments were failures except, in the end, tobacco, and in the much longer run, rice and cotton.

Second, the North American colonies could supplement commodities which England produced herself but in quantities insufficient for her own needs, or which she could in turn export herself. Fish and timber were the chief of these. Both timber production and fishing did indeed occupy the lives of many of the early settlers—the fishing settlement at Richmond Island, Maine, and the Newfoundland settlements are examples. Although few settlers made fortunes, some did find in them a way not only to provide for their own needs, but also to trade with some profit.[38] Furs and skins lay rather between the first and second categories; they were of some importance to English settlers in Virginia and Maryland, and especially in certain parts of New England (where they provided incentives to expand settlement in, for example, the Connecticut valley), but furs were scarcely enough in themselves to lead people to leave England for America. They occupied a very different role in the seventeenth century for the French and the Dutch.

The third and final major economic advantage to be gained from colonies, it was urged, was freedom from population pressure. This, people were told, was why there was unemployment in England (sturdy beggars, accused of being idlers, were often mainly able-bodied men and women out of work and going from place to place looking for it).[39] The state was urged to encourage emigration to colonies because its burden would thereby be lightened; propaganda was there-fore directed to potential settlers to suggest that overpopula-tion was causing them to become poorer and that they would inevitably be better off in places like North America, where there would be plenty of space for them. Continuing (though less severe) inflation made the population argument more plausible, especially when it was combined with downward pressure on real wages.

Modern economic historians tell us that unless agricul-tural production per head of those employed in it rose appre-ciably, there could be no substantial population rise in gen-eral, or growth in the urban population in particular, without some hardship. Towns, though they were congested, dirty, smelly, and disease-ridden by the lowest of modern stan-dards, were nevertheless expanding. London doubled in size in the sixteenth century and had almost doubled again by the middle of the seventeenth century, though it is true that her growth was exceptionally large. London's growth did encour-age more intensive use of agricultural land in southeast En-gland, but not sufficiently to meet the rise in population. There were also many interesting attempts from 1540 to 1640 to diversify and expand industrial production in the coun-try.[40] Many failed, some succeeded, but cloth export indus-tries, even if the content altered from unfinished to finished goods, remained both dominant and inelastic, often being on the edge of depression. The amount of additional employ-ment provided by new ventures was not nearly enough to take up the population increase of several million within the century.

There was, then, some basis for the argument that En-gland was overpopulated, and certainly the idea that to get out was to get on because there would be less pressure from one's neighbors was to some extent effective. It combined with the more strictly commercial arguments into a fairly attractive set of incentives: land, easily grown or gathered products, easy subsistence when in America, and good profits from an assured market in England. We can see now that North America had the potential for meeting these criteria, but as it existed in the period before white exploitation and as it was to exist in the early stages of white settlement, it could not and did not universally offer these rewards. Good health, good fortune, and hard work might bring them to a few, though only a few, of the early settlers. Most of the rest might well find that the likelihood of death or disease, the sheer hard physical labor of creating a homestead, the power that a handful of men with large holdings of land could exercise over them (so that their working conditions could be as bad as in England) and, finally, the economic hold of English merchants on the prices they got for their produce made many of the alleged incentives look like lies told to the unwary. Optimistic colonists hoped to exploit the land; instead they were frequently exploited themselves.

There were other influential incentives which arose from people's attitudes in matters of politics and religion. Many Englishmen felt unhappy at the rule of the foreign Scottish dynasty after 1603 (as others were to feel unhappy at the rule of a German dynasty after 1714), and neither James I nor Charles I did very much to placate English nationalistic—almost xenophobic—feelings, but it is not clear that this in itself provided any great incentive to emigrate, though some people did go to the Netherlands for this kind of reason. The Stuarts were soon to quarrel with their parliaments, which in the end produced a political crisis and then a revolution. But there is little evidence in the first part of the century that ordinary people cared very much (Parliament was something that concerned the rich, not the common people), though it became so gradually after 1629, when Parliament was in abeyance.[41]

Religion was more important. A considerable number of people in England felt either insecure or unhappy about the religious situation as it affected them and became pessimistic about the possibility of it improving in the way they wished it to improve; these individuals were inclined to leave England for North America so as to have greater opportunities to develop their views on church organization and religious life. On the other hand, it must be remembered that sixteenth-century England was one of the least intolerant countries in Europe. The state demanded a somewhat nominal show of conformity from all its citizens; in peacetime a few appearances at the parish church and the taking of communion once a year would be sufficient. In a worldly society these requirements were much less onerous than the interrogations, threats of death, and frequent executions which hung over Protestants in most Catholic countries and which in a comparable form characterized the few highly integrated Calvinist centers like Geneva. In England nonattendance at church involved fines, though those who went to church irregularly were scarcely troubled. Persistent refusal to attend could lead in the end to confiscatory fines for Catholics (though in the early Stuart period they were enforced only where local judges were vindictive or when there was a real or imagined threat of treason), or even when the right to levy them in a particular area had been leased to a courtier. Catholics were, officially, not allowed to have the services of their priests (who could be executed if identified); unofficially, so long as the priests were kept discreetly disguised as servants or craftsmen, neither they nor their sponsors were systematically persecuted. (After all, the two queens of the period 1603–40 were both Catholics, had private chapels, and could admit to their services the Catholic aristocrats who were in favor at court.) Protestants who refused wholly to conform were more systematically punished, though this depended very much on the local authorities of the established church, but they were harassed rather than threatened with extreme penalties. Unless there was a treason scare (and there were treasonable plots by Catholics), or unless some Protestant extremist gave public utterance to outrageous sentiments (for example, attacked the existence of the Trinity or preached the expropriation of all wealth on religious grounds), no one,

137

except for priests in periods of tension, had the threat of death hanging over him as he might well have done in most parts of the Continent.[42]

But we must recall too that it was a religious age. Very many people considered their religious allegiance and practices their strongest emotional and intellectual tie to their country. It seemed to an increasing number of Protestants that England had never had a Protestant Reformation. The state church was reputably Christian, but it was neutral or negative about things which many people felt vitally needed reform. The Church of England was the nearest of the Protestant churches to the Lutherans in its organization and relationship to the civil powers, but it lacked the evangelical touch which Luther had given to his church, the emphasis on personal contact with God and with the Scriptures. The Church of England was inclined to leave enthusiasm out; the Book of Common Prayer and the two sacraments were enough; preaching was a matter of putting forward state policies or academic theology, but not of inspiring people to heights of religious emotion. The label "Puritan," when it is extended to all those people who wished to introduce a Protestant reformation into the Church of England, is somewhat misleading. Nor were there, until Arminianism attracted the Stuarts and their bishops, mainly after 1620, any deep theological divisions. Most of the bishops and clergy accepted the basic Calvinist tenets on predestination, even if they did not apply them to society quite as Jean Calvin or John Knox had done. Reducing the status and power of the bishops and reducing or eliminating the remaining traditional Catholic symbols and liturgical practices were topics constantly being brought up in Parliament between 1604 and 1629 (as they had been under Elizabeth) and rejected by the crown. But the biggest desire was for an emotional drive, based on sermons and on Bible readings and interpretations; many of the local clergy shared this desire, but not the hierarchy or the crown. It was despair at attaining reformation and the intense desire to carry it out themselves which played an important—some would say vital—part in leading to the first mass emigration of Englishmen to North America, that to New England. Between 1630 and 1640 some 20,000 people left England to settle there.[43]

The opening of the Bible to individual interpretation had produced, quite early in the Reformation period, radical groups who hung closely together, perhaps because of some common tenet (adult baptism was one such), or because they felt that they could live a holy, God-fearing life only inside the bounds of a single, untrammeled congregation, "a gathered church" separated from all others. Such Protestants were self-regarding; they were rarely evangelical once they had built up their little congregation; they disliked state churches of any sort; they wanted to be left alone; they insisted on being so. Of all recalcitrants, it was they whom Queen Elizabeth disliked most. The Brownists were persecuted from 1593 onwards, while James I's clergy stepped up the persecution after 1604. The little group who pathetically turned to ideas of a colony on the Magdalen Islands in 1597 (whom I have called "the first Pilgrims") formed a congregation which had been imprisoned wholesale between 1593 and 1597. When walrus and cod in the Gulf of St. Lawrence were found to be monopolized by hostile Catholic fishermen, they turned instead to tolerant Dutch Amsterdam, where as "the Ancient Church" they were an inspiration to the congregation that migrated to Leiden from Scrooby in Lincolnshire in 1607.[44] They were moved in turn in 1618 to consider emigrating to America, and some eventually did so in 1620 to form the Pilgrim colony of New Plymouth. A village community, centered on the religious services and experiences which were its core and raison d'être, with fishing and fur-trading as incidental economic necessities, produced the first surviving, self-sustaining settlement in New England. The prime incentive was the desire for religious community in a free environment. They never quite achieved it, but on the whole their incentive proved powerful enough for them to succeed in doing most of what they wanted.

A good deal of what was put forward in the sixteenth century in the way of incentives to go to North America was based on guesswork or promotional exaggeration arising from brief summertime visits. Only a few people caught on relatively fast to the realities of the situation in the seventeenth century. The hopes of most of the people who went to Virginia in the first ten years were not realized. Very often they died, or went home, or continued barely to exist. Yet a few tough old hands, we now know, did survive from the beginning and probably made a better living than they would have done in England, but they were very few indeed.[45] They paved the way for the cleverer people who followed. By the time individuals could acquire land in quantity in Virginia, the way to use it profitably by exploiting white indentured labor (or, appreciably later, black labor) to cultivate tobacco had been learned. E. S. Morgan has shown how, within half-a-dozen years from the time land was thrown open to speculation by the Virginia Company, many large holdings had been grabbed by a handful of resourceful operators who proved able to grow crops for their own use, to sell them inside the colony, and to get most of the profitable new export crop, tobacco, into their own hands. However, they never blocked the opportunities for small landholders to establish themselves, even if they had to reach out into frontier territory to do so. The later arrivals, if they were also resourceful, efficient, and, maybe, unscrupulous could make a living and perhaps a success out of moving to Virginia. Of course this possibility attracted others to imitate the great land accumulators, but only a very small proportion succeeded in doing so. The prospects for mixed agriculture and animal husbandry were enough, for example, to lead to the foundation of Maryland. The Calverts and their friends and dependents hoped to be more comfortable in their religion by settling in Maryland, but they also expected to make their fortunes as successful planters, just as a handful of Virginians were doing; they were quite prepared to exploit other settlers in order to do so, whether they were Catholic or Protestant, white or, eventually, black. They had sincere doubts about the fluctuating and speculative nature of the tobacco market, though they soon overcame them in practice.

The incentives to success in New England were somewhat different. In the early seventeenth century, the idea slowly caught on that this was a place where there was less chance of encountering strange diseases, and where crops could be grown and animals kept on lines almost identical with those of England itself, but supplemented by indigenous cultivars such as maize. Realistic views of climate, of soils, and of the possible means of settling the land began to develop after John Smith's productive tour of 1614 (when he contributed the considerable incentive of renaming the old Norumbega "New England"). The Pilgrim colony's attractions for nonseparatist Englishmen were not great, but the publications that emerged from it made clear a way of life not substantially differing from that of England was perfectly feasible there.[46] Several other small fishing settlements farther north on Massachusetts Bay in the 1620s provided adequate evidence that this was so.

One major asset was that, though there were plenty of trees, there were also considerable tracts of open land. Partly this was a matter of geology, but also of historical accident, since so much Indian-cleared land lay vacant. Conservatively minded Englishmen who did not wish to risk the novelties of Virginia (or of the West Indian islands, which were just being opened for settlement) could regard New England as a sensible place in which to invest their capital and to which to emigrate. The reforming Protestants of East Anglia and other places in the south and southeast of England, despairing of church reform and of the curbing of the monarchy, could therefore regard New England as providing sufficient incentives to move. These considerations produced the great migration to Massachusetts Bay in 1630 and after.

Many of the emigrants had property in England and intended to exchange it for property in America; they could afford to bring their whole families and to pay passages for servants who would remain with them for some years. The Winthrops and their friends did not think in terms of great plantation estates, but of substantial English farms or modest estates. This was what most of the leaders soon acquired,

141

though some were to add to them very considerably a little later on.[47] Moreover, coming over in large groups and from a fairly wide social spectrum, they were able to envisage an urban element in the colony almost from the beginning.[48] John Winthrop's "City upon a Hill" was not the vision which created Boston, but it was one element in its emergence. The settlers were not going to spread themselves widely, but rather create village nuclei and move outward slowly from such of them as offered the best opportunities. They were people who brought a good deal of capital equipment with them, including tools, furniture and books; some of them were able to leave part of their resources in money, land, or credit behind them in England and send for necessities and luxuries to help them adjust more comfortably to the new setting.

However, almost everybody seems to have worked hard enough in the early days (the Protestant work ethic, much derided as a concept by professional historians today, had something in it). They were not distracted by frivolities, even if their puritanism was not as narrow as it used to be depicted. On the whole, the greatest incentive New England provided lay in the fact that the anticipations of the earliest settlers—apart from those of the Pilgrims—had been found to be realistic. People could live traditional English-style lives, however reformed in religion and social habits, in New England, and increasing numbers of people wished to try to do so. Indeed, the New England township tended to become more a traditional community than more rapidly changing England itself. The stream of emigrants slowed after 1635 only because of restraints imposed in England, but a sympathetic Parliament, on the eve of the Civil War, was willing to send out children to be cared for and to swell Puritan households.

Virginia's attractions, mostly the wealth or at least the competence to be derived from tobacco, also acted as incentives to bring out more people once the initial trials of the Virginia Company period has passed. But Virginia's high death rates and the fear of Indian attacks such as that of 1622 were partial disincentives. Virginia's population in the years

1624–40 rose more slowly than New England's, though it did grow substantially—from little more than one thousand to eight or perhaps ten thousand, though remaining chronically short of women.[49] Maryland too did not have any spectacular population growth to record, even though a minority of complete families with their dependents did go there. New England attracted something like twenty thousand people in its first six years; Maryland, as the latest research has shown, had not many more than four hundred survivors at the end of the same period.[50]

It will, I think, be clear that, as North America emerged from myth to reality, so the incentives for leaving Europe to attempt a new kind of life there became more specific and realistic. As they did so, they attracted more people to follow the pioneers. Success, or the news of success, in settling in North America was the best incentive of all. Of course, there were many who were unlucky or who were more optimistic about their prospects than they might have been if they had not believed too much of the propaganda which circulated in England. Most of those who came were sensible, clear-sighted, and prepared to work hard to improve their positions above those they had had in England, either in respect to religious and political freedom or to economic circumstance. But they could not wholly escape from England; social and class differences crossed the Atlantic, and the majority of settlers became subject in some measure to those who started with initial advantages of birth, wealth, or education. Yet it became clear also that there were opportunities in America for men and women with the initiative to seize them. In Virginia most of the aristocrats gave place to more efficient entrepreneurs. Most of all, it gradually became apparent that North America, if not the Eldorado or Utopia of some of the early pamphleteers, was a good place for Europeans to live. They could push aside the original inhabitants, the Indians, and turn their lands into extensions of England and France; many of them could, by about 1640, already consider that North America was not after all so different from their homeland. It was an extension of Europe rather than a wholly new world.

143

NOTES

1. Our understanding of this relationship has been greatly assisted by a recent work revealing the symbiotic relationship between the Indians and animal life, a relationship gradually weakened and broken down in the period after white contact. See Calvin Martin, *Keepers of the Game: Indian-Animal Relationships and the Fur Trade* (Berkeley, 1980), esp. chaps. 1, 2.

2. The most recent work on this topic, Bernard W. Sheehan, *Savagism and Civility* (Cambridge, 1980), however, appears to go much too far in asserting that this attitude, though it was prevalent, was solely responsible for Englishmen's actions toward Indians in Virginia from 1607 to 1622.

3. A figure of 200,000 persons who came to, survived in, and remained in the Spanish empire in the sixteenth century is given by Woodrow Borah, "The Mixing of Populations," in Fredi Chiapelli, ed., *First Images of America*, 2 vols. (Berkeley, 1976), 2:709.

4. The many-sided impact of the Americas on the rest of the world in the century after 1492 can best be traced in Chiapelli, ed., *First Images*.

5. There are impressive figures in Pierre Chaunu, *Conquête et exploitation des nouveaux mondes* (Paris, 1969).

6. Diffused from materials in G. B. Ramusio, *Navigationi et viaggi*, 3 vols. (Venice, 1550–59), the North American materials being first published in vol. 3 in 1556. For Verrazzano, see D. B. Quinn, ed., *New American World: A Documentary History of North America to 1612*, 5 vols. (New York, 1979), 1:281; for Cartier and Roberval, see H. P. Biggar, ed., *The Voyages of Jacques Cartier* (Ottawa, 1924). Richard Hakluyt was the main diffusing agent in England, for whose works see D. B. Quinn, ed., *The Hakluyt Handbook*, 2 vols. (London, 1974).

7. *A brief and true report of Virginia* (London, 1588).

8. There are lists of commodities known or supposed to exist in Richard Hakluyt, *Divers voyages touching the discoverie of America* (London, 1582); George Peckham, *A true reporte* (London, 1583), in Quinn, ed., *New American World*, 3:51–52; and in John Brereton, *The discoverie of the north part of Virginia* (London, 1602).

9. See Quinn, ed., *New American World*, 3:143, 285, and the drawings of West Indian fruits and other items made by John White

144

on the Virginia voyage of 1585, in Paul Hulton and D. B. Quinn, *The American Drawings of John White,* 2 vols. (London and Chapel Hill, N.C., 1964).

10. See the evidence for this in Paul Hulton, ed., *The Work of Jacques Le Moyne,* 2 vols. (London, 1977).

11. Vilhjalmur Stefansson and Eloise McCaskill, eds., *The Three Voyages of Martin Frobisher,* 2 vols. (London, 1938).

12. Quinn, ed., *New American World,* 3:300.

13. This was at Great Falls, on the Maryland side of the river. It was worked out in the late nineteenth century (personal information from Dr. P. L. Barbour).

14. See Quinn, ed., *New American World,* 4:34–35; Gillian T. Cell, *English Enterprise in Newfoundland* (Toronto, 1969), pp. 59, 63, 72 (for Bell Island).

15. Replacement of Baltic commodities by North American ones was constantly advocated between 1583 and 1612 (Quinn, ed., *New American World,* 3:28, 64, 75, 76, 174; 4:34; 5:242, 351).

16. Ibid., 3:425–26; 5:286, 293, 296.

17. Ibid., 3:442–54, passim; 5:357.

18. Ibid., 5:358; Edmund S. Morgan, *American Slavery—American Freedom* (New York, 1975), pp. 45, 85, 87, 95, 100, 109; Susan M. Kingsbury, ed., *Records of the Virginia Company of London,* 4 vols. (Washington, D.C., 1906–35), 3:612–13; 4:11–12, 23.

19. Jean C. Harrington, *A Tryal of Glasse* (Richmond, Va., 1972).

20. See Morgan, *American Freedom—American Slavery,* pp. 93–97.

21. See D. B. Quinn, ed., *The Voyages and Colonising Enterprises of Sir Humphrey Gilbert,* 2 vols. (London, 1940). vol. 2; D. B. Quinn and Neil M. Cheshire, eds., *The New Found Land of Stephen Parmenius* (Toronto, 1972); and documents (still unclassified) of June 1582, acquired in 1978 by the Public Archives of Canada, Ottawa.

22. Most grants were made to proprietors of towns, who were expected to dispose of at least fifty acres to each household in the township. But there were major grants, if not so great as in Virginia and Maryland, to the principal investors. Sylvia D. Fries, *The Urban Idea in Colonial America* (Philadelphia, 1977), p. 47, says that "the basis was laid for a landed gentry in New England" between 1630 and 1640. Of grants to individuals in this decade, she traced sixty ranging from fifty to fifteen hundred acres.

23. See Richard C. Harris, *The Seigneurial System in Early Canada* (Madison, Wis., and Quebec, 1968).

24. See, for example, Quinn, ed., *New American World*, 3:31, 104 ("the planting of younger brethren").

25. D. B. Quinn, *North America from Earliest Discovery to First Settlements* (New York, 1977), pp. 104, 123, 162, 167, 211, 222, 293, 306; Elizabeth A. H. John, *Storms Brewed in Other Men's Worlds* (College Station, Tex., 1975), pp. 58–97, passim.

26. Abbot E. Smith, *Colonists in Bondage* (Chapel Hill, N.C., 1947) remains the standard authority.

27. Wesley F. Craven, *White, Red, and Black* (New York, 1977), pp. 77–85, examines the exiguous evidence.

28. James P. Baxter, *Sir Ferdinando Gorges and His Province of Maine*, 3 vols. (Boston, 1890) and Robert E. Moody, ed., *Letters of Thomas Gorges, 1640–1643* (Portland, Maine, 1978) contain all the documentary materials.

29. Charles E. Hatch, "Mulberry Trees and Silkworms in Virginia," *Virginia Magazine of History and Biography* 65 (1967) :1–61.

30. There is, of course, a large literature on tobacco. The essentials are made clear in Morgan, *American Freedom—American Slavery*, but see Richard S. Dunn, "Masters, Servants, and Slaves in the Colonial Chesapeake and the Caribbean" in this volume.

31. There is little realistic material on climate, though there is some in John Smith's works. Edward Hayes attempted to account for the weather in Newfoundland (Quinn, ed., *New American World*, 4:32–33), while weather diaries were kept in Newfoundland 1611–13 (that for 1612–13 is printed ibid., pp. 157–78). See also Geoffrey Parker, *Europe in Crisis, 1598–1648* (London, 1979), pp. 17–22.

32. See D. B. Quinn, *England and the Discovery of America* (New York, 1974), pp. 316–33.

33. Gustave Lanctot, *Réalisations françaises de Cartier à Montcalm* (Montreal, 1951), pp. 29–50.

34. D. B. Quinn, "The Preliminaries to New France. Site Selection for the Fur Trade by the French, 1604–1608," *Wirtschaftskräfte und Wirtschaftswege. Festschrift für Hermann Kellenbenz,* 4 vols. (Nuremberg, 1979), 4:1–25; see also Samuel Eliot Morison, *Samuel de Champlain* (Boston, 1974) and Douglas R. McManis, *A Historical Geography of New England* (New York, 1975).

35. See Thomas Harriot on failed English colonists in Quinn, ed.,

New American World, 3:140–41; for Spanish ones, ibid., 2:590–92; 5:15–17.

36. For San Agustín ca. 1612, see Antonio Vásquez de Espinosa, *The Compendium and Description of the West Indies* (Washington, D.C., 1947), pp. 106–9.
37. This theme is developed in D. B. Quinn, "Renaissance Influences in English Colonization," *Transactions of the Royal Historical Society,* ser. 5, 25 (1976) :73–93.
38. See Harold A. Innis, *The Fur Trade in Canada,* 2d ed. (Toronto, 1956); Quinn, *North America from Earliest Discovery,* pp. 533–36; Van Cleaf Bachman, *Peltries or Plantations* (Baltimore, 1970); Martin, *Keepers of the Game.*
39. Edward Hayes and Richard Hakluyt thought England's population was too great to avoid unemployment, but Hakluyt considered that developing colonies would encourage home employment (Quinn, ed., *New American World,* 3:82, 84, 127).
40. Joan Thirsk, *Economic Policy and Projects: The Development of a Consumer Society in Early Modern England* (Oxford, 1978) shows how population growth from about 2.25 million in the 1520s to 3.5 million in 1603, and a rise continuing to 1640 (p. 159), was partly met by the development of consumer industries in England, but even so there were incentives to go elsewhere to look for economic prosperity or to avoid abject poverty (cf. Andrew B. Appleby, *Famine in Tudor and Stuart England* [Stanford, Calif., 1978], for the subsistence crises of the period). There was a push-pull relationship among emigration, external commerce, and internal development (see Carole Shammas, "English Commercial Development and American Colonization, 1560–1620," in K. R. Andrews, H. P. Canny, and P. E. H. Hair, eds., *The Westward Enterprise* [Detroit, 1979], pp. 151–74).
41. The range of public and private grievances is best developed in Carl Bridenbaugh, *Vexed and Troubled Englishmen, 1590–1640,* rev. ed. (New York, 1976).
42. Ibid., pp. 374–410, gives a good conspectus.
43. There is still no agreed figure for pre-1640 emigration to New England. Russell Menard, "Immigrants and Their Increase," in Aubrey C. Land, Lois Green Carr, and Edward C. Papenfuse, eds., *Land, Society, and Politics in Early Maryland* (Baltimore, 1977), p. 109, accepts the traditional figure of 21,200 in Edward Johnson, *Wonder-Working Providence,* ed. J. Franklin Jameson

(New York, 1910), p. 58, while McManis, *Colonial New England,*
pp. 41–81, in the course of an extended demographic analysis, is
prepared to accept the United States Census Bureau, *Historical
Statistics of the United States* (Washington, D.C., 1960), p. 2,
which has 13,700, a figure almost certainly too low. Twenty thousand has been taken as a reasonable approximation.
44. Quinn, *England and the Discovery of America,* pp. 316–33.
45. Compare Irene W. D. Hecht, "The Virginia Muster of 1624/5 as a
Source for Demographic History," *William and Mary Quarterly*
30 (1973):65–92, and Morgan, *American Slavery—American
Freedom,* pp. 115, 395–97. Though information is incomplete, it
is clear that a minority survived from the period of crisis, 1607–
12, until 1625.
46. George D. Langdon, Jr., *Pilgrim Colony* (New Haven, Conn.,
1966) gives the basic information.
47. See n. 22, above.
48. Rutman, *Winthrop's Boston* (1965) and Fries, *Urban Idea* give
convincing evidence of the urban impulse, but Rutman tends to
stress that most settlers came from nucleated villages in England
and not from developed urban communities. Hugh Kearney,
"The Problem of Perspective in the History of Colonial Society,"
in Andrews, Canny, and Hair, eds., *Westward Enterprise,* pp.
290–302, suggests that these township communities tended to
become fossilized into rigid traditional patterns.
49. Craven, *White, Red, and Black,* p. 33, is inclined to be skeptical
about population figures, preferring the reported 2,500 of 1630
to the estimated 3,000 of 1628, but he reports the 15,000 estimate of 1649 as acceptable, though with some caution. Menard,
"Immigrants and Their Increase," pp. 88–110, prefers a figure
of ca. 11,000 for 1640 which seems somewhat high.
50. Estimates of Maryland's population growth from 1634 to 1650
have tended to be considerably reduced as the result of recent
research. Lois G. Carr and Lorena S. Walsh, "The Planter's
Wife," *William and Mary Quarterly* 34 (1977) :543 and Menard,
"Immigrants and Their Increase" give the latest views on the
subject.

RELUCTANT COLONISTS:
THE ENGLISH CATHOLICS
CONFRONT THE ATLANTIC

John Bossy

The state of the English Catholic community, when the *Ark* and the *Dove* set sail from the Isle of Wight on 22 November 1633, was one in which good and bad fortune were mixed. It was not a very large body of people—by my reckoning, something like 50,000–60,000 people. It contained, however, a considerable proportion of the landowning classes and was served by about 600 priests. Its relations with English society in general were governed by the extremely firm hold which Protestant opinions had obtained upon the population of England during the previous century; by a feeling that Catholics had taken the enemy's side in England's conflict with Spain at the close of the sixteenth century, and if given another chance would do so again; and by a system of legal restraint embodied in a series of anti-Catholic statutes which often sounded worse than they were, but which were serious enough. In principle, being a Catholic involved people in severe financial penalties, exclusion from most official positions, and difficulties of various kinds; for Catholic priests, it was a treasonable act to appear upon English soil, entailing, upon conviction, a particularly nasty kind of death.

But the actual situation was not quite as it appeared.

King Charles I, who had been on the throne for eight years, was a man who felt a certain respect, a certain degree of esthetic and political approbation, for Catholicism in general, and who had a Catholic wife. Their court and immediate entourage were notorious for the number of men and women with Catholic opinions, openly or secretly professed, who were to be found there; the king's administration, which included some of them, had devoted itself to the task of making practical arrangements with Catholic subjects which amounted to de facto toleration of the private practice of Catholicism, given assurances of political reliability and some contribution to the king's finances. More generally, it had become evident over the previous century that English political, ecclesiastical, and social institutions were not designed to extirpate a form of Christianity practiced by a significant section of the landowning class (or indeed of any class). Moreover, they were not designed to prevent such a community from growing to the extent that otherwise responsible members of the landowning class felt it necessary to the maintenance and security of their own persuasion that it should. They did not prevent, for example, a Catholic landowner from having his children educated in his own faith, or from ensuring, by the normal operation of the labor market, that this could be shared by servants and others who lived in his house; or even, to an extent which was more debatable, from influencing the beliefs of those who held or worked on his land, or who depended upon him in some way. They were not designed, finally, to prevent him, in spite of the most explicit and formidable statutes to the contrary, from retaining, for himself and others to whom he might feel entitled to make them available, the spiritual, sacramental, and instructional services of a Catholic priest of his own choosing. Since, therefore, the presence of Catholic priests in England was de facto accepted, there was also de facto acceptance of the fact that these priests would possess such forms of government, organization, and financial resources as were necessary to ensure their continuing performance of their duties. These forms were well established among the various kinds of priests who worked in England, notably among the secular clergy, the Jesuits and the Benedictines. On the financial side, it was well established in practice that bodies of clergy were entitled to own such property as they might be endowed with by their flocks, though the arrangements for holding it would naturally include a complicated set of trusts, designed not so much to conceal their purpose as to maintain the fiction that nothing of the kind was occurring.

Within these conditions, the English Catholic community had in fact been modestly expanding since the days of Queen Elizabeth. The fact had been observed with alarm by many Protestant Englishmen, and—as long as Parliament was sitting, which in 1633 it had not been for four years or so—by their representatives in the House of Commons, but there was little they could do about it. Nor was their assumption correct that the only reason popery persisted in England was that King Charles showed a deplorably sympathetic attitude toward it, as was to be evident a decade or so later, when the type of royal government which prevailed in 1633, and then the monarchy itself, were in fact dismantled. The English Catholic community proved to be little affected by the temporary disappearance of monarchy from the English constitution, and indeed there proved to be not a few Catholics who found a kingless constitution more convenient for them than a monarchy.

One advantage which vexed and troubled Englishmen possessed in the reign of Charles I was that it was possible for them to seek a solution for their vexations on the shores of North America. The feelings of English Protestants about the state of their country had recently inspired the settlements at Plymouth and Massachusetts Bay; their creation was relevant to the arrival of a modest number of English Catholics at the mouth of the Potomac. I do not mean to say that Catholics, for whom the government of Charles I was not necessarily more ideal than it was for Protestants, were simply inspired by imitation to go and do likewise, though they clearly were. I mean that the existence of an English Catholic community had become a *fait accompli,* but in circumstances which were likely

151

to make Catholics of average enterprise and ambition feel that their condition was a frustrating one. The point is true in two separate ways; both of which were relevant to the settlement of Maryland, and I propose to consider them separately.

The first concerns the Catholic clergy. The English Catholic community, such as it was in the 1630s, was the result of an enterprise of missionary priests which had been launched some sixty years before. As such, it was an effect of one of the features of the Roman Catholic church of the Counter-Reformation period which most distinguished it from the pre-Reformation church, and to a fair extent distinguished it from the Protestant churches of the sixteenth and seventeenth centuries: its commitment to the spiritual virtues of the life of action, and in particular to wide-ranging missionary enterprises in both the New and the Old worlds. This commitment had been most clearly exemplified in the career of Saint Ignatius of Loyola and in the Society of Jesus which he founded. The mission launched in the 1570s to recover England for Catholicism had not been a Jesuit creation, but from an early date Jesuit influences had been important and active in it, notably in the person of Robert Parsons, who had been himself a missioner in England in 1580–81, and who continued for the next thirty years to play a dominating role in its affairs.

Parsons was a pretty radical activist. "The things that a man hath to believe," he wrote in the *Book of Resolution*, a work of advice on the Christian life widely read in the seventeenth century among both English Catholics and English Protestants, "are much fewer, than the things he hath to do."[1] Parsons, an Oxford don by profession, was one of a considerable group of Elizabethan clergymen who had found the Church of England inadequate to fulfill the vocation of a spiritually active ministry. In consequence they had gone abroad, many of them to join the Society of Jesus. Before the English mission was organized, these men were to be found working as Jesuits in various parts of the world: in Portuguese settlements in India and Brazil, in central and eastern Europe, in Scandinavia, and in Ireland. Parsons himself would have liked to have been employed in such an enterprise, the farther flung the better, and he would probably have been more successful overseas than he was in the English mission, which did not necessarily bring out the best in him. When he drew up a plan for a reconstruction of the English church which would follow a Catholic restoration, he did not give himself the role of supervising affairs at home, but of running a grand seaborne mission which, following the routes of English trade, would carry a revitalized, English-inspired, activist Catholicism to Scandinavia, the Baltic, and Russia, as well as Scotland. Thus, when he was invited in 1605 to consider a scheme for settling an English Catholic colony in North America, he expressed, at the age of over sixty, a personal enthusaism which I am sure was genuine. "The intention of converting those people [the Indians] liketh me so well . . . as for that onely I would desire my self to go on the jorney shuttinge my eyes to all other difficulties if it were possible to obtayne it but for that we do not deal here [on this earth] for ourselves only, but for others also, we must look to all the necessary circumstances."[2] Those circumstances, for various reasons, did not seem to him to be propitious for the venture. Looking back over Parsons's career between his arrival with Edmund Campion in England in 1580 and his death in 1610, it is possible to feel that England was ultimately a frustrating field for the exercise of talents whose natural employment lay elsewhere; the imaginary picture of so intelligent, vigorous, serious, and inventive a man let loose as a missionary in the virgin lands of North America has, for me, enormous fascination.

That was not the way things worked out, and yet the missionary vocation embodied in Robert Parsons did, by various channels, ultimately find a modest degree of fulfillment on the shores of the Potomac. As he organized the transcontinental operations in support of the English mission during the 1580s and 1590s, he brought it closely in touch with the world of merchants and seamen who carried on their business on the Atlantic edge of Europe, from Amsterdam to Seville, from London to Cork. His involvement in this world, with the passage of priests, the transfer of money, and the clandestine import of books, was something which he obviously enjoyed. He ceased to be directly concerned with it on being moved to Rome in 1597, but by then he had got the English Catholic community a footing in the Atlantic world which the indigenous geography and sociology of the group would not have provided. How much effect this involvement may have had in solidifying or extending Catholic belief and practice in the English mercantile and maritime milieu is a matter of speculation. I think it had some effect, though perhaps a temporary one.

However, even if mercantile opportunities were a principal factor in inspiring the English in general to penetrate the continent of North America in the seventeenth century, I do not think they played a large part in the calculations of English Catholics. Though English soldiers who had served in the Spanish army needed to find an occupation after the Anglo-Spanish peace of 1604, it proved easier to recruit them for the Gunpowder Plot than for a crossing of the Atlantic. The lure of the western hemisphere, such as it was, remained in the first place an invitation to the missionary ambitions of the English Catholic clergy, and to the extent that Parsons's enterprise was to issue in the settlement of Maryland, it was through his work in the training of priests, which had led to the foundation of seminaries and clerical establishments in or convenient to the ports of the European Atlantic coast. He himself was responsible for the colleges founded at Valladolid and Seville, the focus of the Spanish Atlantic trade, in the 1590s, and for the Jesuit school at Saint-Omer in the Netherlands; in the 1630s the secular clergy followed suit with a seminary at Lisbon. Out of this Atlantic environment came the priests who ultimately turned up in Maryland. Andrew White came via Valladolid to Seville in the 1590s, and we may perhaps suppose that before his return to the English mission in 1604 the Atlantic had presented itself to him as something more than the means of passage between Seville and London. Thomas Copley came from an émigré family which had wandered around the Atlantic coast of Europe

before he was born in Madrid in 1595. Francis Fitzherbert
had worked in Madeira before coming to Maryland. The English Jesuit mission to North America, like the first successful
Jesuit mission to Ireland from 1596 onward, was a natural
effect of the cultivation of this milieu.

One way and another, then, the Catholic mission in England grew out of and encouraged wider missionary ambitions. The difficulty was that, increasingly as the seventeenth
century wore on, it failed to satisfy them. Although the mission was still an expanding field until the middle of the seventeenth century, its expansion was distinctly limited, governed both by the terms of the unwritten relationship
between the English Catholic gentry and the king's government and by the natural wishes of the gentry themselves.
They were free to practice their religion in private and to
persuade to it those who might come within their private
sphere of influence, provided they did nothing which might
tend to upset the state or the Church of England. Their concern over the limitations thus imposed on them became particularly acute after the Gunpowder Plot, which, like the future Maryland enterprise, was the work of English Catholics
with Jesuit connections. The effect was to turn missionary
priests into chaplains of the gentry. Furthermore, missionary
leaders like Parsons had tended to view the mission as a step
toward a radical reconstruction of English society that would
put every existing social and political institution in the country to the test of its utility for the glory of God, which had
alarmed the Catholic gentry exceedingly and had made Parsons in particular especially unpopular among them until the
end of his life. In order to overcome this unpopularity, the
Jesuits from the early seventeenth century had taken the line
that it was necessary to go out of their way to placate the
gentry.

The growth of the Jesuit mission in England after 1600,
then, a growth completed in 1623 when the English segment
of the Society of Jesus was erected into a separate province
with Richard Blount as provincial, had gone along with a
progressive subordination to the gentry's wishes, and a limi-

tation of the Jesuit role to the rather narrow conditions which they were anxious to impose. In itself this operation was a success. But it entailed, as one may read in contemporary descriptions of their situation by Jesuits working in England, a considerable degree of corporate self-discipline, and it left unsatisfied the thirst for grand spiritual adventures—and even for the opportunities of traveling to faraway places—which had caused many of them to join the society in the first place. In short, as the reign of James I passed into that of Charles I, it was natural that some of the English Catholic clergy, notably the Jesuits, should get restless and look for something more exciting, particularly as the news of the adventures of the French Jesuits in North America began to get about Europe. There was also, as it happened, a growing number of priests who were surplus to requirements and would be available to work elsewhere; in addition, there was a difficulty about the quite considerable funds which the policy of accommodation wih the gentry had brought the Jesuits, but which they had trouble putting to effective use in England. Many of these problems, as well as others which I shall be considering later, emerge from a petition to the Jesuit General made by the English Jesuit Nathaniel Southwell in Rome at the feast of Saint Ignatius in 1634. He asks to be sent on the mission to the Indies, east or west, wherever there is greater need.

> Now the reasons which impel me to this are chiefly the following: first because this always comes up before my mind . . . as the most perfect oblation of all and the greatest sacrifice of myself which I can offer in this life to the Lord . . . ; and likewise a most complete act of self-abnegation, since it is a separation in fact from all things that are dear to me in this life, without any hope of ever seeing them again; and so it is morally a kind of death suffered for Christ. Secondly, because, though the mission of England is certainly one of great merit, on account of the perils of imprisonment and death which confront one there, nevertheless that vineyard is not so destitute of workmen as some parts of India are; and this appears by the mission which, in point of fact, our Fathers are now fitting out from England for the

156

northern parts of America. Besides, since I feel a very strong inclination of nature towards England as toward my native country, friends, etc., I have held this propensity in suspicion, doubting whether it came from God, and not rather from nature. So I have never yet ventured to ask for the mission to England; though, on the other hand, I am not so averse to it but that, if holy obedience bade me, I should be ready to go thither.... May it please your Paternity to consider the whole matter, and to determine as shall seem best in the Lord. I shall hope that good Jesus will incline you to my desires for his greater glory and the closer imitation of Him in what is hard to nature, and for the greater security of my salvation in eternity.[3]

One final element in the clerical situation of English Catholics around the close of the reign of James I is relevant. Since the last years of the reign of Elizabeth, the priests of the English mission had been in a state of endemic dispute about questions of ecclesiastical order and organization. The main question was whether the form of authority to obtain among them should be a traditional one, with bishops and a hierarchy, or not. By around 1620 the dispute had become a fairly simple one between the secular clergy, who wanted episcopal government, and the religious orders, notably the Jesuits and the Benedictines, who did not. There were selfish interests involved, but there was also a fundamental issue of principle. On the whole, the religious orders agreed with the Catholic gentry, who did not want episcopal government in a traditional form, either. Between 1625 and 1631 the question had come to a head during the residence in England of Richard Smith, bishop of Chalcedon *in partibus,* who had finally been defeated in the attempt to establish an episcopal regime. At a time when prospects in America seemed to be opening up, it was natural for both parties to see it as a field for visible achievements which would help to vindicate their cause.

So much, I think, for the clerical side. If there are any general reflections to make at this point, they would point to the predominance of cultural and ideological factors in English Catholic interest in North America over economic or

157

demographic ones, though perhaps also to some kind of Weberian view of the interaction of intramundane ascetics with the entire complex of human activities on which this interaction depends if it is to express itself in visible action. As for the lay side, one should distinguish between the motives which might lead one to want to organize a colonial enterprise and those which might make one want to become a settler oneself. In the second respect, it seems exceptionally clear that English Catholics simply did not want to move out of England. In the 1580s, when the legal repression of Catholicism in England was becoming severe, two Catholic gentlemen developed a scheme to take up a patent of colonization and make a settlement on the New England coast which would in fact be a refuge for Catholics; the history of the idea has recently been written by David Quinn.[4] The main reason why the idea failed to materialize does not seem to have been that Queen Elizabeth's government opposed it; indeed, even so strict a Protestant as Sir Francis Walsingham (perhaps, indeed, because he was so strict a Protestant) seems to have thought it quite a good idea. The real problem, it seems to me, was that Catholics did not want to go. According to Parsons, they viewed the project as a disguised form of forcible transportation—an "exportation to a barbarous country"—and as a kind of cowardly flight for which Protestants would sneer at them. The idea, he says, "became presently most odious to the Catholic party."[5] This tells us a good deal about the Catholic frame of mind, at least among the gentry; for men of honor, it was a dishonorable thing to consider; for men with a heavy stake in their country, deeply embedded in its civilization, it was a brutal uprooting from which they flinched with atavistic instinct.

The fact that no such proposal was, so far as we know, made during the last two decades of Queen Elizabeth's reign, when Catholics were often really being persecuted, says a great deal for the strength of these instincts, and I do not think they got much weaker during the seventeenth century. It would, of course, be natural to suppose that Catholics from the poorer classes, having neither honor nor property to

158

lose, would be less affected by such considerations. Parsons rather supposed it, and so presumably did Tristram Winslade, author or conveyor of the proposal of 1605, who alleged that he could produce a thousand "husbandmen, labourers and craftsmen" for it.[6] Probably in some theoretical sense the men existed—he could have hoped to do so, though the history of Maryland suggests some doubt. Parsons was also probably correct to suggest that in such matters Catholics would be guided by their betters, and that a rejection of the idea by the gentry would entail its rejection by the entire community. It seems pretty clear that here we are touching on some fundamental differences of psychology which distinguished English Catholics from at least some contemporary Protestants. Beyond questions of property and honor, lay Catholics seem to have identified their religious beliefs and practices with the persons, places, and objects which formed their daily environment in a way which could not be quite the same in the more transcendental form of Christianity promoted by the Reformation. A community which invested so much of its emotional capital in rituals concerned with eating, in the construction of human relations by the performance of sacramental acts, in its duties towards the dead, in the holiness of particular places, and perhaps in some vague sense of the country itself was not psychologically well adapted for transplanting itself across the Atlantic. Its allegiances did not draw it toward some ideal state of affairs embodying the radical sovereignty of God which could, if no prospect offered of erecting it in England's green and pleasant land, be created from scratch in the wilderness.

I do not suggest that no Catholics felt this way: after all, Thomas More's *Utopia* offered some kind of model. Clearly Parsons had such feelings and he wrote down his vision in his *Memorial for the reformation of England.*[7] But Parsons was a priest, and it seems to me that at this time conceptions of some ideal Christian society were, among Catholics, a clerical prerogative and somehow presupposed the segregation from common human experience which priestly ordination or the religious life provided. We have seen this sense of

159

segregation from the normal, of doing violence to one's instincts, in Nathaniel Southwell's reflections on the prospect of going to America. You may note that my argument presupposes that the religious frame of mind of English Catholics in the early seventeenth century was still very traditional, and that is certainly an oversimplification. At least since the 1570s, they had been exposed to influences which must have tended to transfer the weight of their religious emotions away from the environmental aspects of Catholic practice of which I have spoken, and toward experiences more individual and interior, comparatively desocialized, which would make leaving England easier. If they all had, let us say, Saint Ignatius's *Spiritual Exercises* (as he set them out) and absorbed his teaching totally into their systems, they would have been more inclined toward the prospect of transplanting themselves to the New World. The fact that they did not then seem to have been so inclined suggests that they were still by 1630 more traditionally minded than one had supposed. My impression is that a change in their general mentality—a conversion, if you like, from a traditionalist to a modernist view of the world—did occur, but that it was not anything like complete until perhaps fifty years after the occasion had passed for them to launch as a substantial body into a colonial venture.

What of that opportunity, and the position of the colonial entrepreneur rather than of the reluctant colonist? George Calvert was a client of Robert Cecil, earl of Salisbury, and was making a promising career for himself on the English political scene during the reign of James I. From 1619 he was one of the secretaries of state, and as such he became a partisan in the great political issue of the end of the reign, the proposed marriage between Prince Charles and the king of Spain's daughter. The marriage did not come off, partly because the Thirty Years' War broke out. Calvert was in favor of the match, and in pursuit of it he seems to have made contacts in Catholic circles which ended in his conversion and the marriage of his son and heir to Anne Arundell, the daughter of a Catholic nobleman, Thomas, Lord Arundell of

Wardour. He resigned his secretaryship, an action which the failure of the Spanish marriage probably made inevitable, but did not fall into disgrace. On the contrary, he received an Irish peerage and very favorable consideration in the grant of patents for colonization in North America, which had become objects of competition among the more enterprising members of the English aristocracy. Entrepreneurial activity of this kind, one may add, was not uncommon among the Catholic gentry and aristocracy of the period. Calvert's father-in-law had been connected with the abortive scheme of 1605 and had sent out a small expedition to New England; other Catholic gentlemen, with whom Calvert was shortly to be connected in internal Catholic affairs, were prominent in various business activities, as, for example, in the development of the iron industry in the West Midlands. This type of activity was partly a consequence of their exclusion from political careers and partly of the court contacts which enabled them to acquire such lucrative and unpopular privileges as the monopoly of soap.

Calvert had acquired a charter to settle part of Newfoundland in 1623, visited it in 1627, and settled there in 1628. He spent the winter there, found it too cold, and returned to England by way of Virginia late in 1629, where he then began negotiating to have his rights transferred to part of Virginia. The king and the privy council proved agreeable, but the arrangements were not completed until after his death in 1632. They were carried out by his son Cecilius: the *Ark* and the *Dove*, which had left London sometime in September 1633 and Cowes on 22 November, arrived at St. Clement's Island in the Potomac on 25 March 1634. Ironically, the colony was named after the French queen whose arrival in England Calvert had done his best to prevent, and it would have been called "Mariana" had not Calvert pointed out to the king that this was "the name of a Jesuit that wrote against monarchy."[8]

When the two ships set sail, they carried with them seventeen Catholic gentlemen and something less than ten times as many "servants," most of them Protestants, at least at the time of departure, though some became Catholics subsequently. It also carried two Jesuit priests, Andrew White and John Altham, and a Jesuit lay brother or odd-job man. Among the gentry on board, all seem to have been from families associated with the Jesuits; so were the other Catholics who invested in but did not go on the voyage. The Jesuits also provided some thirty of the servants, and it looks as if a large proportion of the investment involved had come either from the funds of the Jesuits themselves or from lay men and women whom, as their spiritual advisers, they had persuaded to contribute. It was, in short, not just a Catholic venture, but a specifically Jesuit one. This fact is partly explained by the ideological factors mentioned above, and partly by the schism which had occurred in the Catholic community since the first Lord Baltimore's conversion, and by the part he had played in that schism. Baltimore had taken two priests on his Newfoundland voyage in 1628 who seem to have been hostile to the Jesuits; since then, however, he had come out as one of the foremost among the Catholic gentry in opposition to Richard Smith and the episcopal pretensions of the secular clergy, and he had been largely responsible for getting Smith run out of the country.

Thus Calvert had two reasons for collaborating with the Jesuits. First, they had missionary ambitions which might make it easier to attract them from England than the secular clergy, who saw themselves essentially as the heirs of the English medieval church. Second, they disliked claims for Catholic episcopal authority in England. On the other hand, the Jesuits' sense of and need for an active missionary role was not one which, as a rule, commended itself to English Catholic gentlemen, and in resisting it they were used to playing one sector of the clergy off against the other, as Baltimore's son tried at one point to do in Maryland.

It looks as if it was in the course of pursuing their common campaign against Catholic episcopacy in England that Baltimore and Richard Blount, the Jesuit provincial, had met; and at this point, sometime in 1629, Baltimore seems to have raised the proposition that he and the Jesuits might collabo-

rate in his colonial enterprise. Calvert was interested in getting the kind of support in men and money which the Jesuits
and their influence could give him; Blount was interested in
a possible refuge for English Jesuits if their campaign against
Bishop Smith should fail, as well as in the missionary prospects, both among the settlers and the Indians, which might
offer. It looks very much as if a deal was struck whereby
Baltimore traded his support of the Jesuits against Smith for
their support of investment in his colony. Each of them, I
think, was rather wary of the other, which explains some of
the difficulties which arose on the American side of the Atlantic between the Jesuits and Baltimore's son Leonard. Both
their common interests and the things which were likely to
divide them appear in the terms of the colony's original
charter, which reflect the conflicts among contemporary English Catholics. The relevant terms were these. First, the proprietor had absolute freedom to erect churches in the territory and absolute patronage of them. Here the terms reflect
the successful assertion by the Catholic gentry of their control of the clergy. Second, the Statutes of Mortmain were not
to apply; it was to be possible to make grants of property to
ecclesiastical bodies and persons without getting a royal license for it. The point was evidently put in by Blount or
White, who had failed to persuade Calvert to support the
priests himself, and subsequently retracted by Calvert's son.
Third, the colony was to make no provision of maintenance
for an established clergy, and there was to be no ecclesiastical jurisdiction or spiritual courts. Here both Calvert and
Blount were expressing a common interest in excluding from
the colony the kind of traditional church structure which
Richard Smith had been trying to erect in England; they
were perhaps fortunate in getting a seal on their charter before William Laud's translation to the see of Canterbury. No
English penal laws, or laws including discrimination against
Catholics, were to apply, but in a supplementary instruction
from the second Lord Baltimore (which arrived on board just
before the *Ark* and the *Dove* set sail), it was required that the
exercise of Catholicism in the colony be private, not public,

or rather "as private as may be"; that Protestants were not to be abused or discriminated against; and that everybody was to take an oath of allegiance to the king.[9] These instructions no doubt reflected the anxieties of Charles I about public opinion in England, but they also generally conformed with the Catholic gentry's view.

In such ways the original ecclesiastical constitution of Maryland, which like the venture itself represented a conjunction of the interests of Lord Baltimore, the provincial of the English Jesuits, and King Charles I, was also a kind of encapsulated model of the situation of the English Catholic community as it stood on the day the enterprise set sail. In some respects the situation was precarious, as the events of the next decade or so, on both sides of the Atlantic, were to demonstrate; in others, it was built to last, and if it survives until 1984 will have done so, on both sides of the Atlantic, for 350 years.

NOTES

1. Robert Parsons, *The first booke of the Christian exercises appertayning to resolution* ([Rouen], 1582), p. 6.
2. D. B. Quinn, ed., *New American World: A Documentary History of North America to 1612*, 5 vols. (New York, 1979), 3:364–65; Thomas Hughes, S.J., *History of the society of Jesus in North America*, 3 vols. in 4 (London and New York, 1907–17), *Text*, vol. 1 (1907), p. 5.
3. Ibid., pp. 271ff.
4. "The English Catholics and America, 1581–1633," in D. B. Quinn, *England and the Discovery of America, 1481–1620* (New York, 1974), pp. 364–97.
5. As n. 2, above.
6. As n. 2, above.
7. Edward Gee, ed., *The Jesuit's memorial* (London, 1690).
8. Hughes, *History of the Society of Jesus, Text*, 1:234.
9. Document dated 15 November 1633 in *The Calvert Papers, Number One*, Maryland Historical Society Fund Publication no. 28 (Baltimore, 1889), pp. 131–40.

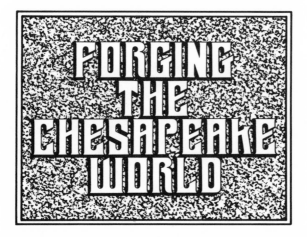

THE LORDS BALTIMORE
AND THE COLONIZATION
OF MARYLAND

Russell R. Menard and Lois Green Carr

I. THE VOYAGE FROM ENGLAND

It was 22 November 1633. The Pilgrims were bracing for their fourteenth New England winter. The new colony at Massachusetts Bay had survived its third year in good condition. In the Virginia colony, first settled over twenty-five years before, disease still brought early death to many, but there was peace and a reasonably orderly life after early troubles, and while the tobacco boom was over, a good living could be obtained. On this morning the first Maryland colonists were assembled on the ship *Ark* and the pinnace *Dove*, anchored at Cowes, England. They were little concerned at the moment with facts about those who had colonized before

An earlier version of this paper was published as Lois Green Carr, Russell R. Menard, and Louis Peddicord, *Maryland at the Beginning* (Annapolis, Md.: Maryland Department of Economic and Community Development for the St. Mary's City Commission, 1978). This revised and expanded version incorporates a substantial part of the original by permission of the department, which retains all rights in the original and any future versions of the pamphlet.

them. They were doubtless consumed with just one thought: the danger of the voyage to the New World and of the life that awaited them in the wilderness.

These 130 to 140 settlers and adventurers were a mixed lot from all walks of seventeenth-century English life. Seventeen were gentlemen who were investing in the enterprise. They were paying the way of the others, who for a while would work for them as servants. A handful of women were aboard, but there is no record of any small children. Most or all of the gentlemen were Roman Catholics; the servants were largely Protestant. Lord Baltimore, the proprietor—that is, the owner of the Maryland grant—was not among the leaders. He had hoped to go, but he had to stay in England to defend the charter that gave him the right to settle a colony in Maryland. He sent a younger brother, Leonard Calvert, as commander of this first expedition.

The *Ark* and the *Dove* had originally been scheduled to leave England by mid-August of 1633, but Lord Baltimore's opponents had caused a delay of several months. His enemies, so he claimed, had "defamed the business all they could both publicly and privately, to over throw it."[1] They had nearly succeeded. King Charles I's privy council had seriously considered revoking the Maryland charter. Not until 3 July 1633 had Lord Baltimore been reasonably certain that he would not lose it altogether.

The departure for Maryland had been scheduled for mid-September, then early October; finally the two ships sailed down the Thames in mid-October. Vessels carrying passengers from London were required to call at Gravesend at the mouth of the Thames so that those leaving the country could take the Oath of Allegiance to the crown as was now required (the stricter imposition of the Oath of Supremacy, which few Catholics would take, had been abandoned).[2] Finally, by 27 October, 128 persons aboard the *Ark* and the *Dove* had taken the oath. The two ships sailed on to Cowes in the Isle of Wight, where it is likely that the three Jesuits who accompanied the first expedition came on board (since it was wise to keep them out of sight of royal officials), and perhaps some other Catholics who found it convenient to do so. The final count of passengers may have been 131 or perhaps a handful more.

Like other seventeenth-century vessels, Lord Baltimore's ship must have been cramped and uncomfortable during the four-month voyage to Maryland. If any passengers had cabins, they were the gentlemen investors. The rest of the men and the few women were confined for the most part to the lower deck of the *Ark*. Although she was a large vessel for her day, of perhaps 350 "tuns burthen," this was a space no more than 90 to 110 feet long and 30 to 40 feet wide at its widest point. Here all slept, ate, and lived side-by-side, with no privacy for the entire voyage. Water-soaked bedding, monotonous food, and the close quarters of so many travelers in a confined space probably made the journey across the Atlantic an ordeal for many of the passengers. But most survived. All had come equipped for new life in America. The advice given to those who would adventure to a New World colony was that supplies be taken to last a year, and the Calvert expedition seems to have been careful to do so. In 1635, Lord Baltimore published a promotional pamphlet that listed what was needed. If Leonard Calvert followed such instructions, quantities of meal, oatmeal, salt, peas, oil, jugs of vinegar, and some sugar, spice, and dried fruit were laid in for each settler before the ships left. Clothing, tools, guns, bullets, fishing lines and nets, and seeds to sow in Maryland soil were also included. For the voyage itself, ships' biscuit and beer were the usual fare, with a little dried meat and cheese. The gentlemen investors no doubt supplied themselves with extras—wines, conserves, pickled meats, lemons, and probably even some live chickens.

Storms and pirates threatened every voyage across the North Atlantic, and passengers nearly always found occasion to pray for God's help. The *Ark* and the *Dove* did not escape. Father Andrew White, a Jesuit priest on board the *Ark*, has left a vivid account of the voyage.[3] During the first days after departing from Cowes, the ships encountered dangerous weather. The first night a calm forced the two vessels to anchor in a nearby harbor. But a strong wind arose and drove another ship upon the *Dove,* which at fifty tons was much the smaller of the two vessels, forcing the *Dove* to cut her anchor and take to sea. The captain of the *Ark* felt that he had no choice but to follow. If the *Dove* sailed on alone, the risk of disaster was high. Turkish pirates might even seize her. So the captain threw off his lines and sailed into the treacherous open sea.

For some days after this inauspicious beginning, the ships had good winds and fair sailing. But on 25 November a fierce winter storm struck, and for an entire night both ships seemed on the verge of foundering. The *Dove* hung distress lights from her mast as a signal to the *Ark* that she was in danger of sinking. When morning came, the smaller ship was nowhere to be seen. Passengers on the *Ark* assumed that the sister ship had been lost. The *Ark* sailed on with great diffi- culty, and on 29 November she encountered a storm so se- vere that it split the mainsail from top to bottom. The master bound up the helm and the *Ark,* in the words of Father White, "left without saile or government to the windes and waves ... floated like a dish till God was pleased to take pitie on her."[4] Luckily, this was the last bad weather.

Five weeks later, after a pirate scare, the *Ark* reached Barbados, a small island in the West Indies where there was already an English colony. Here Leonard Calvert laid in a supply of seed for Indian corn, which did not grow in Eng- land. And here, to the joy of all, the *Dove* reappeared. She had survived the storm by turning back to an English harbor and waiting for better weather. She had been able to accom- pany another ship, eventually overtaking the *Ark* after cross- ing the full breadth of the ocean. The two ships then moved off to another nearby island off the West Indies before finally turning northward up the East Coast of North America.

The next stop was Virginia. Leonard Calvert delivered letters from Charles I to the governor, John Harvey, and the Maryland leaders spent several days meeting with trappers and traders, seeking advice about where to settle. The *Ark* and the *Dove* then sailed up the Chesapeake Bay and into the Potomac River.

The colonists' first landing within Maryland waters was

170

on about 5 March at St. Clement's Island, a small outcropping in the Potomac. "There by the overturning of a shallop we had almost lost our mades which we brought along," Father White relates. "The linnen they went to wash was much of it lost, which is noe small matter in these parts." The Indians were in terror of the *Ark*, a "Canow as bigg as an Island," and "great fires were made by night all over the Country" to spread the alarm.[5] The first order of business was to pacify the Indians.

Leaving the *Ark* behind, Leonard Calvert set off in the *Dove* to find and meet with the Indian "emperor." Accompanying him and his men was Captain Henry Fleet, a Virginia fur trader who offered assistance, although several leaders of the expedition suspected him of warning the Maryland Indians that the new settlers were intent upon war. The party sailed up the Potomac and won an interview with the chief of the native Piscataways, an Algonquian tribe. Captain Fleet, who had dealt with the Indians regularly, helped interpret for Governor Calvert and acted as intermediary in the preliminary negotiations for a peaceful settlement on Indian lands. The Indian chief was wary, but he evidently thought the English might provide protection against the hostile Susquehannocks to the north and the even more dangerous Iroquois "Senecas" or "Sinniquos," who from time to time conducted raids. He granted Calvert permission to settle where he would. The governor and his group then returned down the Potomac to rejoin the expedition anchored off St. Clement's Island. On 25 March 1634, the Jesuit priests offered a mass of thanksgiving on the island—the first mass said within the new colony of Maryland. The day is still celebrated as Maryland Day.

Governor Calvert, with his men and Captain Fleet, immediately embarked on another short voyage of exploration, this time sailing back down the Potomac River to a site known to Captain Fleet. Located very near the mouth of the Potomac was a broad and deep river curving north. Calvert, after naming the river St. George's (it was later renamed the St. Mary's River), sailed about six miles upstream toward a

171

small Yaocomico village. The Yaocomicos, a peaceful farming and hunting tribal group, had settled a village within view of the river some years before. They were already planning to abandon the site because of their fear of the Susquehannocks. Bartering with a supply of hatchets, hoes, and cloth, Calvert was able to strike a bargain whereby the Indians would surrender half of their village site immediately to the settlers and pass on the other half over the coming year. Thus it happened on 27 March 1634, after four months at sea and more than two weeks of exploration up and down the Potomac River, Maryland's first official settlement expedition had found a home. The *Ark* and the *Dove* arrived three days later.

The settlers began at once to construct a storehouse and a guardhouse; they then unloaded the ships and moved ashore. According to accounts of the participants, they fired cannons, flew flags and banners, and staged a full-dress ceremony in honor of the occasion. The Maryland party took possession of the land in the name of the king, Charles I, and the Lord Baltimore, Cecilius Calvert. Leonard Calvert immediately named the place "Saint Maries," or, as we prefer, St. Mary's, in honor of Henrietta Maria, queen of England, and of the Virgin.[6] For some sixty-one years thereafter, St. Mary's was the capital of Maryland. It was never to become a real town, remaining more a settlement of convenience, which all too soon was relegated to a position of little importance. Nevertheless, at the time, this broad, rolling stretch of verdant land fronting on the St. Mary's River seemed to the debarking colonists to be the promised land of the New World.

How did the settlers begin the arduous task of hewing a patch of civilization from the Maryland wilderness? An answer must begin with a look at the Calvert plan to establish a New World colony.

II. THE CALVERT VISION

George Calvert, the first Lord Baltimore, brought more than twenty years of experience with colonies and colonizers to the Maryland enterprise. The son of a Catholic Yorkshire gentleman of small means, he had made a major success as an official of the English crown until he foundered in the mid-1620s because of his support for a pro-Spanish policy, which was followed by his conversion, or reconversion, to the Roman Catholic religion. Over his office-holding years his location in London and his immersion in affairs of state had exposed him to a variety of opportunities to invest in colonizing ventures, and the profits of his offices had given him the means. At first he had probably aimed primarily at easy profits. As early as 1609 he had invested twenty-five pounds in the Virginia Company, and a few months later he had begun a series of profitable investments in the East India Company. By 1620 he had begun to participate more actively in colonizing enterprise. That year he purchased an interest in part of Newfoundland, and in 1621 he financed a fishing settlement at Ferryland on the Avalon peninsula. The following year he joined the Council for New England and began plans—never completed—to take up a large grant in New Albion on the coast of Maine. He was also developing estates in Ireland on lands granted to him, beginning in 1619, in County Longford, which had recently been seized from its Irish inhabitants and opened to English settlement. These Irish grants eventually came to 5,000 acres, part of them in County Wexford.[7] All these colonizing adventures of the early 1620s involved George Calvert in schemes for establishing settlements outside England that left their mark on his plans for Maryland.

There were several basic similarities in all these early projects. All relied on attracting men with the necessary capital and capacity for leadership by means of large land grants and through offers of special status and political power. These leaders were to bring in settlers who would develop the land as servants or as tenants. By this means the traditional structure of English society could be transplanted to regions which had hitherto not been settled or were being resettled. As an official of the crown, Calvert had become familiar with plans for settling Englishmen in Ireland which were based on these or comparable principles. He was encouraged to put them in practice there when, in 1625, he was created baron of Baltimore in the Irish peerage, which was being enlarged to induce Englishmen and Scotsmen with capital to participate in Irish settlement. He supported similar schemes as a member of the Council for New England. In the early 1620s, the council sought changes in its charter to allow it to make grants in which rights to subinfeudate and to establish manorial courts would be included. The council also hoped to acquire the power to grant titles of honor. Calvert saw to it that the charter for his Newfoundland colony, Avalon, contained both these elements.

Avalon was Calvert's main colonizing venture before he undertook to settle Maryland. In 1621 he sent a small group of men and women, who were followed by others the next year. They built a small fleet of fishing boats and added the production of salt for curing fish to their activities. Encouraged by the reports they sent him, Calvert decided to ask the crown to grant him a charter that would give him complete jurisdiction over his colony. This he obtained in 1623. It was the direct ancestor of the charter he obtained for Maryland in 1632 and served as a model for a number of other proprietary grants.

In the middle 1620s, a crisis in both Calvert's career and his personal life caused him to turn more to colonization. His strong support for the Spanish marriage project made his position at court more and more untenable after the collapse of the marriage negotiations. Early in 1625 he resigned his secretaryship, although he was simultaneously created baron of Baltimore in part compensation. He then announced his adhesion to the Roman Catholic church and, in consequence, could no longer take the Oath of Supremacy, which denied the temporal power of the papacy. The result was his exclusion from Charles I's privy council and an end to his career as a royal official. He could then devote himself to colonizing projects, though with the gradual infusion into them of a religious as well as an economic objective.

The new Lord Baltimore turned his attentions to Newfoundland. A visit to Avalon in 1627 was followed by the development of a full-scale plantation at Ferryland in 1628, where he, his wife and children, his servants, and his planters barely survived a severe winter. He wrote to Charles I that Newfoundland, where "my house hath beene an hospital all this wynter, of 100 persons, 50 sick at a time, myself being one and nyne to ten of them dyed," was not the place for him; he desired a grant of land in Virginia, with all his Avalon privileges, instead.[8] With some of his settlers and his wife, he sailed for the Chesapeake, arriving in Virginia in October 1629, but he was repulsed by the planters because he would not take the Oath of Supremacy and was not wanted. He returned to England to press for a grant from the King, preferably south of the James River. But this area had already been assigned to Sir Robert Heath as "Carolana." Virginia planters, London tobacco merchants, and former members of the Virginia Company combined to oppose any concession to Calvert. Finally Charles made him a grant in the northern Chesapeake. Opposition to this continued, and George Calvert died on 15 April 1632 before achieving victory. He handed on most of his estate and his vision of the colony to his eldest son, Cecilius. The young second Lord Baltimore successfully guided the charter forward so that it passed the Great Seal on 30 June 1632.

The charter for Maryland was in large part identical with the one granted for Avalon.[9] Both granted regal powers, enabling the proprietor to declare war, raise a militia, pass laws with the assent of an assembly of freemen, establish courts of justice, punish and pardon, and appoint all government officials. He was authorized to regulate trade, impose taxes and customs duties, and incorporate cities. He could also create honors and titles, so long as they did not duplicate those of England. The proprietor's subjects were guaranteed the rights of Englishmen, and all laws were to conform as much as possible to those of England. But no specific right of appeal to the crown was mentioned. Lord Baltimore was to be the ruler of his colony.

Some changes from the Avalon charter appear in the Maryland patent, and one represented a considerable concession. It altered the terms of Calvert's tenure from knight service, which could carry heavy feudal burdens, to free and common socage, a tenure that carried minimal obligations. Other new language merely made explicit powers implied in the Avalon charter via its famous "bishop of Durham" clause. A new section expressly permitted the Maryland proprietor to make land grants that would be held of him, not the crown, and allowed him to erect manors, with rights to hold courts baron and view of frankpledge. Both powers were essential to Calvert's plan of settlement. Taken together, these changes made the Maryland charter stronger than its predecessor. It gave the Calverts the safety of fully stated rights in a charter that put few limits on proprietary authority, yet no longer required compensatory payments for the extraordinary powers it granted.

George Calvert's vision of Maryland was now matured and ready to be made actual by his son. It was rooted in what had become traditional in English colonization. First, colonists of means and status were to be attracted to Maryland by offering any who would transport sufficient numbers of settlers manorial estates, powerful offices, and noble titles. Such men were to form the core of a New World gentry and provide the leadership required to establish a well-ordered community in the wilderness. This part of the plan was familiar to men acquainted with past promotions. A second part Calvert had developed after his conversion to Roman Catholicism in the mid-1620s. He and his son were determined to make Maryland a refuge for Catholic Englishmen, who in England could not practice their religion without violating the law, and whose belief in papal supremacy was considered treasonous by many Englishmen. The idea of a religious refuge in the New World was not itself new. By 1632 English Protestant dissenters had established two successful colonies in New England. Nor was this the first time that the idea of a Catholic refuge had been proposed. The possibility had been considered as early as 1569, when Sir Thomas Gerard—two members of whose family played a significant role in the founding of Maryland—had proposed an English Cath-

176

olic plantation in Ireland. In George Calvert and his son the idea of a Catholic refuge found champions with sufficient ability, energy, resources, and experience to make such a vision a reality on the shores of the Chesapeake.

Colonization required heavy investment, and the first Lord Baltimore had already put much of his fortune into the abortive Avalon colony. Armed with his new charter, the second Lord Baltimore and first proprietor of Maryland set out to attract wealthy English gentlemen to his colony, out of financial necessity as well as ideological conviction. He proposed to make liberal grants of land in return for a small yearly quitrent. His first "Conditions of Plantation," drawn up a year or more before the first expedition, offered favorable terms, especially to large investors.[10] Men willing to participate were to be granted 2,000 acres of land for every five men between the ages of sixteen and fifty brought into the province—that is, 400 acres per man. If an investor brought in fewer than five men he could claim 100 acres per man. The estimated cost of transporting and supplying a servant was twenty pounds; hence the cost to the large investor was less than five pence per acre. The first adventurers were also told that they would be assured ten acres of town land for each person they transported to Maryland. Cecilius planned a city, and this offer of land within it to the first adventurers was seen as a particularly advantageous inducement. The projected city was to serve Maryland as the center of commerce and seat of government. The second Lord Baltimore undoubtedly expected that, as the colony grew, the value of the town land would increase rapidly. Landowners could then turn a profit by leasing or selling lots to a growing town population. Judging from the numbers who took up town land and paid rent on it, many early investors shared his expectation.

The most distinctive feature of Lord Baltimore's land policy was his offer of special privileges to substantial investors in the colony's future. Anyone transporting enough men to receive a grant of at least 1,000 acres (later, 3,000 acres) could have the tract erected into a manor, with the right to

177

hold courts and with all other privileges usually attached to a manor in England. Potential lords of manors were also offered the possibility of provincial office, titles of honor, and "no small share in the profits of trade."[11] From the start of the Maryland venture, the plan of "raising some nobility," a proposal central to the ventures that had attracted George Calvert, was a primary recruiting device.

Cecilius Calvert expected that political leaders in the new colony would be drawn from the ranks of these adventurer investors. He foresaw that their control of large blocks of land, together with their partnership roles in the colony's trade, would enable them to dominate the provincial economy. The lords of the manors, he hoped, would form a core of trusted lieutenants through whom he could direct the colony's economy and government. In theory, at least, their dependence on Calvert for land and status would guarantee their loyalty; their wealth and the prestige of their new titles would ensure the deference and dependence of more ordinary settlers. The manor was intended to become a central institution in the life of the province, both as an instrument for social control and as a focal point for community loyalties.

In this manner, Cecilius Calvert hoped to distribute the heavy burden of funding a new settlement. Colonization, he knew from his father's experience with the colony in Newfoundland, required substantial capital outlays over a long period before a profitable return could be expected. The offer of manors would allow him to finance the passage and supply of a larger number of settlers than would be possible if he depended on his own limited resources. In addition, the lords of the manors presumably would work hard at protecting and developing their investments, to the benefit of the province as well as to themselves.

However, Cecilius Calvert feared that in the first stages of settlement these incentives would be insufficient to attract the necessary large investment. Returns would not be immediate, and Englishmen at that time were reluctant to invest in long-term, high-risk ventures. Something more was needed: a cooperative enterprise promising immediate returns. In

178

Newfoundland, George Calvert had tried to use the fishery he developed to this purpose; in Maryland, Cecilius hoped the fur trade would serve. He therefore organized a joint-stock company to control this trade, and he offered "a portion and Share thereof unto such as Should adventure their persons and Estates for the beginning of a Plantation."[12]

Despite these trading opportunities and despite his promise to create landed gentry in the New World, replete with feudal trappings and rents from a New World peasantry, Calvert's recruitment campaign was not an unqualified success. Probably because of the Roman Catholic associations of the enterprise, few men of means and position responded to his proposals. Furthermore, the men who did invest represented a very narrow segment of English society, the Roman Catholic landed gentry. The promotional campaign turned up enough support to get the colony started, but it failed to generate adequate financial backing or to recruit Protestant settlers of substance. These failures had serious consequences for Maryland's early history. The colony was not sufficiently funded, a fact that placed a severe strain on Lord Baltimore's personal fortune. Above all, the inability to extend Maryland's English leadership beyond the Catholic community left Cecilius in a weakened political position, open to attacks based on anti-Catholic prejudice and hard-pressed to counter charges of discrimination against Protestants.

Because he failed to attract enough financial backers, Lord Baltimore was forced to provide a considerable share of the necessary funds himself. He owned a share of the *Dove* and about half of the shares in the joint-stock company. He also financed the passages of twenty-five of the servants who went to Maryland in the first expedition. Throughout all this, it was his money that oiled the wheels of England's bureaucracy, both to ease his charter through official and nonofficial channels and to defend it from its numerous and formidable enemies. Even given that Baltimore had the support of several "silent partners," his statement of May 1637 that "he hath employed the greatest part of his fortune" in the venture was probably true. In less than a decade, Cecilius Calvert's

179

heavy expenditures on the colony had turned his once substantial inheritance into what his father-in-law accurately described as a "weak fortune."[13]

Several members of Baltimore's immediate family also
invested in Maryland. His younger brother Leonard, in a
partnership with Sir Richard Lechford, invested just over
four hundred pounds in 1633, an amount he supplemented
occasionally in the years that followed. Another brother,
George, one of the first settlers, probably also ventured some
of his inheritance. His brother-in-law William Peasly invested in the fur trade and may have been one of Baltimore's
silent partners, as well as serving as treasurer of the joint-
stock company and helping with the recruitment effort by
maintaining a London office for Lord Baltimore. Brother-in-
law Ralph Eure probably financed the passage of several servants on the first expedition. Even Lady Baltimore made an
investment.[14]

Apart from the Calvert family, the main investors were
the Jesuit order and a few Roman Catholic gentlemen. Because many Catholics showed "great liberality" towards the
Jesuit mission to Maryland, the Society of Jesus could make a
significant contribution to the colony's founding; Jesuits both
aided the promotional campaign and made a substantial capital investment in the province. The society financed the
transportation and supply of about twenty persons in 1633
and imported nearly thirty more servants before the end of
the decade. The properties the Jesuits developed supported
missions that ministered to the religious needs of the Catholic population over the whole colonial period. The principal
Catholic gentlemen were Thomas Cornwallis, Edward and
Frederick Winter, Jerome Hawley, Richard Gerard, and John
Saunders, who owned shares in the joint-stock company and
in the *Dove*. All went to Maryland with the first expedition,
and all took advantage of Calvert's liberal land policy by
transporting enough servants to become eligible for manorial
grants.[15] Unfortunately, only Thomas Cornwallis left even an
implicit description of his motives for his commitment to the
Calvert colony.

Although not a rich man by contemporary standards, Cornwallis was the second heaviest investor in the Maryland venture. He owned an eighth share of the *Dove* and a substantial interest in the joint-stock company. He invested heavily in the retail provisions trade, built Maryland's first mill, and quickly established himself as one of the Chesapeake's leading tobacco merchants. Cornwallis also transported twelve servants on the first expedition and over the next ten years brought in forty-five more. Because he committed himself to the limits of his ability and perhaps beyond, he later complained of seeing his fortune run "almost out of breathe" in supporting the colony.[16]

Cornwallis's reasons for making such a great commitment shed light on those of the other investors. Above all, he was a devout Roman Catholic, and it is clear that he was attracted by the unique promise of refuge. He also saw an opportunity to create a flourishing church in the New World. "Securety of Contiens [conscience]," Cornwallis wrote Lord Baltimore, "was the first Condition that I expected from this Government." So strong, in fact, was Cornwallis's religious motivation that at one time in the course of various conflicts that arose he threatened to leave Maryland rather than "Consent to anything that may not stand for the good Contiens of A Real Catholick."[17] Also significant was a long-standing Cornwallis family interest in the emerging English empire. Both his father, Sir William, and his grandfather, Sir Charles, had invested in colonial adventures. Furthermore, the Calvert and Cornwallis families were well known to each other. Sir Charles Cornwallis had accompanied the first Lord Baltimore on a mission to Ireland in 1613, and Sir William had sat in Parliament with him. Thomas Cornwallis and Cecil Calvert were cousins by marriage.[18] This heritage of connections with empire and the Calvert efforts to extend it helped to lead Cornwallis to Maryland.

Finally, ambition was important. As a Roman Catholic and a younger son, Cornwallis's horizons in England were limited. He could not expect to inherit a major part of the family estate, which by English law would go to his oldest

181

brother, nor, because of his religion, could he make his mark in the professions or in politics. Cornwallis was devout, but he saw no conflict between piety and profit. Maryland promised an opportunity to improve his "Poore younger brothers fortune" and to gain at least some of the power and position denied him in England.[19] The vast landed estate available on the Chesapeake appealed to a man forced to the fringes of English landed society by an accident of birth and a profession of faith. Furthermore, Lord Baltimore gave him special encouragement. In addition to the conditions extended all adventurers, Cornwallis was offered a seat on the council which was to rule Maryland, special trading privileges, and a license to build a mill. The opportunity to serve his faith, share in the glory of building a new colony for England's empire, and improve his fortune made Cornwallis one of Maryland's most active early developers.

The other five major investors shared several characteristics with Cornwallis. They were, with the possible exception of Cornwallis's business partner, John Saunders, all Roman Catholics. All belonged to families of sufficient status in England to appear in the visitations of the College of Heralds, and, with the exception of Hawley, all were younger sons. Four—again Saunders may have been an exception—came from families with a history of interest in colonization and with some connections to the first Lord Baltimore. These characteristics were also shared, of course, by Baltimore's two younger brothers, Leonard and George, and by several of the relatively minor investors in the first expedition, such as Thomas Greene and Henry Wiseman.[20] In the later 1630s and early 1640s, this initial band was joined by several others—James Neale, Giles Brent, Thomas Gerard, and John Langford, for example—who fit the general pattern.[21]

Throughout the first decade of Maryland's existence, then, Baltimore's most prominent supporters were recruited primarily from sons of English gentry families, men who saw in the settlement on the Chesapeake an opportunity to serve their church and make their mark in the world. However, the very nature of the group was a danger in that it was limited to

Roman Catholics. In a colony largely peopled by Protestants and belonging to a Protestant kingdom, Protestant investors and leaders were necessary. Lord Baltimore's efforts to recruit them eventually would meet with success, yet here lay danger too. Protestant leaders could be a source of instability and conflict in a colony where Catholics had power. A policy was needed that would account for such difficulties if Maryland was to become and remain a Catholic refuge.

To solve this problem of political stability, the Calverts planned in Maryland a religious toleration based on separation of church and state. Men were to share power and decisions without regard to their religious differences, even though elsewhere men were fighting wars to force everyone to accept the same religion. This was an experiment in social relations, yet there is no evidence that experimentation was a conscious intention. The Calverts found it necessary to build a colony in which Catholics and Protestants would share political power; they backed into social pioneering from political necessity.

Neither George nor Cecilius Calvert left any precise statement that tells how they developed the policy they finally adopted. However, their plan was based on a body of Catholic opinion which was then emerging in England. By the 1630s many English Catholics had accepted the fact that in England they would be only one religious group among many; they would be a sect like other groups that refused to worship in the Church of England. There was no hope that the Roman Catholic church would ever again be the church of the English state or that other religions would be suppressed. If Catholicism were to survive in England, it must support the king, not the pope, as the ruler of the civil polity, and Catholics must endorse toleration of other sects. Religion, these Catholics argued, was a private matter that should not affect one's civil role and status. The state's proper concern was preserving harmonious civil relations, not coercing belief. "Moreover," according to a Maryland colonization tract, "Conversion in matters of Religion, if it bee forced, should give little satisfaction to a State of the fidelity of such convertites, for those who for worldly respects will breake their faith with God will doubtless doe it, upon fit occasion, much sooner with men."[22] The tract argued that the surest way for the state to win the loyalty of dissenters was to end discrimination and persecution. Religious men would defend a government that allowed them freedom of worship. "Let every religion take what spiritual head they please," argued one anonymous English Catholic of the day, "for so they will, whether wee will or no, but the matter imports not, so they obey the king as temporal head, and humbly submit to the state and civil lawes, and live quietly together."[23]

Cecilius Calvert, as proprietor of a new colony, was in a position to extend these principles and transform them into a public policy that would work in the New World. As practiced in Maryland, toleration was primarily intended to prevent differences between Protestants and Catholics from disrupting the civil order. Christians could follow their faith in private, without persecution, discrimination, or exclusion from the ruling groups. But they were not free to proselytize or debate doctrine publicly if such activities promised to threaten the peace. They certainly could not use unflattering epithets or in other ways publicly criticize someone of a different religious persuasion. In fact, the government was to act with special vigor to contain or suppress such activities. Cecilius Calvert denied that government had a right or need to regulate opinion, but affirmed its authority over public expressions of belief that affected the peace. He also understood that his precarious political position demanded especially circumspect behavior on the part of Catholic colonists. This understanding of the requirements of toleration is clearly expressed in Baltimore's instructions to his brother Leonard on the conduct of the first expedition. He ordered that Governor Calvert and his councillors should be "very carefull to preserve unity and peace amongst all . . . and that they suffer no scandall nor offence to be given to any of the Protestants . . . and that for that end, they cause all Acts of Romane Catholique Religion to be done as privately as may be, and that they instruct all the Roman Catholicques to be silent upon all occasions of discourse concerning matters of religion."[24] This essentially negative view of toleration, framed as much with an eye toward the reactions of English officials as with an appreciation of the needs of the colonists, had a failing. Calvert had not thoroughly confronted the problem of toleration among essentially intolerant men. Something more positive than the occasional suppression of controversy was needed. Protestant Englishmen were too distrustful of Catholics to accept their participation in the polity with equanimity. Marylanders needed to be taught the virtues of toleration if it were to succeed. Baltimore did not perceive this educational necessity, and even if he had, he lacked the institutional means for carrying out the task. Toleration lasted, with some interruptions, for fifty-five years, but the potential for serious conflict over religion was always present and ultimately ended the experiment. Nevertheless, the early colonists made toleration work. Catholics and Protestants, together, founded Maryland.

III. THE FIRST SETTLEMENT

In April 1634, Leonard Calvert wrote, "We have seated ourselves within one half mile of the river, within a pallizado of one hundred and twentie yeards square."[25] The former Yaocomico village, about six miles up from the Potomac on what was to be known as the St. Mary's River, was an ideal spot for the expedition borne in the *Ark* and the *Dove*. The first authoritative account, *A relation of Maryland* (1635), described it as "a very comodious situation for a Towne, in regard the land is good, the ayre wholesome and pleasant, the river affords a safe harbour for ships of any burthen, and a very bould shoare; fresh water and wood there is in great plenty, and the place so naturally fortified, as with little difficulties it will be defended from any enemy."[26] Governor Calvert was seeking fields already cleared by the Indians so that his party might quickly sow their crops and avoid a first disastrous winter such as earlier colonists had experienced. The voyage had been scheduled to allow for a spring arrival and a full growing season. Hearing that the Yaocomicos were more than willing to turn their homes over, Leonard Calvert wasted no time in bringing his settlers to the site. About half of the resident Yaocomicos moved away upon the arrival of the English, and the bark houses they left behind probably served as temporary homes for the colonists.

Work was immediately begun on the "pallizado," the ditched, banked, and palisaded enclosure of the strong point or "fort" which was thought to be necessary as protection against the Indians—not only those nearby, but also the Susquehannocks and marauding bands of Iroquois from the north. The governor was aware from his meetings with his Indian neighbors that only a few years previously a band of such invading "Senecas" had massacred the inhabitants of nearby Moyoane, a Piscataway village that had existed for at least three hundred years. For the first months the Maryland colony probably existed within or near this crudely built fort. Meanwhile, work surely went on as fast as possible to build more permanent dwellings, clear more fields, and sow the anxiously awaited crops.

According to members of this first expedition, the colonists found a bountiful nature at St. Mary's. Bears, elk, deer, wildcats, wolves, and beaver were within the woods on all sides of the early village. Small game, such as foxes, squirrels, and rabbits, abounded. Cranes, ducks, geese, and even wild pigeons flew in flocks so dense that by one account they threatened to block the sunlight from the earth. Wild turkey was a favorite of the Yaocomicos, and terrapin, crabs, and oysters were abundant. The huge virgin woods of cedar, poplar, oak, elm, ash, chestnut, and walnut provided seemingly inexhaustible supplies of building materials and fuel. According to Father Andrew White, these woods were almost completely free of undergrowth or scrub. The countryside abounded with color and beauty. Sorrel and violets, strawberries and raspberries, and all kinds of herbs for "sallets" were there in profusion. So too was a plant grown by the Yaocomicos for their own enjoyment. The first colonists were not encouraged to grow tobacco, but Maryland would soon be relying upon it as the primary cash crop.

It was assumed in the seventeenth century that cities were necessary to both commerce and civilization. Lord Baltimore had therefore decreed that a close, clustered settlement must be built at once in his projected colony. His instructions called for houses "neere adjoining one to another and for that purpose to cause streets to be marked out where they intend to place the towne and to oblige every man to buyld one by another according to the rule."[27] But the town was not built. By 1637, and probably much sooner, the settlers had scattered. The colony's leaders had taken up land at a distance from the fort and had carried their servants with them. The fort was left to destruction born of neglect, for despite occasional alarms, the Indians were largely peaceful.

The Maryland leaders made a conscious effort to avoid conflicts with the local Indians that might lead to warfare such as the Jamestown settlements had faced. The English paid the Indians for their land and supplies and the leaders wrote of the natives with respect. The natives responded with a willingness to teach the English how to make corn bread and hominy, to show them what herbs and roots could be used for medicines and dyes, to make them log canoes, and to help in other ways. If the Indians had decided on war, the infant colony might not have survived. As it was, while relationships were often uneasy, no major hostilities broke out.

Thus the first settlements had a good start. The Indians knew how to select good land, and today's soil maps show that the Yaocomico village occupied the very best site on the east side of the St. Mary's River. The rich soil, spotted with tree trunks the Indians had never removed, provided a good growing medium. The first garden and corn crop, thanks to the temperate spring and summer of 1634, "prospered exceeding well."[28] All seemed to be right, with "God's favour," for the Calvert expedition. But as the time went on, the strains and conflicts inherent in Lord Baltimore's colonization scheme would come to the surface.

187

IV. GROWTH AND DEVELOPMENT OF THE
NEW COLONY

Early Maryland was politically fragile from the beginning. Although essential to the Calvert plan, the prominent immigrants who joined the first expedition were a threat to the colony's well-being, and particularly to the proprietor's influence there. Precisely because the half-dozen major investors had a status independent of the proprietary favor, Lord Baltimore's ability to control them was to prove limited. Cooperation between the proprietor and Maryland's new landed gentry depended upon a convergence of interests that never came about. Given the ambitions of the leading immigrants, contrasted with Lord Baltimore's pressing need to improve his depleted finances, quarrels over privileges and trade were inevitable.

Contributing to these difficulties was the fact that the anticipated fur trade enterprise was a failure. The supply of furs was limited. Furthermore, the master of the *Dove* abandoned his vessel after a quarrel with the owners; it became worm-eaten and repairs delayed its departure. By the time it could set out for England, most of the first year's furs had rotted. The ship itself then disappeared at sea. The initial investment was entirely lost, and the business enterprise never recovered. This failure was disheartening. Baltimore had expected quick returns to shore up his sagging fortunes, and the other investors had shared his expectations. Had the adventure into the fur trade been a success, relations between the leading colonists and Calvert might have been easier. The result instead was continued financial strain, discouragement, and a bitter struggle for control of what little fur trade was coming out of the Maryland colony. Fortunately for Calvert and his settlers, tobacco was available as an alternative economic resource. It did not immediately create wealth, but it provided a sustaining income.

In other ways Lord Baltimore's plans collapsed. The manorial system failed to function as intended. In part it fell victim to his need for both men and money. Abundant labor was necessary to make vast wilderness tracts productive, yet Baltimore, in order to attract investors, had set a man-land ratio too low to bring lands into profitable cultivation. Five men per 2,000—later 1,000—acres could not accomplish much. Nor could the manorial lords obtain easy riches. The manpower shortage was too great. Servants were usually bound to their masters for only four or five years. The offer of opportunity to acquire land was essential to the recruitment of servants, and when they were free they were given rights to their own land. They might need to continue as laborers or tenants for a while before they could pay the expenses of establishing an independent plantation, but since wages were high and rents were low where land was plentiful and people scarce, labor in this form was expensive. In the long run the large landowners would do very well, but get-rich-quick profits were impossible.

In addition, the manors did not provide the institutional stability that Lord Baltimore had envisioned. There was no realistic way to confine settlement to the areas covered by these large grants. Few ex-servants were content for long to be tenants. Though the manorial lords were not making fortunes, the small profits which their tenants were making allowed these poorer men to better their condition. From the time of its founding, Maryland was potentially a colony in which independent owner-operators, not tenants or manorial lords, would constitute a majority among the planters. The early Maryland society was, therefore, short-lived. Over the first decade it was as planned, a hierarchical community based on firm distinctions of status, a society dominated by a handful of English gentlemen who owned nearly all the land and financial resources. But a very different society soon emerged.

Throughout the 1630s the fledgling community on the St. Mary's River grew at a steady but unspectacular pace. As Father White reported in 1639, five years after the landing of the *Ark* and the *Dove*, the colony was "every day bettering itself by increase of Planters and plantations."[29] By 1642, a year for which tax lists survive that make possible a crude estimate of population, there were perhaps 340 to 390 resi-

189

dents in or near St. Mary's. Nevertheless, there should have been more. High mortality, characteristic of the Chesapeake region, had cut back population growth considerably. Nearly every newcomer sickened soon after arrival and many died— what proportion we can only surmise. Malaria and dysentery appear to have been the chief causes of illness, and those who recovered were weakened for other diseases. It is likely that at least 500 persons had immigrated since 1634. More than a fifth of those who sought opportunity in a settlement had met their deaths instead.

However many had come, there were not yet many settlers in 1642. The St. Mary's region revealed few traces of the impact of English culture eight years after the arrival of the *Ark* and the *Dove*. Over 37,000 acres of land had been surveyed by the end of 1642, but most of them were still unimproved. Even if one assumes that each taxable resident (males of twelve years and older) had about 10 acres under cultivation, well over 90 percent of the patented land remained untouched virgin soil. At most, the colonists had improved only three square miles. Maryland had just barely begun.

The St. Mary's settlement was not the only one in Maryland. Kent Island, across Chesapeake Bay, had been colonized in 1631. Lord Baltimore claimed it as part of his grant, but William Claiborne and his settlers considered themselves part of Virginia. Leonard Calvert and the St. Mary's colonists had to spend valuable energy establishing Calvert authority on the island. They had succeeded by 1638, and men from Kent attended the Maryland Assembly. But isolated Kent remained an area of doubtful loyalty for many years to come.

There were three major settlement clusters in the St. Mary's River area by 1642. Most of the inhabitants still lived around the St. Mary's River within a few miles of the original landing site and fort. This group of settlers was divided into three administrative units, or "hundreds": St. Michael's Hundred, St. Mary's Hundred, and St. George's Hundred. St. Michael's, the largest, stretched from Point Lookout at the

190

mouth of the Potomac River to St. Inigoes Creek and had perhaps 120 inhabitants. St. Mary's Hundred, situated on the east bank of the St. Mary's River just north of St. Michael's, included the landing site; its smaller area was probably the most densely settled, with about 80 to 90 residents. Finally, about 70 people lived within St. George's Hundred, on the west bank of the river. In all, some 270 people lived in the major settlement cluster on or near the St. Mary's River.

Two additional settlements had been established by 1642 at a considerable distance from the original landing site. St. Clement's Hundred, bounded by the Wicomico River on the west, had about 60 inhabitants. Mattapanient Hundred, the other major outlying settlement cluster, had about 30 to 40 inhabitants. It was located on the Patuxent River, about five miles north of the St. Mary's fort. All five hundreds were organized as St. Mary's County.

Although the concept of clustering is useful in describing the settlement pattern of early St. Mary's County, the term is somewhat misleading. In no way were these population clusters dense villagelike pockets. Rather, each of the groupings was a loose dispersal of houses and settlers. Plantations were not concentrated around a village square or common, but strung out along the river banks, on the necks of peninsulas between rivers, and on other navigable streams. The settlement pattern that was to dominate American tobacco areas throughout the colonial period emerged almost immediately in St. Mary's County.

There were various reasons for the spread of first settlement along the water. The Chesapeake Bay's many water highways, feeder rivers, and creeks provided convenient transportation of goods and services at a time when roads were nonexistent. Profitable tobacco culture required easy access to these navigable waterways, as the "sotte weed" was found to be too bulky and too delicate to travel well over land. Immediate dependence on England for goods and services and a system of marketing and supply which often entailed direct exchange between planters and ships' captains also encouraged settlement along the rivers and larger

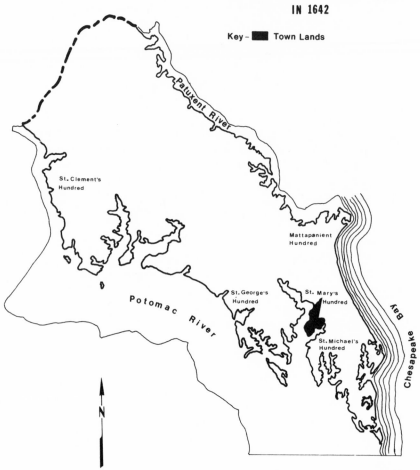

Courtesy of the St. Mary's City Commission

creeks. Doubtless important, too, was the desire of these voluntarily exiled colonists to maintain some communication with visitors from the mother country; Englishmen were to be seen and spoken to when the occasional ship from England anchored to load and unload goods. In 1656, to keep waterfront land available for newcomers, Lord Baltimore placed limits on the amount of such land that could be taken up. Interior settlement did not begin until waterfront land was gone later in the seventeenth century.

Evidence also suggests that traditional English agricultural wisdom helped shape the emerging settlement pattern. All of the sites chosen for cultivation by 1642 were good for tobacco production, but they were also well suited for other crops, performing well with Indian corn and English grains and garden produce. Many contained some wet, marshy lands which formed a natural meadow base usable for grazing livestock, although cattle could be mired and lost in these marshes. In addition, many sites contained some low land that was "subject to drown" and some land with a slightly higher elevation that was well drained. Thus, by planting some of his crops on low lands and some on high, the early Maryland farmer could take precautions against both drought and excessive rainfall; he could spread his risks. In so doing he was following the practices of his forefathers.

These considerations, based on the need for access to water and the spreading of risks, affected the decisions of planters wherever men settled in the Tidewater Chesapeake. But in St. Mary's County manorial grants also profoundly influenced the pattern. By 1642, sixteen private manors had been surveyed. Together they contained 31,000 acres, or a full 83.1 percent of the total patented land in the area. There was, furthermore, a pronounced tendency for small landowners to take up land close to the manorial grants. As the map (p. 192) makes clear, manors dominated four of the five major settlement clusters. In St. Michael's Hundred, there were six manors. Three belonged to Leonard Calvert, two to Thomas Cornwallis, and one to the Jesuits. St. George's Hundred contained West St. Mary's Manor, which had been surveyed for Cornwallis in 1640, but which belonged to the proprietor by 1642. Another, St. George's Manor, owned by Thomas Weston, was not formally patented until 1643, but Weston had probably been living on the site for nearly a year before. Four manors accounted for all the patented land in the Mattapanient Hundred. All inhabitants there must have been living and working on a manor. Thomas Gerard's 6,000-acre tract included most of the settled area in St. Clement's Hundred. Only St. Mary's Hundred, where settlement still centered loosely on lands intended for town development, escaped manorial domination. Even there most of the land was owned by the very men who had large manorial holdings elsewhere.

Thus the manorial lords in effect made the basic choices as to where inhabitants settled. They directed the locations in which their servants and hired men would work and determined what lands would be leased to men beginning life as planters. And since the lords were the main source of credit, supplies, and marketing services for men with little capital, smaller landowners chose land near them. However, this concentration on the manor was not to last. At first the Calvert vision of well-knit manorial communities might have seemed to be coming into being, but economic forces were pushing in the opposite direction. Manorial laborers and tenants expected to leave the manor to establish their own holdings, and those who had done so soon outnumbered those who remained.

The proprietor may have intended that the lords of the manors would establish manorial courts that would constitute local governments. So far as is known, however, only one ever functioned in this way. A few records for 1659–72 remain for Thomas Gerard's St. Clements Manor, but the business considered was trifling. Most lords probably did not try to enforce recognition of their judicial powers. There were an increasing number of small landowners, furthermore, who did not live on manors. The colony leaders soon established the hundreds and the county instead. As in nearby Virginia, the county court, with its justices of the peace and sheriff

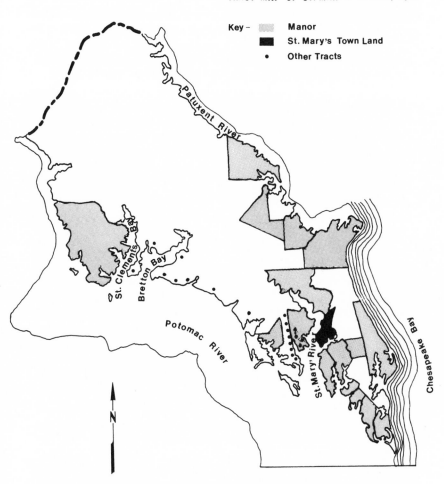

Key –   Manor
         St. Mary's Town Land
    •   Other Tracts

Patuxent River

St. Clements Bay

Bretton Bay

Potomac River

St. Mary's River

Chesapeake Bay

N

Courtesy of the St. Mary's City Commission

195

appointed by the governor, became the chief unit of local government.

Over the first ten years, there was probably little distinction made between the St. Mary's County court and the provincial government. The governor and his councillors—who were mostly manorial lords—ran the day-to-day affairs of the colony and sat as the provincial court. These men, who were appointed by the proprietor, took up every kind of business. In a colony so small and new, they probably paid little attention to jurisdictional lines. There was overlapping membership on county court and provincial court that in any case blurred distinctions.

There was a check on the power of these leaders. The charter required that laws be passed in an assembly of freemen or their delegates. Such assemblies were established in all the New World English colonies. Until 1670, a freeman in Maryland was literally any man who was not a servant, and for several sessions in the early years every freeman was called to attend in person or by proxy. The reason that so many could participate—nothing like it was to be found in England and soon would not be found in Maryland—doubtless lies in the fragile nature of authority in a new and isolated settlement. It was necessary that the colonists work together if a well-ordered society in the wilderness were to be created. The governor and council could not enforce laws or policies not based on widespread agreement. The economic and political power of the gentry was great, and they occupied all important offices. But in these early assemblies, every free male settler had some chance to influence the policies such officers enforced.

Nevertheless, leadership of the colony remained in the hands of the few. Lords of manors may not have had their own courts, but they sat as judges and councillors. What did not function as Lord Baltimore had hoped was a community of interest between him and these distant rulers. Upon this community of interest depended the development of political order. This failure was to prove a serious weakness.

Lord Baltimore had planned that his seat of government

would be a flourishing town. But as elsewhere in the Chesapeake, the marked tendency towards scattered settlement frustrated any hope that a town would soon develop. His belief that a city was essential to the prosperity of his colony could not command one into being. Important market functions were in the hands of English merchants and ships' captains. There was no need for a provincial town as a center of commerce. The manorial system in itself, moreover, undermined urban development. The manors offered several additional centers of credit and services and hence competed for settlers. Finally, the distribution pattern that appeared for the land set aside for a town did not encourage its development. Lord Baltimore had intended that the Town Land—about 1,500 acres around the original landing site—be distributed in 5- or 10-acre lots. But the headright system he simultaneously developed permitted the colony's leading investors to take up much larger parcels than he had anticipated. Thirteen tracts were actually surveyed on the site before 1642. Holdings ranged, not from 5 to 10 acres, but from 30 to 400, the average being 115. Leasing may have led to some further subdivision, but the St. Mary's Town Land little resembled a village. A dozen households, perhaps, were spread out over five square miles.

Eventually a village did arise, because the Town Land remained the seat of government. The governor and council, the courts, and the assembly met in the fort while it lasted, or at the nearby home of the provincial secretary, John Lewger, which had been built by 1638. By the 1660s the population had grown enough to require and finance construction of public buildings, and enough people were coming from a distance to encourage the opening of inns and stables. At a late stage, the development of St. Mary's City had come about. However, when the capital was moved to Annapolis in 1695, the reason for a town on this site disappeared. Within a few years the St. Mary's Town Lands had returned to the density of the 1640s.

The needs of the tobacco economy were the main influence on settlement patterns, yet when the Lords Baltimore

197

began their promotion of the new Maryland enterprise, tobacco was mentioned almost as an afterthought. Neither George nor Cecilius Calvert saw the increasingly popular substance as an integral part of Maryland's future. They treated it as just one of several crops in a diversified agriculture. Their lack of foresight is surprising, given that the adjacent Virginia economy was already dependent on tobacco. The Calverts and their friends kept well informed about their neighbors to the south; they must have known how important tobacco was there. Possibly the late King James's aversion to tobacco (an aversion shared, incidentally, by Thomas Cornwallis, Maryland's key backer aside from the Calvert family) had led to a tactical decision to deemphasize the crop in the recruitment campaign. In any case, the price of tobacco had declined sharply in the years just prior to settlement of the Maryland colony. The luxury prices paid Virginia planters for the weed in the early 1620s had not lasted. By 1629, tobacco prices had fallen so low that the Virginia Assembly had restricted production. It is likely, therefore, that the promotors of the Maryland enterprise hoped to avoid dependence on a crop with such an uncertain future.

Yet, despite what the promotors may have throught about the "sotte weed," the colonists were soon engrossed in producing it. The adventurers did not grow tobacco at St. Mary's during the first year of settlement, but thereafter the crop quickly emerged as the staple of the Maryland economy. By 1637, a mere three years after the *Ark* and the *Dove* sailed up the St. Mary's River, tobacco had become the money of account. Colonists traded with it and priced other goods according to its value. By one estimate, Maryland exported 100,000 pounds of tobacco in 1639, an average of more than 600 pounds for each male old enough to engage in production.[30]

There should be little mystery about why Marylanders turned with one mind to tobacco production. While promoters may have expected successful production of grain, meat, hemp, flax, and wood products, tobacco was the only crop with a fully developed marketing network extending from England to the Chesapeake. And while tobacco prices

198

admittedly fluctuated, creating recurrent booms and busts in the trade, profits over the long run paid returns sufficient to make the investment worthwhile. The first Marylanders found a readily available market for tobacco with English and Dutch merchants who were already trading with Virginia tobacco growers, and these early planters found rising prices. By 1635 planters were receiving between four and six pence for a pound of tobacco, up from a penny a pound a few years earlier. Such a dramatic increase in profitability was a large inducement to abandon all other forms of agriculture.

The price boom of the mid-1630s proved to be short-lived. By 1638 the price per pound Marylanders were receiving had fallen to three pence, and it continued to fall well into the early 1640s. But having tasted the prosperity that tobacco could bring, Marylanders were not about to give up the crop. Instead, price depression served to spur them to action. In 1640 they joined with their Virginia neighbors in an attempt to raise the price. Leading tobacco merchants induced Virginia planters to rush an act through their assembly in January of that year requiring that "all rotten and unmerchantable and half of good" tobacco of each planter be burned for the next three years. The idea was to raise the price by limiting the supply. The Maryland Assembly was not willing to go this far, but it did pass an act providing for the appointment of tobacco "viewers." These inspectors were to forbid the export of any damaged leaves. There is no evidence that the Maryland legislation was ever seriously enforced, and the law lapsed two years later.[31] But it was the first effort (though not the last) to keep tobacco prices from falling.

While tobacco was the staple crop, other crops, of course, had to be grown. As a means of ensuring adequate food supplies, the Maryland Assembly adopted Virginia's well-established two-acre rule. Each farmhand working to plant and harvest tobacco had also to tend at least two acres of corn. Livestock was also necessary, and at first cattle and hogs were imported from Virginia. But as early as 1635, prospective immigrants were advised that whatever corn, poultry, or

199

swine they would need on arrival could be purchased in Maryland. Four years later, an influential colonist reported that "for swine we need not much care though virginea be shutt up to us hereafter." Nor was there need for the proprietor to import additional cattle, since his herd would soon include "as many as can bee well looked after and provided for in the winter as yet."[32] Thus Maryland early developed two assets: self-sufficiency in food production and a staple crop, tobacco, that would attract investment and bring in settlers to people the land.

V. THE FRONTIER SOCIETY

The social structure of the St. Mary's settlements changed little over the first decade. There was some turnover in the Maryland leadership, but nothing that produced basic change. Several of the gentlemen adventurers died. In fact, only four of the original seventeen principal backers were still living in Maryland in 1642. But as men had left the colony, the proprietor had been successful in recruiting a number of new backers, including a handful of Protestants.

Unlike the first adventurers, those coming later were not clearly divided into gentlemen on the one hand and servants on the other. In the late 1630s and early 1640s, a few men of middling means and social standing had settled in Maryland. For instance, Thomas Passmore, an illiterate carpenter, had moved to Maryland from Virginia with his wife, children, and four servants in the summer of 1634. In 1636, Randall Revell, a cooper who also could not write his name, had arrived in the province with his wife, son, and one servant. Another individual typical of this free immigrant group was John Cockshott, a wood craftsman who had brought his wife, two daughters, and four servants to the new colony in 1641.[33] Other men had no capital but at least had managed to pay their own way to Maryland. They had soon taken advantage of the opportunities to purchase land cheaply and to improve their place in society.

200

But such immigrants had not much altered the structure of the early St. Mary's County settlements. Tax lists, headright entries, and court records reveal the status of 260 men who lived there in 1642. Of these, 172 were free, but the great majority had come as Protestant servants indentured to Catholic masters of means and status, and most were still dependent on major investors for employment of land to raise a crop. In addition, there were at least 53 servants, while another 35 men transported since 1638 perhaps were still under indenture.

Surviving records show that these Marylanders shared several characteristics usually associated with frontier populations, and particularly with new settlements organized around the production of a single crop that required a great deal of labor. First, young unmarried males who came to work in the fields contributed most of the population growth. They hoped to acquire a farm and a family, but for the time being there was little opportunity to marry. A rough count of the settlers living in early St. Mary's suggests that there were about four men for each woman living in the county. Families were few, and produced few children before death claimed one or both of the parents. Where the variety of crops and activities was greater, as in Pennsylvania and New England, families helped establish the first settlements and produced children that swelled their numbers. In Maryland and similar one-crop regions, such as Virginia and South Carolina, a settled and family-structured population that could increase from births took much longer to develop. Wills written in the early years demonstrate these characteristics of early Maryland society. Of the thirty-two men whose wills were probated between 1635 and 1650, twenty (62.5 percent) were single. Eight were married, and four were widowers. Of these twelve men, furthermore, six were childless, and among them all, they had only nine children. Clearly, large families in the new colony were exceptional. The population could not grow much from births; immigration provided the increase.

The general standard of living in the early years of the

province was also what might be expected in a frontier settlement. Thomas Cornwallis reported about four years after the first landing that all the inhabitants still lived in "Cottages."[34] These were at best crude, one-story, wood-framed enclosures with sidings of riven boards, perhaps filled with wattle and daub (clay impressed on a network of twigs). Roofs were covered either with boards similar to the sidings or with thatch. These structures had one, or at most two, rooms, with a space above reached by a ladder. The chimney was made of wood or wattle and daub. Brick construction came later, when the Maryland subsoil and rich clay deposits could be mined. Poor planters were still building houses like these a century later, but even the rich did not do better the first few years. To be sure, Cornwallis was at that point building a good brick house, and a surviving list of its contents shows rich furnishings for the day. Tapestries hung on his walls and fine china graced his table.[35] But it is clear that his house was extraordinary. The few surviving estate inventories point to a rude, rough life even for the prominent and wealthy.

None of the highly specialized or unusual crafts of seventeenth-century English life were so far represented in the New World civilization. There were no artisans to serve the tastes of the wealthy. Most of the inhabitants worked at raising tobacco, and the skills represented were those essential to the task of carving plantations out of the wilderness. Among the 172 free men living in the county in 1642, there were 28 identifiable artisans: 12 carpenters, 3 coopers, 3 tailors, 2 boat builders, 2 mariners, 2 barber-surgeons, 1 joiner, 1 sawyer, 1 blacksmith, and 1 brick mason. Housing and clothing for people and casks for the crop were the main requirements, and all that most of these skills could serve. Even the men who used them were probably planters or agricultural laborers who pursued their crafts part-time.

Six "Esquires" and thirteen "Gentlemen" can also be identified in the population of 1642. Such titles did not distinguish a class of the idle rich, as they may have in the mother country. In the New World, these esquires and gentlemen pursued callings as merchants, planters, Indian traders, land speculators, moneylenders, and estate developers. Thomas Cornwallis, for example, built the colony's first mill, engaged in the Indian trade and retail provision trade, exported enough tobacco to England to be included in the top 10 percent of British tobacco merchants, and was the leading creditor of early St. Mary's.[36] Even the richest in this society could not be men of leisure.

If disparities in wealth and power were not much reflected in living standards or leisure, they appeared in educational advantages. While perhaps not as illustrious as some of the men of Massachusetts Bay or even of Virginia, a few of the settlers possessed impressive cultural credentials. John Lewger, for instance, was an Oxford M.A. and later the author of tracts on church-state relations. The Jesuit Andrew White was a former professor of divinity, while other Jesuits in the colony were certainly well-versed theologians.[37] Leonard Calvert doubtless shared with a number of other Maryland backers a standard classical education. A wide gulf separated these men from the majority of the Maryland colonists. Rudimentary reading, writing, and a smattering of arithmetic were usually the upper limit for most settlers, and the majority probably fell well short of even so modest an educational achievement. Most culture was oral culture at early St. Mary's. Nearly all the affairs of the daily life were conducted by word of mouth. In fact, surviving election returns of 1639 show that only twenty-five of the fifty-two voters were able to sign their names; the others made marks on their ballots. Thus it is reasonable to assume that at least half of the settlers who were not gentlemen or priests lacked even basic literacy.

This society of gentlemen with education and capital, who held economic and political sway over laborers and small planters, resembled what the Calverts had intended. But it would not continue to do so. These social arrangements did not envision the rapid rise of poor men to landowning status, much less to wealth and power. Such changes were already underway, although not yet very visible. Their nature can be seen by looking more closely at the ways in which servants became freemen, freemen became planters, and planters became freeholders—that is, landowners—in the growing tobacco economy.

Indentured servants were at the very bottom of the social structure in the first decade. Most were little more than boys. Among those whose ages are known, the mean age on arrival was seventeen. They came from families that represented a broad range of English society below the gentry: farmers, artisans, tradesmen, and laborers. Even by seventeenth-century standards, their lives in Maryland were difficult. It is reasonable to conclude that they worked anywhere from ten to fourteen hours a day, six days a week. Unlike servants in England, they could be bought and sold, and the penalties for running away were severe. At all times they were subject to the discipline of their masters, including corporal punishment. On the other hand, servants had rights. They were entitled to adequate food, clothing, shelter, and a Sunday free from hard labor. They could not bring an action at common law, but they could protest ill-treatment in the courts. Most important of all, if the indentured servant escaped premature death, he could look forward to being a free man in a society that offered great opportunities for advancement.

A model indenture contract, as printed in a publication of 1635, specifies that a servant was to work at whatever his master "shall there imploy him, according to the custome of the Country."[38] In return, the master was to pay for his passage and provide food, lodging, clothing, and other "necessaries" during his term of service. "At the end of the said term," a master had to give his indentured servant "one whole years provision of Corne, and fifty acres of Land, according to the order of the Country." An act of 1640 passed by the Maryland Assembly specified "order of the Country" to mean that the servant would receive "one good Cloth Suite of Keirsey or Broadcloth, Shift of white linen, one pair of Stockins and Shoes, two hoes, one axe, 3 barrels of corne, and fifty acres of land whereof five at least to be plantable."[39] St. Mary's land records make clear that the fifty-acre requirement need not be taken literally. In practice, custom demanded only that masters provide their freed servants with the headright to fifty acres. This in itself was no great benefit, since a fifty-acre warrant could be purchased for one hundred pounds of tobacco and sometimes even less. Thus, if the servant wished to take advantage of this "gift" of land and actually acquire a tract, he had to locate the land and pay both surveyor's and clerk's fees himself.

The usual term of indenture in Maryland was four years, but occasionally servants were able to work out arrangements with their masters to shorten that time. John Courts and Francis Pope, for example, purchased their remaining time from Fulke Brent, probably arranging to pay him out of whatever money they could earn as free men. Another typical arrangement is seen in the pact Thomas Todd, a glover, worked out with his master, John Lewger. Todd was to dress a number of animal skins and make breeches and gloves for Lewger in return for an early release. George Evelin released three of his servants, Philip West, William Williamson, and John Hopson, a year early on condition that they provided themselves with food, clothing, and lodging and paid him one thousand pounds of tobacco each—in effect, the crop they would otherwise have raised.[40]

Whether released early or on time, the former indentured servants soon were close to a majority in the colony. In 1634 nearly all of the working hands had been bound to service but, by 1642, 50 to 70 percent were free men. Of these as many as 75 to 80 percent had once been indentured. Although the others had paid their own way to Maryland, many of them had no more wealth than the newly freed servants, and their standing was no higher. These were the men who now supplied the greater part of the colony's labor.

For former servants and impoverished free immigrants, there were basically three choices. They could hire out for wages, or for a share of the crop, or they could lease land from a large planter and raise tobacco on their own. Although such men were entitled to headrights, immediate ownership of land was usually impracticable. To acquire that land, not

205

only did a man have to pay surveyor's and clerk's fees for a patent or pay a purchase price to a landowner, but he also had then to clear land and build a house. Tools, seed, and livestock were necessary. Meanwhile, he had to obtain provisions until he could harvest the first crop. All of this took capital, and capital was precisely what he lacked. Wage labor, sharecropping, and leaseholding therefore offered him a chance to accumulate enough wealth to acquire a plantation of his own and to sustain himself in the process.

Daily wages were between 15 and 20 pounds of tobacco. Considering that a man at the time usually produced 800 to 1,000 pounds of tobacco in a year, such wages were extraordinarily high. But labor was scarce, and men with strong backs and willing hands must have found all the work they wanted. Few devoted themselves to full-time wage labor or sharecropping for long periods. As soon as a man could, he usually worked his own crop and hired out only occasionally to supplement his planting income. Some men did sign contracts or enter into verbal agreements for long-term labor, usually by the year. In some ways their status resembled that of indentured servants, since they were subject to the same discipline and suffered the same penalties if they ran away; nevertheless, there were important differences. They probably could not be sold, and they could not bring actions at common law for breach of contract. Wages, furthermore, ranged from 1,100 to 1,500 pounds of tobacco a year, plus shelter, food, and clothing. Thus a long-term labor agreement, although it restricted a man's freedom, could enable him to accumulate sufficient capital to become a planter and even a landowner himself.

The next step on the route from servant to freeholder was formation of a household. The sheer excess of available land made this easy. In 1642 most men who had been free for a year or more had attained the status of "housekeeper." By achieving householder status, even very poor men attained a degree of independence and responsibility denied to those who lived in the households of others. They were masters in their own families, responsible for the discipline, education, and day-to-day maintenance of their subordinates. They also formed the backbone of the political community, serving on juries, sitting in the Assembly, and filling minor offices.

Some households assumed the familiar shape: a man, his wife, their children, and possibly one or two servants. But this pattern was not the norm in the Maryland of 1642. Given the overwhelming predominance of unmarried males, many households were of necessity composed of only one person. Whereas in preindustrial England men first married and then established households, in early Maryland men first established their households and then began the search for a wife. Since potential wives were few, households could remain incomplete for years. The master of the house had no family to rule.

Many men who could not afford to buy servants or pay wages joined with a male "mate." Partnership of this sort may have served as a substitute for marriage in early Maryland. By working together, such mates could create a plantation. The arrangement was occasionally complicated if one of the two men acquired a wife and family. The original mate would sometimes remain, giving the household two heads and certainly altering the master's traditional all-powerful role. In these instances, there was the expected jockeying for power and advantage, agreement being reached through discussion and compromise and a certain diminished authority on all sides. Of course, this two-headed household quickly fell out of favor as the male-female ratio became more equal, and the traditional family-unit household then became the norm.

There were three forms of land tenure available to the householder: ownership in fee, long-term leasehold, and short-term leasehold. Tenure in fee—loosely called "freehold"—was the most secure and the most desirable. Title to the land came directly from the proprietor, or occasionally from the lord of the manor. The owner could sell to another. A small rent was owed the proprietor or the manorial lord, but neither had a right to take back the land unless an owner died without heirs, nor could freehold property be seized to pay a debt. Possibly 20 to 25 percent of the colony's ex-servants and free immigrants had become freeholders by 1642.

In many ways there was little difference between land held in fee and land held under a long-term lease, which was usually for the lives of three people named in the lease. Such leases could be inherited and sold by the tenant. They were purchased for a lump sum, and the yearly rents were often low. A lease for lives, furthermore, carried freehold privileges. But when the lease came to an end, the original owner could reenter the property and demand a new lump-sum payment or a higher rent. The landlord thereby secured for himself some of the benefits of the improvements the tenant had made—housing, fencing, and cleared land. Hence men were understandably reluctant to purchase a leasehold when they could own their land outright for only a small additional cost. Such long-term leases were common in England, where land was less freely available, but they were rare in early Maryland.

In contrast to freehold tenures, short-term leases offered the tenant little security. They could not be sold or inherited, and thus offered him no opportunity to benefit from any increase in the value of the property. Nonetheless, such six- or seven-year leases were undoubtedly the most common form of tenure in the early colony. Their great advantage to the tenant was the absence of an entry fee—that is, the lump-sum payment. This made them particularly attractive to former servants and other immigrants who had come to the New World with little or no capital. The rents assessed for such leases were probably very low, certainly no higher than 500 pounds of tobacco a year for a plantation and maybe even as low as 200 pounds. Rent for the first year, furthermore, was probably not due until after the initial crop was in. If the land were uncleared and no house had been built, there might be no rent due for several years.

Regardless of the terms of a land lease, the arrangements benefited both landlord and tenant. The landlords had their land cleared, housing erected, orchards planted and fenced, and a small income. Tenants, meanwhile, were able to accumulate the capital necessary to acquire a tract of their own, while working the land and harvesting cash crops.

By the end of the first decade, although many ex-servants and poor immigrants were beginning to improve their lot in this manner, most were still subject to the gentry, who provided the employment opportunities, offered land to lease, and supplied credit. They were the manipulators of the entire economic and social structure. However, the time soon came when particularly motivated or fortunate individuals could accumulate enough land and capital to rival the gentry. The former laborer became a master; the former borrower became a lender; the former petitioner in the court became a judge. The cycle continued as new immigrants took their places at the bottom of the economic and social ladder, there to work to better their condition. The social order allowed for far more upward movement than the Lords Baltimore had anticipated, and this upward mobility after a time transformed that order.

VI. THE ST. MARY'S RIVER SETTLEMENTS AFTER THE FIRST DECADE

The hierarchical social order of the first decade had not developed as the Lords Baltimore had hoped. It had not made early St. Mary's a stable community. Instead, a nearly continuous series of disruptive and debilitating struggles had shaken the colony's government. The men who had been expected to provide leadership had instead looked mostly to their own fortunes. The lower orders, furthermore, had not been so ready to be ruled as in more traditional societies. Religious tensions had also contributed to instability. On Governor Leonard Calvert's return to Maryland in September 1644, after a year and a half's absence in England, the government was on the brink of collapse. Some inhabitants, for example, were refusing to pay for or serve in expeditions against the Susquehannock Indians, who had attacked the outlying settlement at Mattapanient. Consequently, when the ship captain Richard Ingle raided St. Mary's in the name of Parliament early in 1645, Calvert and the gentry were unable to mount an effective resistance.

Ingle's Rebellion, as this event is usually called, nearly destroyed the colony. Leonard Calvert fled to Virginia, and Ingle, after looting the St. Mary's settlements, took the Jesuit priests and several Catholic leaders as prisoners to England. Maryland was left without a government for nearly two years. In later times, men referred to the period as "the time of troubles" or "the plundering time." Most of the inhabitants left, many becoming the first settlers in northern Virginia, just across the Potomac River. By the end of 1646, when Calvert reestablished his government, there were probably fewer people in St. Mary's County than had arrived on the *Ark* and the *Dove*. However, the colony revived, perhaps in part because the next few years saw a period of great expansion in the Chesapeake economy. Had there been a depression, the damage might have been irreparable. Toleration also survived the uprising, despite its anti-Catholic character, and was enacted into law in the famous Toleration Act of 1649. What did not reappear was the hierarchical society of Lord Baltimore's plan.

Such a society was bound to disappear. Opportunities for poor men were too great to encourage them to settle permanently on manors and accept the economic and political domination of their lords. If a servant or poor free immigrant did not die early—and admittedly early death was a definite risk—his chances of acquiring land and recognition in his community were excellent. Of 160 men who are known to have arrived as servants before the end of 1642, fewer than 10 percent of those still alive in Maryland ten years after gaining their freedom failed to become landowners. Furthermore, nearly the same proportion held some kind of community office during their lives, and 22 held positions of real authority: justice of the peace, sheriff, delegate to the Assembly, and councillor. Some of these men could not even write their names. They bore no resemblance to the gentlemen

210

investors who had owned most of the land and held all of the major offices during the first ten years.

Over the third quarter of the seventeenth century, the small owner-operated plantation, not the manor worked by laborers and tenants, became the prominent feature of the Maryland landscape. There were, of course, still indentured servants, free laborers, tenants, and sharecroppers, as well as landed gentry who could continue to hold much greater wealth than their neighbors and occupy offices of authority as a matter of course. Nevertheless, the owner of the modest plantation, a yeoman farmer with a fondness for hard work and advancement, became for a while the colony's typical citizen. And for those who were especially fortunate, political office and power was a possibility, despite the fact that they had not been born or educated to hold it. The early arrival who survived shared these opportunities.

The last quarter of the seventeenth century saw the disappearance of this highly mobile, predominantly small planter society in which church and state were separate. About 1680 a long depression in the tobacco industry set in. At the same time, planters' costs began a long-term rise as land and especially labor became more expensive. Planters were turning to black slaves as an answer to ever-present labor shortages, but capital was necessary to pay for slaves. These changes were destructive to poor men's chances. By about 1700, furthermore, the emergence of a native-born white population enabled some men to begin their adult careers with inherited wealth and office, thereby further diminishing opportunity for the poor. And toleration came to an end after a Protestant-led rebellion against the proprietor's authority in 1689. Catholics were barred from holding political office, and all free men were obliged to pay taxes to support the Church of England.

Eighteenth-century Maryland, where Catholics were deprived of political rights and the labor system was based on slavery, was not what the first two Lords Baltimore had envisioned. Nevertheless, its social hierarchy took on something of the shape that they had thought necessary for social stabil-

211

ity. Extremes of wealth increased and mobility slowed down. Men who began with nothing no longer could expect to become freeholders, much less attain a position of leadership. Political authority became concentrated in the hands of men born to wealth and the expectation of power. Small freeholders were still a majority, and the gentry courted their votes, but the deference of men low down in the hierarchy to men in positions above them was a cornerstone of the social order. This Maryland resembled the Calvert ideal far more than had the Maryland that followed the first decade. Most important of all, Maryland survived and grew. Cecilius Calvert's "hopeful Colony" had to struggle at first, but his "Expectation of good Success" became a reality.[41]

NOTES

1. Cecilius Calvert to Thomas Wentworth, 10 January 1634, *The Earl of Strafforde's Letters and Dispatches*, ed. William Knowler, 2 vols. (London, 1739), 1:178–79.
2. Research in recorded departures from England in the 1630s does not show any attempt to impose the Oath of Supremacy or any refusal to take the Oath of Allegiance where offered (personal communication from Mrs. Dinah Saville to D. B. Quinn).
3. "A Briefe Relation of the Voyage unto Maryland," in Clayton Colman Hall, ed., *Narratives of Early Maryland, 1633–1684* [hereafter *Md. Narratives*] (New York, 1910; repr. 1967), pp. 29–45.
4. Ibid., p. 31.
5. Ibid., p. 40.
6. *A relation of Maryland* (London, 1635), repr. in *Md. Narratives*, pp. 70–77.
7. D. B. Quinn, *England and the Discovery of America, 1481–1620* (New York, 1974), p. 394.
8. George Calvert to Charles I, 19 August 1629, in William Hand Browne et al., *Archives of Maryland* [hereafter *Md. Archives*], 73 vols. to date (Baltimore, 1883–), 3:15–16.
9. See above, pp. 23, 26–27, for a more detailed discussion of the Avalon and Maryland charters.
10. *Md. Archives*, 3:47–48; *Md. Narratives*, pp. 91–92, 95–96.

11. *Md. Narratives,* p. 6.
12. *Md. Archives,* 1:43.
13. Ibid., 3:180; Bernard C. Steiner, "More Fragments from the British Archives," *Maryland Historical Magazine* [hereafter *MHM*] 5 (1910):248; L. Leon Bernard, "Some New Light on the Early Years of the Baltimore Plantation," ibid., 44 (1949):93–100.
14. "Articles of Agreement made 7th October, 1633 between Leonard Calvert of London, Esquire, and Sir Richard Lechford of Shellwood in the County of Surrey, Knight," *The Calvert Papers, Number Three,* Maryland Historical Society Fund Publication no. 35 (Baltimore, 1899), pp. 13–14; Leonard Calvert to Lechford, 30 May 1634, ibid., pp. 25–26; *MHM* 1 (1906):363–64; 22 (1927):318–19; Bernard, "Some New Light," ibid, 44 (1949): 93–100; *A relation of Maryland,* p. 70; Alexander Brown, *The Genesis of the United States,* 2 vols. (Boston, 1890; repr. New York, 1964), 2:888; *Md. Archives,* 10:155; Cecilius, Lord Baltimore to Leonard Calvert, 21 November 1642, in *The Calvert Papers, Number One,* Maryland Historical Society Fund Publication no. 28 (Baltimore, 1889), p. 214.
15. "Annual Letter of the Society of Jesus, 1641," in *Md. Narratives,* p. 118; Thomas Hughes, *History of the Society of Jesus in North America,* 4 vols. (New York, 1907–8), *Text,* 1:244–52; Patents, 1:17, 18, 20, 25, 37, MSS, Hall of Records, Annapolis, Md.; Russell R. Menard, "Economy and Society in Early Colonial Maryland" (Ph.D. diss., University of Iowa, 1975), Appendix 1.
16. Thomas Cornwallis to Cecilius, Lord Baltimore, 16 April 1638, in *The Calvert Papers, Number One,* pp. 172, 174–75. For Cornwallis's investment and position, see also Raphael Semmes, "The Ark and the Dove," *MHM* 33 (1938):15–22; Bernard, "Some New Light," ibid., 44 (1949):93–100; Patents, AB&H:243–45, MS, Hall of Records, Annapolis, Md.; Robert P. Brenner, "Commercial Change and Political Conflict: The Merchant Community in Civil War London" (Ph.D. diss., Princeton University, 1970), p. 139; "Instructions to the Colonists by Lord Baltimore," in *Md. Narratives,* p. 16; Leonard Calvert to Cecilius, Lord Baltimore, 25 April 1638, in *The Calvert Papers, Number One,* pp. 190–191.
17. Cornwallis to Cecilius, Lord Baltimore, 16 April 1638, in *The Calvert Papers, Number One,* p. 172.
18. Brown, *Genesis of the United States,* 2:863; *Dictionary of National Biography,* 4:1159, 1169 (biographies of Charles and Wil-

liam Cornwallis); Harry Wright Newman, *The Flowering of the Maryland Palatinate* (Washington, D.C., 1961), passim.

19. Cornwallis to Cecilius, Lord Baltimore, 16 April 1638, in *The Calvert Papers, Number One,* p. 176.

20. See Menard, "Economy and Society," Appendix 1; Newman, *Flowering of the Maryland Palatinate.*

21. Edwin P. Beitzell, "Thomas Gerard of Maryland and Virginia; Old World Roots," *Chronicles of St. Mary's* 7 (1959):53–60; Christopher Johnson, "Neale Family of Charles County," *MHM* 7 (1912):201–18; Julia Cherry Spruill, "Mistress Margaret Brent, Spinster," *MHM* 29 (1943):259–68; W. B. Chilton, "The Brents of Maryland and Virginia," *Virginia Magazine of History and Biography* 16 (1908):96–99.

22. *A moderate and safe expedient* (London, 1646), p. 8. See the discussion of this pamphlet in Lawrence C. Wroth, "The Maryland Colonization Tracts," in William W. Bishop and Andrew Keogh, eds., *Essays Offered to Herbert Putnam* (New Haven, 1929), pp. 539–56; and Wilbur K. Jordan, *The Development of Religious Toleration in England, 1640–1660* (London, 1938), pp. 443–46.

23. Quoted in Jordan, *Religious Toleration,* p. 44.

24. "Instructions to the Colonists by Lord Baltimore," p. 16.

25. Leonard Calvert to Sir Richard Lechford, 30 May 1634, in *The Calvert Papers, Number Three,* p. 21.

26. *A relation of Maryland,* p. 73. The following discussion of the founding of the first settlement is based on this narrative and the sources cited in nn. 3 and 25, above.

27. "Instructions to the Colonists by Lord Baltimore," p. 22.

28. *A relation of Maryland,* p. 76.

29. Father Andrew White to Cecilius, Lord Baltimore, 20 February 1639, in *The Calvert Papers, Number One,* p. 228.

30. V. J. Wycoff, *Tobacco Regulation in Maryland,* John Hopkins University Studies in Historical and Political Science, n.s., no. 22 (Baltimore, 1936), p. 49.

31. W. W. Hening, *Statutes at Large: Being a Collection of All the Laws of Virginia from the First Session of the Legislature in the Year 1619,* 16 vols. (Richmond, Va., 1809–23), 1:224–25, 228; *Md. Archives,* 1:97–99. For tobacco prices, see Russell R. Menard, "A Note on Chesapeake Tobacco Prices, 1618–1660," *Virginia Magazine of History and Biography* 84:401–10.

32. John Lewgar to Cecilius, Lord Baltimore, 5 January 1639, in

The Calvert Papers, Number One, pp. 194–201. The letter gives a valuable conspectus of conditions at this date.

33. Patents, 1:24, 64–65, 100, 107, 129; AB&H:10, 79, 90 MSS, Hall of Records, Annapolis, Md.; Clayton Torrence, *Old Somerset on the Eastern Shore of Maryland: A Study of Foundations and Founders* (Richmond, Va., 1935), pp. 306–10.

34. Cornwallis to Cecilius, Lord Baltimore, 16 April 1638, in *The Calvert Papers, Number One*, p. 174.

35. *Cornwallis* v. *Ingle*, Records of the High Court of Chancery, C24/690/14, MS, Public Record Office, London. We are indebted to Noel Currer Briggs and Southside Historical Sites, Williamsburg, Virginia, for calling our attention to this document.

36. See n. 16, above.

37. Hughes, *History of the Society of Jesus in North America, Text*, 1:155–61, 168–76, 350–53.

38. *A relation of Maryland*, p. 99.

39. *Md. Archives*, 1:97.

40. Ibid., 4:27,283; 5:183; Patents, 2:509.

41. The basic study on which the foregoing essay depends is Menard, "Economy and Society in Early Colonial Maryland," chapters 1, 2, 3, and 5. This is complemented by Russell R. Menard, "From Servant to Freeholder: Status Mobility and Property Accumulation in Seventeenth-Century Maryland," *William and Mary Quarterly*, 3rd ser., 30 (1973):37–64; Lois Green Carr, " 'The Metropolis of Maryland': A Comment on Town Development along the Tobacco Coast," *MHM* 69 (1974): 124–45; Lois Green Carr, "The Foundations of Social Order: Local Government in Colonial Maryland," in Bruce C. Daniels, ed., *Town and County: Essays on the Structure of Local Government in the American Colonies* (Middletown, Conn., 1978), pp. 72–110; Lois Green Carr and Russell R. Menard, "Immigration and Opportunity: The Freeman in Early Colonial Maryland," in Thad W. Tate and David L. Ammerman, eds., *The Chesapeake in the Seventeenth Century: Essays in Anglo-American Society* (Chapel Hill, N.C., 1979), pp. 206–42. The historiography of the Tidewater Chesapeake area in the seventeenth century is fully discussed in Thad W. Tate, "The Seventeenth-Century Chesapeake and Its Modern Historians," ibid., pp. 3–50.

215

INDIANS AND FRONTIERS IN
SEVENTEENTH-CENTURY MARYLAND

Francis Jennings

Our conceptions of what happened on the frontiers of early Maryland depend upon the assumptions we bring to the subject. Changing assumptions require changing interpretations of fact. More traumatically, the discovery or realization of new facts sometimes requires that dearly held assumptions must be cast aside to be replaced by others more consistent with the facts. The latter process is often painful and seldom swift. An example of the process of change, and of the resistance it has encountered, is our understanding of what is familiarly known as "colonial" history. The name itself is misleading. So also is the title of this lecture. Both phrases imply that the only proper concerns of the historian are the people who immigrated to these shores from England, the social institutions they created, and the point of view with which they contemplated their handiwork. Given these assumptions, the historian places himself in imagination in the middle of Maryland's colonial settlements and looks outward from there.

If he limits himself to that one viewpoint, what he sees out yonder is a great unknown: a region of trackless wilderness inhabited by strange, wild, dangerous creatures. Some of these creatures have the shape of human beings, but their speech is unintelligible, their bodies are sinfully naked (and the use of

216

their bodies no less sinful), their beliefs are such as to foreordain them to eternal damnation, and their methods of regulating their communities are invisible. In short, they are savages. Their past excites curiosity only insofar as it seems to hint at a degenerate descent from cursed outcasts of ancient Israel. Their future is to get out of the way of civilization—namely us—either naturally and voluntarily or by being shoved.

The historian who adopts such assumptions sees only one frontier. It is the edge of civilized life, and beyond it is the undifferentiated mass of menacing savagery. As civilized society expands, history records "Progress," and the transformed land then becomes eligible for historical study. This conception of history is what gave birth to the Frontier Theory of Frederick Jackson Turner, but it did not die with Turner. As recently as 1965, Hugh Trevor-Roper, the eminent English historian, dismissed as merely amusing "the unrewarding gyrations of barbarous tribes in picturesque but irrelevant corners of the globe: tribes whose chief function in history, in my opinion, is to show to the present an image of the past from which, by history, it has escaped."[1]

We may, I suppose, take some comfort from Trevor-Roper's concession that the Chesapeake Bay can be picturesque. The irrelevance of this corner of the globe is less gratifying.

It did not seem irrelevant to the interests of Europeans prying into the coasts of North America. There were Frenchmen trading from shipboard with the Powhatan Indians so early as 1546, and Spanish priests became interested in the region when an important Powhatan Indian was captured in 1561. Baptized as Don Luis de Velasco, he guided a band of missionaries to the Chesapeake in 1566 and another in 1570, but then he changed sides. Whether he "reverted to savagery" or patriotically led his own native people in a liberation struggle depends on the way you look at it; what is not open to interpretation is that those priests were killed by those Indians, and Don Luis helped kill them as fervently as if he had been a Huguenot instead of a Catholic Powhatan.[2] The event was highly disturbing to Spanish authorities, who

217

took pains to mount a punitive expedition against the Powhatans. Something more than religious fervor was involved. The mission had received help from secular statesmen because they recognized the strategic value of the Chesapeake. Spanish sensitivity on the subject was sharpened by Ralegh's Roanoke colony of 1585–86 and the war with England so dramatically colored by the Spanish Armada. In 1599 the Spaniards even contrived a plan to build a great fort on the Chesapeake as a base from which to block English colonization along the whole Atlantic coast, but the plan was abandoned when European troubles forced Spain to concentrate attention closer to home. England got in after all, and 1607 saw the founding of Jamestown.[3]

My point is to demonstrate that there were a number of frontiers being created on the Chesapeake before Maryland was even thought of, and when Lord Baltimore's first ship arrived in 1634, it added just one more complication to an already complex situation. These were not merely frontiers of lines on the map—maps in those days were rather vague affairs—and they were not merely social frontiers between people of different cultures. They might perhaps be called overlapping zones of interest groups, but that is a bland sociological way of saying that these were lands for which different empires, nations, tribes, colonies, and freebooters were prepared to fight. Besides being always in danger of raids from the sea by privateers or pirates of European nativity, Maryland immediately became embroiled in bitter dispute with the other Englishmen of Virginia, and in later years extended its antagonisms to New York and Pennsylvania. Having all these frontiers to worry about, early Marylanders were almost casual about the surrounding Indian peoples. The colony's first hostilities began with a Virginian, a big planter named William Claiborne, who had nipped in without a patent to set up a trading post on Kent Island in 1631. When Leonard Calvert arrived with his brother's royal charter in 1634, Claiborne refused to get out; Calvert gained possession of Kent Island by armed force only after four years of bickering and a miniature sea fight.[4]

There is a special significance to Kent Island, for it was from that base that traders sailed up to the head of the bay to trade with the Susquehannock Indians, and this powerful tribe created yet another frontier for Maryland, one which was to become intertwined with all the others and to affect Maryland's destiny in unexpected ways. Until Captain John Smith met a canoe full of them in 1608, we have no record of the Susquehannocks, but Smith reported that they had trade goods in their canoe, so we assume that they must previously have had some contact, direct or indirect, with the traders thronging along the distant St. Lawrence River.[5] We know more certainly that they became very active as traders of peltry and as intermediaries in trade between the tribes of the far interior and the new European colonies along the Atlantic coast.[6] At the dawn of their recorded history, they lived in a single large community on the west bank of the Susquehanna River, about thirty-five miles from its mouth at the head of Chesapeake Bay.[7] The size of that village must be conjectured, but it was much larger than the English population of Maryland. We have an estimate from 1647 that implies a total Susquehannock population of about 6,000 persons at that date, and we know that these were the survivors of a smallpox epidemic that had buried many more.[8]

By contrast, Maryland's numbers were little more than 400 by 1642 and were still fewer than 1,500 by 1650.[9] Yet the Marylanders felt confident enough in their superior arms, armor, and horses to make the Susquehannocks their second adversary in combat. Alleging, perhaps correctly, that William Claiborne had instigated the Indians' hostility, Maryland declared war on the tribe in 1642 and launched two expeditions. The first triumphed in 1643, but the second came to grief a year later, when Marylanders first began to discover the possible complications in their frontier with the Susquehannocks.[10] Against all expectations, the Indians defeated and routed Maryland's force, capturing and brutally killing fifteen prisoners.

Thus Maryland learned that its frontier with the Susquehannocks was also a frontier with New Sweden. The Swedes

219

had founded their tiny colony on nearby Delaware Bay in 1638. Their purpose was single-minded: they wanted to trade with Indians for a profit, and their best trading partners turned out to be the Susquehannocks. The Swedes were acutely aware that a conquest of the Susquehannocks by Maryland would jeopardize their own colony's survival, so they supplied the Indians with firearms and military advisers, and the greatly outnumbered Maryland troops went down to crushing defeat.[11] It was but the first of many encounters that Maryland would have, directly or indirectly, with colonial occupants of Delaware Bay. As that bay later came successively under the jurisdictions of New Netherland and New York, Maryland's proprietary Calvert family tried repeatedly to snatch it away, but all such efforts were made with the chastening memory of the defeat by the Susquehannocks.

New Sweden was a tiny colony, almost forgotten even by its progenitors in old Sweden. At its absolute peak it never amounted to as many as 250 persons, though its alliance with the Susquehannocks gave it what we might now call leverage.[12] This alliance also had its interconnections and limitations. The trade that formed the nexus of relationships on Chesapeake and Delaware bays also extended into the interior for many hundreds of miles, and what happened at one end of it was likely to reverberate all the way to the other end. At the same time that Maryland, New Sweden, and the Susquehannocks had their difficulties in the south, there were similar contentions in the north on a much larger scale, involving New France, New Netherland, the Hurons, and the Iroquois Five Nations. Because the Susquehannocks had an alliance with the distant Hurons, Maryland came to have still another frontier, spread across the Great Lakes.

The Hurons and the Iroquois had been struggling for control of the sources of peltry in the Great Lakes region, and their colonial allies, New France and New Netherland, gave them support. New Netherland sold firearms to the Iroquois who attacked Huronia in 1649 and gained a decisive victory.[13] One after another, the Iroquois shattered the tribes of the old Huron network of allies until, in 1652, they gained another great victory over some people whom we know only as the Atrakwaeronnons. This dimly seen conflict in the wilderness became, strangely enough, a turning point for Maryland, for it seems likely that those Atrakwaeronnons were our friends the Susquehannocks. One of the problems with this kind of history is that different scribes put down different names for the same people, depending upon the language of the scribe and the language of the person from whom he got his information. We read about the defeat of the Atrakwaeronnons in a *Relation* of the Jesuit Fathers in New France, who were quite vague about the location of these people.[14] We have to reach out to archeology for evidence to identify them with the Susquehannocks. Our clue is numbers. Whoever those Atrakwaeronnons were, they lost 500 to 600 prisoners carried off by the Iroquois and suffered an unknown but probably large number of casualties. As I have mentioned, in 1647 the Susquehannocks had a population of roughly 6,000 persons. An archeological dig made at the site of the village they occupied after the battle of 1652 indicates a total population of something between 2,000 and 3,000 persons.[15] The sudden 50 percent drop implies a disaster such as the battle of 1652 surely was for the tribe on the losing side.

More positively, whether or not the Atrakwaeronnons and the Susquehannocks were the same people, the Iroquois conquests definitely caused the Susquehannocks to mend their fences. In that same year, 1652, they concluded a peace treaty with Maryland which enabled them to turn their full attention to the Iroquois.[16] The war ground on in a long series of raids and sieges that made a no-man's-land out of the vast tract of territory between Chesapeake Bay and the Mohawk Valley. What Marylanders were to discover in all this was that by becoming friends to the Susquehannocks they had become enemies to the Iroquois. They had some consolation in the price the Susquehannocks paid for their treaty— the cession of large tracts of territory on both shores of Chesapeake Bay. We cannot tell how the Susquehannocks acquired a right to territories so distant from the upriver land that they actually inhabited, and maybe the local tribes were not too happy about the arrangement, but the treaty was made and the cession was part of it.

Shortly afterward, another turnabout occurred. On Delaware Bay the Swedes forcibly closed down the posts of their Dutch competitors, whereupon the Dutch retaliated in 1655 by closing down all of New Sweden. The conquest was swift, and it forced reconsideration of all alliances. Since England and the Netherlands had already entered upon a protracted struggle for commercial and imperial supremacy, their American colonies knew that a showdown would have to come in the near future. The Dutch were therefore more than slightly apprehensive about all those Englishmen, so near but so un-neighborly, in Virginia and Maryland. The directors of the Dutch West India Company commented that "we cannot expect anything good from this nation, considering their insufferable proceedings in the past," and they advised New Netherland's director-general to keep all Englishmen out of Delaware Bay, by means unspecified.[17]

They had grounds for worry. In 1659, Cecilius Calvert, second Lord Baltimore, sent a delegation to demand the formal surrender of Delaware Bay, giving as authority the terms of his charter from the English Crown. Though Dutch officials stoutly rejected the demand, they could not keep news of it from their people. Panic ensued, and some fled to Maryland. Instead of having to keep individual Englishmen out, the Dutch were kept busy trying to hold their own people in.[18] The air became thick with suspicion. In 1660, five of the Piscataway Indians allied to Maryland were killed by the northern Oneidas. A seemingly simple frontier incident, it became complex when viewed in all the circumstances, for the Oneidas were at war with the Susquehannocks, and, as Maryland's council heard the news, the victims had been killed "for being friends" to Susquehannocks and Maryland.[19] That was the simplest explanation. What made it more dubious was that the Oneidas came from the north, where the Dutch seemed to dominate all trade with Indians. Could the Dutch have instigated the raid, and were more raids to come?

222

Let me say quickly that I have found no evidence that such was the case, but I can speak with hindsight. To Maryland's council the surrounding woods seemed filled with danger, and they immediately took two steps to make themselves secure. They declared war on what they called "Senecas"—by which they meant all the tribes of the Iroquois League, including the Oneidas—and they expanded their nonaggression pact with the Susquehannocks into a full alliance.[20] The propriety of such actions seems above reproach, but there were undercurrents in it.

Lord Baltimore wrote from England to instruct his government to direct hostilities against "certaine Enemies, Pyratts, and Robbers," by which euphonious terms he meant the Dutch.[21] Then another backwoods incident occurred. This time the victims of murder were four Marylanders, and the killers were Lenape Indians from Delaware Bay. Maryland called upon its Susquehannock allies to assist in getting "satisfaction" from the Lenape, and the Dutch became alarmed.[22] They were not concerned about any niceties of due legal process that the Marylanders might be skipping over a little hastily. What bothered them was the simple fact that the Lenape Indians lived on Delaware Bay, within the territory of New Netherland. The Dutch secretary, Beeckman, explained his fears quite clearly. "If the English go to war with these savages . . . all of the territory whence they drive out the same will be seized as taken from their enemies by the sword. The English will most likely come into our jurisdiction to pursue their enemies without having given previous notice; in case of refusal they would suspect us and treat us in the same manner."[23]

The scheme did not come off after all. The Susquehannocks, upon whom it depended, were not about to attack the Lenape, who were also their allies and whose manpower was badly needed for defense against attacks by the northern Iroquois. There was also a certain hesitation in Maryland, where the gentlemen in charge were rather closer to the possibility of retaliation than was Lord Baltimore in his comfortable dwelling in London. How could one be sure where these

223

proceedings would stop, once begun? The council wondered whether "Generall Styvesant at the Manhatans [might] make an advantage by those Indians" allied to the Dutch. Caution replaced belligerence, an explanation of the killings was given by a Lenape chief and accepted—they were in retaliation for the murder of an Indian—and Maryland made peace all round.[24] Nevertheless, the idea of seizing Delaware Bay remained very much alive. The only judgment being made at this moment was that the time was not yet ripe.

War broke out again between England and the Dutch. In September 1664, an English fleet sailed up Delaware Bay, and on the first of October the Dutch colony capitulated. Surely there should have been rejoicing in Maryland. Now, Lord Baltimore's charter could take full effect, and Delaware Bay would become part of the colony without any cost or trouble. There was, however, a catch. Royal commissioners were aboard that conquering English fleet, and they carried royal instructions. Among these was one that proclaimed that "the reduction of the place being at his Majesties expense, you have commands to keep possession thereof for his Majesties own behoof and right."[25] Charter right gave way to rights of conquest. Instead of Maryland swallowing up its frontier with New Netherland, it acquired a new frontier with New York. How vexing!—all the more so as the new frontier in some respects seemed to function in much the same manner as the old one. Though its menace had gone, the new frontier was an even stronger barrier to expansion.

For a few years there was so much confusion, internally and externally, that no new adventures were attempted on the border, but peace came in Europe in 1670, and with it came peace in North America—everywhere except on Maryland's frontiers. In the back country, Susquehannocks continued their wasting war with the Iroquois. At Delaware Bay the truce was broken when Lord Baltimore issued another proclamation in 1672. Once more he asserted that the lower end of Delaware Bay belonged to Maryland. This time there was no shilly-shallying. To enforce the edict thirty horsemen went out from Maryland to attack a community at the mouth of Delaware Bay, then known as the Whorekills, where Lewes, Delaware, now stands. The troop was formally charged to suppress all "mutinies, Insurrections, and Rebellions whatsoever," which was a rather roundabout way of saying that it was to establish Maryland's jurisdiction instead of New York's. The troop picked up some plunder, but the raiders quarreled among themselves and returned without accomplishing lasting results.[26] They did succeed in raising the blood pressure of New York's governor, Francis Lovelace, but this did not matter much because Lovelace was one of the most ineffectual statesmen ever to govern an American colony.[27] In any case, Lovelace was soon put out of action by a revival of the Anglo-Dutch wars. As an English fleet had formerly conquered New Netherland, so now, in 1673, a Dutch fleet conquered New York, and Maryland found itself once again with a Dutch frontier at Delaware Bay.

This merely inflamed Maryland's rulers to greater exertion. In December 1673, they launched another and larger cavalry raid on the Whorekills under the command of Captain Thomas Howell. It was intended to create a final solution to the jurisdictional problem there. Howell dallied for a bit while he tortured a merchant into confessing the location of his treasure, but he then got down to serious business. On Christmas Eve he called all the inhabitants together, relieved them of their arms, and disclosed his instructions from Lord Baltimore. He was to destroy everything on fifteeen minutes' notice; "he must not leave one stick standing." While the helpless inhabitants stood watching under guard, Howell's men put the place to the torch, refusing to permit the salvage of a single possession. Even boats and horses were taken away, as well as arms and food, and Howell rode off, abandoning the inhabitants to face the winter empty-handed, shelterless, and without means of travel to refuge. Neighboring Indians gave them help. Indeed, survivors recalled later that "the Indians that Lived here about wept when they saw the spoil that the Inhabitants had suffered by their owne native Country men." It is an instructive reaction when we contemplate the long history of racist rhetoric about the Indian menace.[28]

When the news reached him, the Dutch governor, General Anthony Colve, also sent help, and he put all the inhabitants of Delaware Bay into a state of military emergency. Ambiguously, he ordered "proper arrangements" to prevent "such cruel tyranny" in the future.[29] Precisely what these arrangements were does not appear in the record, but it is certain that Maryland's frontier with Delaware Bay had ceased to be an easy place to live. Once again, Marylanders drew conclusions also about the implications in that eastern frontier for the security of their northern frontier. On the first day of June 1674, the Maryland Assembly voted unanimously that it was "necessarie that a Peace be Concluded" with the Iroquois Five Nations.[30] It would seem that the assemblymen suspected a connection between Governor Colve's "proper arrangements" and the same governor's alliance with the Iroquois.

By this time, however, a peace with the Iroquois was not going to be easy to achieve. For over a dozen years, Maryland had been inciting the Susquehannocks to ever fiercer war against the Iroquois, and the hostile tribes had settled into a seemingly interminable feud. As the situation was presented by Maryland's council to the Assembly's representative lower house, hatred between the tribes had become so intense that the intended peace with the Iroquois might entail "a Warre with the Sasquahannoughs." How neatly this argument fitted into the stereotype of irrational savage ferocity, and how expertly the Assembly was manipulated by it! Lord Baltimore's council knew well that the Susquehannocks had long been weary of the dreadful raids and counterraids. Ten years earlier they had passed a hint to Maryland that they would welcome peace with the Iroquois, but the only response was increased agitation for continued fighting.[31] As events were to show, the Susquehannocks and Iroquois were ready enough to be reconciled when other parties would let them. I think that Maryland's council knew this. Why, then, did they raise the "savage menace" bogey to frighten the lower house of the Assembly?

The answer seems to lie in what they extracted from that

house by their scare tactics. This was legislation empowering the governor and council to make and finance war outside the colony's boundaries. The justification was the supposed likelihood of war with the Susquehannocks if peace were to be made with the Iroquois, but the language of the act extended beyond the Susquehannocks to include also "their Confederate Indians by them countenanced and protected."[32] The confederates in question were the Lenape Indians of Delaware Bay, and their inclusion makes suddenly clear what this charade was all about. Once more there was to be an invasion of Delaware Bay, this time on a large scale and financed by the provincial treasury. It would appear that the Maryland Assembly was anything but eager to fight a war against the Dutch, so they were manipulated into authorizing a war against the Lenape (which would amount to the same thing).

With the authorization safely in hand, Governor Calvert summoned the Susquehannock chiefs to a conference at Mattapany, and he did a strange thing. To these presumably menacing Indians he issued what was politely called an invitation to bring their entire tribe down into Maryland. What means of persuasion Calvert used are not recorded. An ultimatum, backed by the threat of war, seems likely.[33] The whole tribe did move, taking up new habitation in an abandoned stockaded village where Piscataway Creek flows into the Potomac, just south of present-day Washington. It was odd, surely, that such a location should be assigned, as it was, by Maryland's government, for it was much closer to Maryland's settled communities than the Susquehannocks' former village, and presumably it put them in position to wage war more formidably.[34] The location makes sense, however, when we disregard the propaganda about the Susquehannocks being a danger to Maryland and concentrate on the revealing phrase that they had been countenancing and protecting their Lenape allies. From their new position on the Potomac they would not be able to interpose themselves between the Lenape and an attacking force from Maryland.

But a sudden upset elsewhere forced abandonment of

227

the whole project. England and the Netherlands ended their war, the Dutch ceded New Netherland permanently to the English, and the duke of York sent over a new governor to take charge of Dutch territory at Delaware Bay as well as on the Hudson. He was the energetic and able Edmond Andros. We need not admire his authoritarian ways in order to recognize his intelligence and efficiency. We can infer also that he was informed about the maneuvers in Maryland, for his master, James, duke of York, had been told of the raids at the Whorekills, and it is unlikely that such important information would have been kept from the duke's most important officer on the scene. But whatever the details, the result is plain. Maryland called off its plans. Once again, however, we must add "for the time being." The threat of an attack on Delaware Bay would rise yet once more, even though the place had come under English jurisdiction. Through a strange twist of events, the threat next time would be occasioned by misfortune befalling the Susquehannocks, who had so tractably left their homeland at Calvert's demand.

The Susquehannocks' removal exposed them to a danger they had never anticipated, for it made them into a sort of lightning rod, attracting strikes from would-be conquerors. As the conquest of the Lenape implied seizure by Maryland of territory on Delaware Bay, the conquest of the Susquehannocks at their new location implied seizure by Virginia of choice territory on the Potomac River. As was their normal routine, bands of Susquehannocks scattered from their village to hunt, and one of these bands unwittingly drew Virginia's lightning down upon them all.[35] Late in 1675, some Doeg Indians raided a Virginia plantation and killed its herdsmen. A hue and cry went up, and a party of men seized arms and set out to punish the offenders. As is unfortunately too usual in such cases, they did not stand upon niceties of differentiation between one Indian and another. They came upon a cabin and began shooting. By the time their officer screamed at them to stop because these were friendly Indians, fourteen Susquehannocks lay dead. To complicate matters further, the affray had taken place on Maryland's territory.

228

It is very difficult to ascribe motives for what happened next. Were the Virginians' subsequent actions caused by hysterical panic or cool calculation? Either would be possible in the circumstances. One can assume panic over the possibility that the killing of Susquehannocks would arouse that fighting tribe to retaliate by killing Virginians. In fact, there were Indian raids on the back settlers, but several tribes were embroiled by the time these occurred. Or we can think that, regardless of what officialdom understood, the killing of Susquehannocks proved to the popular mind that they were a guilty people and deserved further punishment. Either assumption would explain the decision in Virginia to organize a large force to campaign against the Susquehannocks, a decision that was made by Colonel John Washington and Major Isaac Allerton in defiance of Governor Berkeley's orders to conduct an investigation instead of a campaign. There is a third possibility: that Washington and Allerton calculated that an attack on the Susquehannocks would enable Virginia to claim, by right of conquest, borderlands that were still in dispute between Virginia and Maryland.

It would seem that the third possibility was much in the minds of the Marylanders. Although they had protested the first incursion on Maryland's soil and the killing of their Indian allies, when Washington and Allerton announced their intention to march again, Maryland mobilized 250 troops to march with them. The combined force laid siege to the Susquehannocks' stockaded village.

The situation seems bizarre nowadays because we no longer appeal so nakedly to conquest as justification for making war. Today all wars are called "defensive" by both sides. But in the seventeenth century, rights of conquest were treated very seriously as a major factor in what passed for international law, and the situation in Maryland was not an isolated example. The New England colonies had much earlier attacked the Pequot tribe for the same reason, and Massachusetts and Connecticut spent decades squabbling over which of them had gained conquest rights over Pequot territory. They were in process of repeating the same performance with an attack upon the Narragansetts while Virginia and Maryland were on the march against the Susquehannocks.[36] Modern historians have preferred to look past what seem now to be fairly sordid affairs, but war was an accepted instrument of policy in those days, and conquest was an accepted goal of policy. The record shows that Maryland troops joined Virginia's without any apparent good reason to do so. The Susquehannocks had behaved as desired and had lived up to the terms of their treaty. Yet now they were being attacked in Maryland by Maryland. The only explanation that makes sense to me is that if conquest rights were going to be claimed, Maryland intended to have as good a claim to them as anyone else.

Whether such inferences are right or wrong, the affair itself was a squalid fiasco. Five Susquehannock chiefs were granted a safe conduct to come out of their stockade and negotiate. The pledge was violated. Instead of being allowed to rejoin their people or even being taken into captivity, the chiefs were seized by order of one or both of the colonial commanders and immediately killed. I suppose the intention was to demoralize the Susquehannocks sufficiently to make them give up, but they fought on, and one black night they emerged secretly from their stockade and stealthily made their way to a clean escape. They killed ten of the besieging militiamen on their way, and soon gave cause to all colonials to regret their treatment. The Susquehannocks valued each of their chiefs' lives at ten Englishmen's lives. Without delay they began to settle the account.

It is worth notice that there was outrage in Maryland over the whole mess. Major Thomas Truman, who had commanded Maryland's troops, stood trial in the Assembly for his complicity in the slaughter of the chiefs and was convicted, but conviction meant little more than opprobrium. Truman's sole punishment was a requirement to give a security bond, and Lord Baltimore quietly lifted that a couple of years later. Only the resentment of the populace had forced him to trial. Baltimore explained, "I have no desire that the said Truman should imagine I have the least malice or prejudice to his person . . . what I formerly did order [that is, the requirement that Truman should stand trial] was only occasioned by the great exigency of affaires att that tyme."[37]

There were no such inconveniences for Washington and Allerton in Virginia. They simply heaped all blame on Truman, producing affidavits from their followers to back them up.[38] In any case, Virginians were preoccupied by matters of more immediate urgency. Nathaniel Bacon presented himself as an unauthorized commander of militiamen and launched a campaign against Virginia's tributary Indians—even against those who had themselves fought against Susquehannocks. Bacon's ostensible reason was that he was going to punish Susuquehannocks, but in fact he never touched them, though he did kill and plunder a great many members of tribes living under subjection to Virginia. "Plunder of Indians" sounds strange to a modern ear, but there was real wealth to be gained in the form of accumulated stocks of peltry. Whether Bacon and his men were actuated more by hatred of Indians or by greed is impossible to say; the killing and plundering are on the record.

Maryland had warded off the rights-of-conquest threat from Virginia only by making enemies of former friends. The Susquehannocks hid in the backwoods and struck when they pleased at both colonies' isolated outposts. Now Maryland had one more frontier, and this one corresponded, within its limits, to the Frontier—the line of racial hate between Indians and whites. But far from being the norm, as Frontier theory has depicted it, this situation was so intolerable to the people actually living in it that several different efforts were immediately made to reestablish peace. The Susquehannocks themselves, having satisfied their ideas of justice by taking ten lives for each of their murdered chiefs, offered peace to Virginia if that colony would pay reparations for its unwarranted attack and withhold aid from Maryland. Precisely those lives, however, had made such a settlement inconceivable. Perhaps if the Susquehannocks had not already taken such a heavy toll of retaliation, Virginia might have paid their price for peace and thought it cheap. There is room

231

for some skepticism. Anyway, it did not happen. Both Virginia and Maryland remained in a state of war.[39]

A peacemaker appeared from an unexpected direction. Far to the north and east, New York's Governor Edmond Andros had watched appalled as the flames of Indian war went up in colonies on both sides of his own. The danger seemed imminent to him that the Wampanoags and Narragansetts of New England would combine with the Susquehannocks and sweep up all the tribes between to launch a general racial war against all English colonies.[40] The thought was intolerable, and Andros was not a man to sit by and wring his hands.

In February 1676, he sent his allied Mohawks against the New England tribes to turn the tide of battle decisively—a feat that New England's historians have never adequately acknowledged. (They have a grudge against Andros for his later domination while governor of the Dominion of New England.) This military success was only the beginning of Andros's arrangements. His true genius lay not in winning the war, but in achieving a peace. Having forced the Indians to recognize defeat, he offered them refuge in his own jurisdiction of New York and protection against the intended vengeance of the furious Puritans. He was as good as his word. When Indian refugees straggled in, as they did by hundreds, he settled them at the village of Schaghticoke, on the Hudson above Albany, and steadfastly denied the demands of Massachusetts and Connecticut for their blood.[41] Perhaps it was mere coincidence that their village was strategically situated to guard the passageway from French Canada to Albany.

In the south his task was easier, for the Susquehannocks had already been made war-weary by their long conflict with the Iroquois and the climactic disaster of colonial attack. Andros's hardest problem, indeed, was to make contact with them. Finally, in February 1677, there came a day when two Susquehannocks were reported to have been seen among the Lenape at Delaware Bay. Andros immediately ordered his deputy there to find and bring them to him in New York.[42] When it was done, he came directly to the point with charac-

232

teristic bluntness. If the Susquehannocks would return to live "anywhere" within his government, he said, "they shall be welcome and protected from their Enemys. . . . They should say whether they will come into the government or no. If they will not, it is well; if they will, he will make provision for them." No strings were attached. The long feud with the Iroquois would end. That would be the easiest part of the peace, as the Mohawks were positively eager to welcome the Susquehannocks as long-lost kinsmen.[43] The Susquehannocks may have been a little doubtful about this sudden turnabout. They did accept Andros's invitation to settle within his jurisdiction, but instead of joining the Mohawks, they chose to attach themselves to their old associates, the Lenape on Delaware Bay.

Here was a difficult situation for Maryland. The Susquehannocks were out of reach of ordinary punitive action. Nothing but a major campaign could be effective against them on the Delaware, and that would entail serious consequences in England even if successful. On the other hand, it was impossible to ignore the danger of the situation while Maryland was still formally at war with both the Susquehannocks and the Iroquois. Andros had made peace within his own jurisdiction, but he could not control these independent tribes further than he could persuade them, and his resources for persuasion, though great, were not without limits. When Maryland contemplated Indian enemies in protected sanctuaries, it seemed advisable to make its own peace.

Complications remained, however. Maryland was allied to other tribes, and those Piscataways and Mattawomans had been conspicuous in hunting down the fugitive Susquehannocks. For Maryland to make its own peace would be to abandon these allies to Susquehannock revenge. They wanted the war continued until their enemies ceased to be an effective threat. Maryland's council scented interesting possibilities. Would these allied tribes march under Maryland's officers against the Susquehannocks? They would.[44]

Lord Baltimore still claimed Delaware Bay by charter right, and once more he seemed to have the possibility of

233

adding conquest rights by invading the place in hot pursuit of Indian enemies. The evidence is all circumstantial, but there is no doubting that Edmond Andros was aware of the possibilities. He moved decisively to eliminate them. He issued a polite ultimatum to Maryland's government: it must make full peace with the Susquehannocks where they were, or else receive them into its own territory. Otherwise Andros might have to let the Iroquois take them to the Mohawk Valley—which might be "of a bad consequence."[45] When Maryland failed to respond, Andros turned to the Susquehannocks themselves. The situation became sticky when they sat tight. They liked Delaware Bay.

It got stickier when Maryland maneuvered to take the initiative away from Andros. Instead of making the peace with the Susquehannocks that Andros had demanded, Maryland's Deputy Governor Thomas Notley projected a peace with "all manner of Indians."[46] This was a little like praising mother love. Who could find fault with it? There was, however, as on so many of these occasions, a small catch. The peacemaking in question was to be directed primarily toward the Iroquois, and it would have the effect of detaching them from Andros's domination. It is evident from the proposals that Maryland tried to work into its treaty that the objective was to make the Susquehannocks responsible to the Iroquois and the Iroquois subject to Maryland. Maryland could sit comfortably on top of such a structure.

The same sort of effort was being made simultaneously in New England as Massachusetts and Connecticut tried to wheedle Andros into letting them go directly to the Iroquois to make treaties independently of his controls. There were quarrels over territory as the duke of York claimed all the land formerly disputed between New Netherland and the Puritan colonies; and in New England also the power of the Iroquois seemed to be the key element in strategy for supremacy.[47] Andros was as much aware of this as any of his adversaries, and he was not caught napping.[48] Before Maryland could get its Iroquois plan into operation, Andros sent these same Iroquois down into Delaware Bay to talk to the stubborn Susquehannocks, and, when the Iroquois returned to their own country, most of the Susquehannocks went with them. In that position, instead of being a hazard, they were an addition to Iroquois strength, and Iroquois strength was Andros's strength. Thus, when Maryland's emissary Henry Coursey journeyed to New York to persuade Andros to accept the Maryland project for what would have been a somewhat lopsided peace treaty, he faced a series of unpleasant surprises. He traveled by way of New Castle on Delaware Bay, with an escort of mounted gentlemen, and at the very outset they received a most inhospitable welcome. As they approached the town an alarm was sounded and the local militia was summoned to man the fort, "there to bee uppon their Garde and Receive such further order as shall be found necessary." Vigilant New Castle had no intention of becoming another Whorekills.

This flurry past, Coursey found in New York that Andros was proof against all persuasion, even the hundred pounds sterling that Lord Baltimore offered "as a token of his Lordshipps thankfulness for [Andros's] care and kindness to Maryland." Though a treaty was finally made, its terms were dictated by Andros; all of Coursey's efforts to acquire hegemony over the Indians were rejected. What Coursey got was peace and no more; the Susquehannocks remained safe and sound, beyond Maryland's reach, in Iroquoia. It was not even a completely comprehensive peace. By the Indians' interpretation it left them free to strike at will against Maryland's allied tribes, and complaints to New York were ignored or rebuffed. Finally the turbulence in Maryland's back country compelled the colony to send another treaty mission, in 1682. Then, at last, the frontier between Maryland and the Susquehannocks ceased to be an active problem.

This is not to say that the back country became peaceful and quiet—there was always nervousness about prowling Indians allied to New France—or that the Calvert proprietaries of Maryland gave up their claim to Delaware Bay. That frontier was reactivated in a new form, and an entirely new frontier came into being in the north after William Penn carved the new fief of Pennsylvania out of New York. A whole new series of threats and battles and lawsuits commenced over the boundaries between the colonies, but that is a very long story in itself. It is sufficient here to note only that it continued for another eighty years, until the Mason and Dixon Line finally settled it—*almost* completely.

What is the significance of tales such as this? I don't think it is a matter of good guys and bad guys so much as of traditions and circumstances. As the saying goes, almost everyone has a little larceny in his heart. If he lives in a time and place where a particular sort of predation is acceptable behavior, he will probably try to grab what he can. Community mores set our limits and determine whom we may regard as legitimate prey and whom we must respect as though he were a member of the family. In the seventeenth century most Englishmen could not conceive of Indians as kin. One had to respect the Indians' power to retaliate for injury, but the law of moral obligation coincided with the bounds of ethnicity. Now *there* is a frontier for you!

Traditions that contributed strongly to this state of affairs were those of Christianity and conquest. I do not speak of the Christianity of the Sermon on the Mount, but rather of the religion of warrior lords of crusade, the Inquisition, and holy wars of Reformation and Counter-Reformation—the Christianity that ordered men to kill or enslave those other men whom they could not convert. It was a tradition still very much alive in seventeenth-century Europe, and it went hand-in-glove with the tradition of conquest. Englishmen accepted both traditions as normal and displayed their acceptance with peculiar intensity in the Elizabethan and Cromwellian conquests of Catholic Ireland. How should Indians expect more humane or respectful treatment than Irishmen?

There was still another tradition inherited from medieval Europe in the history of struggle and private war between noblemen over possession of estates. The English crown had gained only an uncertain ascendancy over such struggles within the realm, and it lacked means to control them in the colonies, as the colonists understood, When the Calvert family acted on the principle that possession would enable them to win at law, they held the same assumptions as a large proportion of the medieval baronage of England. It was a widely held tradition: while the Catholic Calverts demonstrated it on Delaware Bay, the Puritans of Massachusetts Bay and Connecticut struggled simultaneously to gobble up Rhode Island with the same sort of devices. The Indians also, it may be noticed, could not have been manipulated if they had not been ready, for their own reasons, to go along with the game. The Susquehnanocks would fight the Iroquois because their interest in the fur trade was at stake, and so it did not matter that they were acting at the same time as Maryland's cat's-paws, but they would not fight their allied Delawares when Maryland egged them on. They could and did draw the line there, and their doing so frustrated Maryland's schemes. When it finally became advantageous, the Susquehannocks made peace with the Iroquois and joined their old enemies.

The prime lesson I would draw from all this is to look with open eyes at what happened in history and let that determine our theories, instead of selecting data to demonstrate theories. As for the role of frontiers in our history, I will conclude with a quotation from an unimpeachably objective publication, the *Dictionary Catalog of the History of the Americas: The New York Public Library Reference Department.* Page 1 of its introduction summarizes the contents of those enormous tomes—and of that great library—with a dryly unambiguous comment: "The amount of material concerning boundary disputes is so extensive in the catalog that the subject must be regarded as a characteristic element of American history."

NOTES

1. Hugh Trevor-Roper, *The Rise of Christian Europe* (New York, 1965), p. 9.
2. Woodbury Lowery, *The Spanish Settlements within the Present*

Limits of the United States, 1513–1561 (New York, 1901), pp. 360–64; D. B. Quinn, *North America from Earliest Discovery to First Settlements: The Norse Voyages to 1612* (New York, 1977), pp. 281–83.

3. Quinn, *North America*, pp. 283–87, chaps. 13, 18.
4. William Hand Browne et al., eds., *Archives of Maryland* [hereafter *Md. Archives*], 73 vols. to date (Baltimore, 1883–), 3:64–73.
5. John Smith, *A map of Virginia* (Oxford, 1612), in Philip L. Barbour, ed., *The Jamestown Voyages under the First Charter*, 2 vols., Works Issued by the Hakluyt Society, ser. 2, vols. 136, 137 (Cambridge, 1969), 2:342.
6. William A. Hunter, "The Historic Role of the Susquehannocks," in John Witthoft and W. Fred Kinsey, ed., *Susquehannock Miscellany*, vol. 3 (Harrisburg, Pa., 1959), pp. 8–18; Francis Jennings, "Susquehannock," in William C. Sturtevant, ed., *Handbook of North American Indians*, to be completed in 20 vols. (Washington, D.C., 1978–), vol. 15, *Northeast*, ed. Bruce G. Trigger, pp. 362–67.
7. D. H. Landis, "The Location of Susquehannock Fort," *Publications of the Lancaster County [Pa.] Historical Society* 14 (March 1910): 81–117; John Witthoft, "Ancestry of the Susquehannocks," in *Susquehannock Miscellany*, p. 29.
8. Reuben Gold Thwaites, ed., *The Jesuit Relations and Allied Documents*, 73 vols. (Cleveland, Ohio, 1896–1901), 33:129. The Jesuits reported an estimated 1,300 Susquehannock warriors; multiplying by 4 implies a total population of 5,200, and by 5 a total population of 6,500. For the epidemic, see Bruce G. Trigger, *The Children of Aataentsic*, 2 vols. (Montreal and London, 1976), 2:528; *Jesuit Relations*, 14:9.
9. Arthur E. Karinen, "Maryland Population: 1631–1730: Numerical and Distributional Aspects," *Maryland Historical Magazine* [hereafter *MHM*] 54 (1959): 370; table 2, p. 405.
10. *Md. Archives*, 35:64, 66, 116–17, 127–28, 130–32, 148–51; Beauchamp Plantagenet, *A Description of the Province of New-Albion*, 2d ed. (London, 1650, p. 14; Report of Governor Johan Printz, 1644, in Albert Cook Myers, ed., *Narratives of Early Pennsylvania, West New Jersey, and Delaware, 1630–1707*, Original Narratives of Early American History (New York, 1912), p. 102; Peter Lindeström, *Geographia Americae*, trans. and ed. Amandus Johnson (Philadelphia, Pa., 1925), pp. 241–44.

Lindeström used the term "Virginians" for all Englishmen on Chesapeake Bay. It is significant that Maryland's defeat does not appear in the colony's official records—it would not have looked well when they came to the crown's attention.

11. Plantagenet, *Description of New-Albion*, pp. 10, 14.
12. List of inhabitants, 1654–55, in Amandus Johnson, *The Swedish Settlements on the Delaware, 1638–1664*, 2 vols. (Philadelphia, Pa., 1911), 2:716–22.
13. The best account of the Iroquois wars is in Trigger, *Children of Aataentsic*, 2:629–33, chap. 11.
14. *Jesuit Relations*, 37:97, 111. On p. 105 is a report that the Iroquois had gone against "the Atra'kwae'ronnons" or "Andasto, e'ronnons." The Andastoeronnons were the Susquehannocks (as known to the French by way of the Huron language). The quoted phrase is ambiguous: it could mean that there were two distinct tribes and that the reporter was uncertain which had been attacked, or it could mean that "Atrakwaeronnon" was simply another name for Andastoeronnon.
15. Interview with Barry C. Kent, 23 August 1972, about unpublished findings of the Division of Archaeology, Pennsylvania Historical and Museum Commission, Harrisburg, Pennsylvania.
16. *Md. Archives*, 3:276–78.
17. E. B. O'Callaghan and Berthold Fernow, eds., *Documents Relative to the Colonial History of the State of New York* [hereafter *N.Y. Colonial Documents*], 15 vols. (Albany, N.Y., 1856–87), 12:215–16.
18. *Md. Archives*, 3:365–78, 426–31; *N.Y. Colonial Documents*, 12:248–55, esp. p. 255; Alrichs to De Graaff, ibid., 2:70.
19. *Md. Archives*, 3:403.
20. Ibid., pp. 406–7, 420–21, 453.
21. Baltimore to Captain James Neale, 20 July 1660, ibid., p. 427; council minutes, 1 July 1661, ibid., p. 426.
22. Ibid., pp. 414–15; clause 9 of treaty, 16 May 1661, ibid., p. 421. Other violence by Indians identified as Susquehannocks had purportedly taken place in April, but the treaty does not demand their surrender; instead, Maryland sent troops to build a fort for the Susquehannocks with instructions "upon all occasions to assist against the Assaults of their Ennemies" (ibid., p. 417).
23. William Beeckman to Stuyvesant, 27 May 1661, *N.Y. Colonial Documents*, 12:343–44.

24. *Md. Archives,* 3:433; *N.Y. Colonial Documents,* 12:356–57. The Delawares' explanation of the killings as retaliation is confirmed by the account given to Maryland's council before it made an issue of the case. Five Delawares had been killed by Marylanders in an affray in which they lost one of their own men (*Md. Archives,* 3:414).
25. *N.Y. Colonial Documents,* 12:457–58.
26. Whorekills inhabitants' affidavits in *Pennsylvania Magazine of History and Biography* 74 (1950):477; *Md. Archives,* 45:50–55; 5:106–11.
27. Victor Hugo Paltsits, ed., *Minutes of the Executive Council of the Province of New York: Administration of Francis Lovelace, 1668–1673,* 2 vols. (Albany, N.Y., 1910), 2:678–82.
28. Leon de Valinger, J., "The Burning of the Whorekill, 1673," *Pennsylvania Magazine of History and Biography* 74 (1950): 473–87; *Md. Archives,* 15:27–29.
29. *N.Y. Colonial Documents,* 12:511.
30. *Md. Archives,* 2:377–78.
31. Ibid., 3:498–502.
32. Ibid., 2:462–63.
33. Ibid., pp. 428–30; 17:98; conference between Penn and Talbot, New Castle, 1684, in *MHM* 3 (1908):25.
34. Alice L. L. Ferguson, "The Susquehannock Fort on Piscataway Creek," *MHM* 36 (1941):1–9.
35. The facts of what follows are drawn from Wilcomb E. Washburn, *The Governor and the Rebel: A History of Bacon's Rebellion in Virginia* (Chapel Hill, N.C., 1957), chap. 2.
36. Francis Jennings, *The Invasion of America: Indians, Colonialism, and the Cant of Conquest* (Chapel Hill, N.C., 1975), chaps. 12, 13, 17, 18.
37. *Md. Archives,* 15:182–83.
38. See, for instance, those in Lyon G. Tyler, "Col. John Washington: Further Details of His Life from the Records of Westmoreland Co., Virginia," *William and Mary Quarterly,* ser. 1, 2 (July 1893):38–49. A Marylander deposed that Captain Truman had been "overswayed" by the Virginia officers (*Md. Archives,* 2:482–83).
39. Washburn, *Governor and Rebel,* p. 25.
40. *N.Y. Colonial Documents,* 12:543.
41. Jennings, *Invasion of America,* pp. 314–16, 318, 321–23.
42. Andros to Cantwell, 22 February 1676, Dreer MSS Collection,

Governors of Colonies, 1:2, Historical Society of Pennsylvania, Philadelphia.

43. *N.Y. Colonial Documents,* 13:497–98; 12:558.
44. *Md. Archives,* 15:120–26.
45. *N.Y. Colonial Documents,* 12:558.
46. *Md. Archives,* 5:152–53; 15:149.
47. Jennings, *Invasion of America,* chap. 18.
48. What follows is recounted in greater detail and with full documentation in Francis Jennings, "Glory, Death, and Transfiguration: The Susquehannock Indians in the Seventeenth Century," *Proceedings of the American Philosophical Society* 112 (January 1968):39–45.

MASTERS, SERVANTS, AND SLAVES
IN THE COLONIAL CHESAPEAKE
AND THE CARIBBEAN

Richard S. Dunn

What is the point, one may ask, of comparing the Chesapeake pattern of colonial settlement with that of the British West Indies? These two regions are physically remote from each other, they are geographically distinct, and they developed into entirely different societies. Yet we should remember that they were founded by much the same people at much the same time. The earliest English islands—Barbados, St. Kitt's, Nevis, Antigua, and Montserrat—were colonized between 1624 and 1634, only a few years after Virginia was started and contemporaneously with Maryland. The people who went out to these two regions of the New World, unable to discover gold mines, quickly settled into growing tobacco. Chesapeake tobacco was much better than Caribbean tobacco, but both groups of pioneer settlers encountered the same problems in getting this crop going, both suffered heavy mortality from strange diseases, both initially utilized a white labor force composed of indentured servants, and both switched from white servant labor to black slave labor during the seventeenth century.

Yet it is obvious that these comparisons cannot be carried too far. In the mid-seventeenth century the Caribbean planters switched from tobacco to sugar, from a marginally profitable crop to an immensely profitable one. They plunged into slave-holding earlier and more vigorously than their Chesapeake counterparts. And as the sugar and tobacco economies matured, the island planters became more dependent on home support, while the Chesapeake planters came to feel increasingly independent. By the time of the American Revolution, the two regions had diverged very strikingly. In the Chesapeake were rebels against the crown, founders of a new republic, Americans who thought of the New World as home. In the Caribbean were loyalists to the crown, many of whom were absentee proprietors, and who thought of England rather than the islands as home.

The people from the two regions even turned into somewhat different physical types. Visitors to the Chesapeake, such as Ebenezer Cook, made fun of the crude tobacco farmers, decked out

> In Shirts and Drawers of *Scotch-cloth* Blue.
> With neither Stockings, Hat, nor Shooe.
> These *Sot-weed* Planters Crowd the Shoar,
> In Hue as tawny as a Moor.

Native writers, such as Robert Beverley, upbraided the Chesapeake folk for their lazy habits.[1] But in fact the colonial inhabitants of Maryland and Virginia pursued intensely active lives. If they were not toiling in the fields, they were constantly on horseback. Eighteenth-century diaries show that Chesapeake horsemen covered nearly as many miles annually as modern motorists. Robert Rose, a Tidewater parson, slept under his own roof only half the nights of the year and made three or four round trips annually between the Rappahannock and the Blue Ridge.[2] And when Chesapeake people wanted to relax, their favorite recreation was boisterous dancing: jigs, reels, and other hearty country dances. It was the West Indian planters who really practiced the fine art of laziness. Some of these West Indians, disdaining to work or even to walk in the tropical heat, made their slaves carry them from place to place in litters and confined their physical exertions to the lifting of punch cups. When visitors from the islands showed up, North Americans looked askance at their carbuncled faces, slender legs and thighs, and large, prominent bellies.[3]

Why did these societies, having started in important respects at the same base point, move so swiftly in opposite directions? Edmund Morgan recently has offered a new interpretation of the development of the colonial Chesapeake in his provocative book, *American Slavery—American Freedom*.[4] Morgan talks about Virginia, but his argument is also meant to apply to Maryland. He emphasizes the long, slow process of conversion in the Chesapeake from a white servant labor force to a black slave labor force. The Virginians, he contends, struggled hard for almost a century to erect a society based on white labor, but they failed because the Chesapeake white laborers felt so exploited and became so dangerously restive. The only solution the Chesapeake people could find was to switch to black African slave labor. Morgan argues that this creation of black slavery was symbiotically related to the emergence of an American doctrine of freedom. The Virginians' concept of equality, of liberty, and of republicanism—the concepts that we honor the founding fathers for—were rooted in their experience as slaveholders. They believed in freedom with special ardor because they held slaves. They valued republican self-government because they kept their black workers in shackles. How does this intriguing and unsettling thesis, this insistence on the mutual development of America's most creative and destructive institutions, apply to those other Englishmen in the Caribbean, who likewise switched from white to black labor, from servants to slaves? And how does the Caribbean experience in general throw light on the Chesapeake transfer from white to black labor?

In order to understand the situation in the early seventeenth century, when both the Chesapeake and the Caribbean planters got started by employing white indentured servants, it is necessary to inquire into the labor system in England, from whence these pioneers came. In the early seventeenth century, over half of the English population

244

was in a state of servile labor. Most of these servile laborers were permanently employed by others, either as wage laborers or as tenant farmers; they owned little or no property of their own beyond the clothes on their backs; they were unable to save for the future or provide for their children; and they were socialized to expect such circumstances as their permanent, unalterable fate. But there were also a large number of servile laborers of a temporary sort; these more fortunate people were the young apprentices or indentured servants who contracted to work without wages throughout adolescence and then graduated into independent status as adults. For these people, servile labor was a stage in education and career training. But whether these servile laborers were permanent or temporary, they performed most of the hard work in seventeenth-century England, receiving minimal or no wages, and their work earned them no share in society's meager stock of surplus wealth. In this system the apprentices and indentured servants could expect eventually to improve themselves, but the permanent drudges who constituted the bottom half of society knew that they would never have anything beyond bare subsistence.[5]

The first English colonists, whether they came to the Caribbean or to the Chesapeake, naturally expected to transfer this system of servile labor to America. It did not occur to Sir Walter Ralegh that he was thwarting the ambitions of the colonists he sent to Roanoke by employing them as servants. The investors in the Virginia Company saw nothing odd about shipping contract laborers to Jamestown. The early investors in the Chesapeake and the Caribbean saw these areas as stages for economic exploitation. They were not really looking for new places to live, but for new sources of profit. They were hoping of course to find gold and silver, like the Spaniards, but they were willing to settle for trade with the Indians or for some kind of profitable cash crop which would be attractive at home. In the 1620s and 1630s they settled for tobacco. In staking out tobacco farms they thought automatically of two categories of colonists: owners and workers, or managers and servants. In early Barbados or Virginia, one finds a small cohort of gentry to supervise affairs, the agents of absentee gentry, and a much larger class of servants to do the work.

These servants, both in the Chesapeake and in the Caribbean, seem to have been drawn largely from the ranks of the temporary servile laborers at home. Permanent drudges in England did not have the incentive to sign up for contract labor abroad. Some of them were certainly kidnapped and shipped over involuntarily. To be "barbadosed" in the seventeenth century was equivalent to being "shanghaied" in the twentieth. A good many military prisoners were sent over during the civil wars of the 1640s and 1650s. But the majority of the indentured servants in the Chesapeake and in the Caribbean appear to have signed up voluntarily. They were young males for the most part; the shipping lists we have show them to be between the ages of fifteen and twenty-five. In England such youngsters were in a transitional state, being old enough to perform heavy labor but too young to marry or establish independent lives as farmers or craftsmen. We can think of them as migratory laborers, who might stay on in America if the chances looked good, or who might prefer to return home when their indentures expired.[6] Of course, many of them died shortly after arrival, before they had this choice to make. The fact that most of them were males is another indication of their temporary tenure in America. There was little provision in the early Chesapeake or Caribbean colonies for settled family life or for permanent households.

Servants everywhere in the seventeenth century were subjected to a great deal of physical discipline and public humiliation. They knew the whip, the pillory, the stocks, and in extreme cases the gallows. By such means the young were socialized into keeping their proper place as dependent workers. Back home in England, the servant lived and worked in a household where his master and mistress were substitute parents. The parish parson watched over his spiritual state, and the neighbors noticed irregular extracurricular activities. But in the Caribbean and in the Chesapeake, these social and moral constraints were largely missing. There were few clergy, few household mistresses, few spying neighbors. The servants were so numerous and so restive that even when masters exerted semimilitary discipline they had trouble keeping these young men and boys in line. One big trouble was that they had no sexual outlets, though we may exaggerate the importance of this point, since the court records in seventeenth-century England show that young people were rarely charged with premarital or extramarital fornication.

Morgan accuses the Virginia servants of being lazy—suicidally lazy. The young men at Jamestown seem to have spent their time bowling in the streets rather than planting something to eat, with the consequence that some of them literally starved. It is very evident that the Virginia servants were not liberally endowed with the Protestant work ethic. They worked unwillingly because they could see no personal gain in their work, and there is reason to suppose that this was generally the attitude of servile laborers in seventeenth-century England. The early Virginia servant did have incentives unobtainable at home; he was promised enough free land at the expiration of his service to set himself up as a small farmer. But to people who knew firsthand the difficulties in clearing American land, the prevalence of disease, and the scarcity of marriage partners, such incentives may not have seemed particularly alluring. In Virginia, as Morgan shows, the servants found themselves victimized by exploitive masters. In Morgan's view, Virginia servants, because of the combination of laziness and exploitation, developed into a class of "terrible young men" who ripped the place apart in their frustration. Trouble climaxed in 1676 with Bacon's Rebellion, which he sees as a colonywide protest movement by servants and ex-servants against a handful of domineering grandees. Virginia's search for a labor force thus triggered the biggest colonial revolt of the century.[7]

Morgan's assessment may be unduly harsh. The scholars who have so far done the most detailed work on early Mary-

247

land, such as Lois Carr, Russell Menard, Lorena Walsh, and David Jordan, tend to argue a rather different way. They do not find so many terrible young men in Maryland. They do not believe that the Maryland rebellion of 1689 was provoked by restless servants and ex-servants. They argue that Maryland servants in the seventeenth century had considerable opportunities for upward mobility.[8] It is possible that the people who came to Maryland were qualitatively superior to the people who came to Virginia, but this seems unlikely. Ebenezer Cook's scarecrowlike sot-weed planters, flocking to the Maryland shore in their Scotch-cloth blue, do not seem to be the makers of a Great Society.

If one cannot altogether reconcile the Morgan view of Virginia with the St. Mary's view of Maryland, one can say with assurance that there were plenty of terrible young men in the seventeenth-century Caribbean. Contemporary accounts are quite emphatic on this point. For instance, in 1629, when a Spanish fleet attacked St. Kitt's and Nevis just after the English settled these islands, the servants who constituted the militia threw away their muskets, cried out "liberty, joyful liberty," and swam out to the Spanish ships to tell the invaders where the English masters had hidden their wealth. Two years later, in 1631, the diarist Sir Henry Colt arrived at Barbados and commented on the great number of servants who immediately overran his ship, staying there in order to avoid working in the tobacco fields. Colt says he never saw anybody at work in the fields during his two weeks in Barbados, and when his ship was ready to leave, the captain had to spend a full day clearing the servant visitors away before he could embark. A few years later, in the late 1640s, the Barbados servants staged an islandwide rebellion, which was just nipped in the bud, with a number of rebel leaders executed. Later in the century a good many servants escaped from field work by joining the buccaneers— a far more roisterous group of deviants than could be found anywhere in the Chesapeake. From the 1660s through the 1680s, the buccaneers, led by an ex-servant, Henry Morgan, made Jamaica their special playground.[9]

248

If indentured servants constituted a fractious element in both the Chesapeake and the Caribbean, the crucial difference between the two cases is that the Chesapeake planters clung to this white servant system for nearly a century, not converting to extensive black slave labor until the 1680s, whereas the Caribbean planters abandoned the white servant system much sooner, in the 1640s and 1650s. The reason for the switch from white to black labor in the Caribbean is, I think, very obvious and fairly simple. The Barbadians discovered how to grow sugar around 1640. This was quite a difficult task, for sugar is a complicated crop to manage. It requires a great deal of intensive labor, with closely synchronized squads to cut the cane just when it is ripe, grind it before it dries up, and boil the cane juice into syrup before it spoils. All this requires three to six months of steady, hard, exacting labor. Out of crop time there is still little chance to relax, for this is when the new fields must be prepared and cane holes dug—the hardest labor of all—in order to plant the next crop. If the Barbadian indentured servants disliked cultivating tobacco in the tropical sun, they disliked sugar work far more, and so the West Indian labor problem was greatly intensified. But the sugar planters reaped such sensational profits from their first crops that they could afford to buy slaves, and they also had convenient help from the Dutch, who not only taught them how to grow and process the cane, but also supplied them with slaves from Africa. It was already known, from the experience of Portuguese and Dutch sugar planters in Brazil, that African slaves could be forced to perform the taxing labor required for effective sugar production. The Barbadians soon found that a handful of white masters, overseers, and drivers could keep hundreds of blacks at work and under control.[10]

Very quickly several thousand slaves a year were pouring into Barbados; by 1660 the island was half black, by 1680 it was two-thirds black, and by 1700 it was three-quarters black. In Jamaica, a much larger island, where sugar estates and slave gangs were correspondingly larger than in Barbados, the population was nine-tenths black by the time of the

American Revolution. Obviously the adoption of sugar and the massive importation of slaves intensified the Caribbean division into masters and workers. A starkly segregated two-class society quickly took shape. In my *Sugar and Slaves* I endeavor to describe the remarkably hierarchical social pattern in Barbados as of 1680, as illustrated by a detailed census taken that year. There were plenty of small landholders on this island; 2,500 persons held land, and the island contains only 100,000 acres. But a very small number of these landholders dominated the scene. The 175 biggest planters, those with 60 or more slaves apiece, held more than half the acreage (which was also the richest and best-watered cane land) and more than half of the slaves and servants on the island. These big planters had all the top jobs: they were the councillors, the legislators, the judges, and the militia colonels. Smaller planters served as lieutenants and ensigns in the militia, and white servants made up the rank and file. The masters occupied the tip of the social and political pyramid; the 40,000 slaves formed the base, supporting the full weight of the system.[11]

The hierarchical system made this tight little island a much more rigidly ordered and disciplined place than Virginia or Maryland would ever be. At the time of the Barbados census of 1680, there really were no big planters in Virginia or Maryland. Sir William Berkeley of Virginia, the target in Bacon's Rebellion, was the best-known seventeenth-century Chesapeake grandee, but Berkeley had less liquid wealth than any of the top 175 Barbados planters of his day. Nathaniel Bacon, the Virginia rebel leader, was a would-be grandee with 1,300 acres—a larger estate than any in crowded Barbados. But Bacon had only 13 laborers to work this land, and 6 of them were children. He held 5 Negro and 6 Indian slaves.[12] And when the Chesapeake planters began to adopt slaveholding on a large scale in the generation after Bacon's Rebellion, they never matched the Barbados planters' concentrated economic and social dominance. By 1790 the Maryland slave population was 100,000—compared with 40,000 in Barbados in 1680—but these slaves were dispersed widely among the white planters. Only about 100 Marylanders in this year of the first federal census held 60 or more slaves, compared with 175 Barbadians a century earlier.[13] Though the big planters are very conspicuous in our memory of the colonial Chesapeake, they were never as dominant as their counterparts in Barbados, Jamaica, and Antigua.

Why did the Chesapeake planters stick so long with their labor system of white indentured servants? In Morgan's view, they clung to indentured servitude because it worked reasonably well from the planters' viewpoint—until Bacon's Rebellion exposed the dangers inherent in the system. Other historians offer alternate explanations. Winthrop Jordan, in his *White over Black*, suggests that the Chesapeake planters wanted to preserve their white man's world.[14] They considered Africans to be apelike and primitive and uncivilized and ugly and smelly. As they came to equate "black" with "bad," they hesitated to inundate Virginia and Maryland with slaves, especially since they could not afford to escape to England, as the West Indian sugar planters were doing. Wesley Frank Craven, in his *White, Red, and Black,* a study of seventeenth-century Virginia somewhat parallel to Morgan's, suggests that the Chesapeake planters imported servants as long as they were easy to obtain, but that around 1675 employment opportunities improved in England and servants stopped coming over.[15]

There is yet another explanation, which strikes me as perhaps the most important one: before the 1680s the Chesapeake planters could not get slaves in any numbers, even if they wanted them, and so they had to stick to servants. Slaves were in scarce supply up to the Glorious Revolution of 1688–89. The slave traders preferred to ship the few thousand Africans they peddled each year to the closest and surest market, the Caribbean sugar islands. In the 1670s and 1680s one could sell a shipload of slaves in Barbados in a few days, before too many of them died. A few big planters might get together and contract for an entire shipload, for the big planters were always needing replacements. In a gang of 200 Barbados blacks, the death rate was so much higher than the

251

birth rate that the planter found it necessary to bring in ten or twenty new slaves per year just to keep his labor force at full strength. But in the Chesapeake, no planter in the 1670s and 1680s had the money or credit to buy so many slaves at one time. Even in the eighteenth century, when the Chesapeake slave trade was well established, Maryland and Virginia planters preferred to buy new slaves one or two at a time. The typical slave ship needed about a month to dispose of its cargo in the Chesapeake, and the captain had to engage in protracted haggling with hundreds of prospective customers.[16] From the slave trader's viewpoint, the Chesapeake was always a marginal market. Before 1680 it was too marginal to be worth bothering with.

The turning point in the Chesapeake came just after the Glorious Revolution, when the monopoly of the inefficient Royal African Company was broken, new slavers entered the business, and the search was on along the African coast for new supplies of slaves and along the American coast for new markets. The volume of business quickly doubled. In the 1680s the Royal African Company had delivered 5,000 slaves per year, almost all of them to the West Indies. By 1700 English slavers were delivering 11,000 Africans per year, including a steady stream of shipments to the Chesapeake.[17] This sudden new enthusiasm for slavery seems to have been purely a business matter. Englishmen had never seriously objected to the African traffic; now, after half a century's experience in the trade, they were meeting the American demand. At first the Chesapeake black population grew slowly, and all growth was attributable to importations. But after about 1720 blacks began to increase naturally in Maryland and Virginia, with much the same growth rate as the white population. After the middle of the eighteenth century, it was easier for prospective purchasers to buy from fellow planters than from the slave ships.

Here, of course, is one of the strongest contrasts between slavery in the Chesapeake and in the Caribbean. In sugar islands like Jamaica, the black population continued to decrease naturally right down to Emancipation in the 1830s.

252

The slave system was only kept going by massive African imports. Altogether, the Jamaicans imported some 750,000 slaves from Africa—about five times the total Chesapeake importation—yet the Jamaican black population in 1808, the year that marked the end of the African slave trade, was 350,000, some 200,000 less than the black population of Maryland and Virginia at that date. Any effort at comparing developments in the two regions has to endeavor to explain why West Indian slaves died faster than they were born, while the Chesapeake slaves increased and multiplied. One other general point of contrast needs to be kept in mind. While the black population grew impressively in the Chesapeake, it never matched the white population: Maryland and Virginia were about 40 percent black at the time of the Revolution. In the islands, as we have seen, the black-white ratio was far different—about 90 percent black at the same date. A slave system in which the slaves greatly outnumber their masters naturally differs in many respects from a system in which the slaves constitute the minority.[18]

Undoubtedly the best way to get some sense of a slave system in action is to look at case studies. There is danger in this approach, to be sure, for the examples one can study are not likely to be typical. In my searches through American and British archives, I have almost always found slave records only for large estates. The small farmers who held most of the Chesapeake slaves have left little or no trace. Still, even the records of big planters show significant differences between conditions in the Chesapeake and those in the Caribbean. To illustrate this point, let us observe three pairs of slaveholding planters: Cary Helyar from Jamaica as compared with William Fitzhugh from Virginia during the late seventeenth century; Christopher Codrington's Barbados estate as compared with Robert Carter's Virginia estate during the eighteenth century; and the Mesopotamia slave community in Jamaica compared with the Mount Airy slave community in Virginia during the early nineteenth century.

Our first pair of planters, Helyar and Fitzhugh, were both just getting started in the slaveholding business at a time when slavery was taking root in Jamaica and Virginia. Cary Helyar came to Jamaica in 1664, a younger son without good prospects at home. He staked out a tract of 1,200 acres—the same size as Nathaniel Bacon's contemporaneous tobacco farm in Virginia—but Helyar wanted to cultivate cocoa and sugar, and he needed a far larger, more permanent work force than Bacon's thirteen indentured servants. In three years he laid out £1,200 for fifty-five slaves and another £650 on additional plantation expenses. Everything seemed to be going well when suddenly, in 1672, before he had actually produced his first sugar crop, Cary Helyar took sick and died. That is not an atypical Caribbean story. Helyar's investment was too large to be abandoned, so his older brother, who lived in England, took over and tried to carry on by sending over relatives or working through Jamaican agents. The slave force was doubled in size, plentiful sugar crops were produced, yet the Helyars always felt that they were losing money and the slaves on the estate died at an alarming rate. Eventually the Helyars gave up. They sold their Jamaican estate in 1713. These absentee owners, who might have held one of the great Jamaican sugar fortunes had Cary Helyar lived a few years longer, gave up after forty years of mismanagement.[19]

Contrast the story of Cary Helyar with that of William Fitzhugh, who came to Virginia at very much the same time, in 1671, and like Helyar was a young man with good English connections but little money. Fitzhugh married in 1674 and through this marriage obtained his first two slaves. We can tell from Fitzhugh's letterbook that he bought new slaves, one or two at a time, until he had twenty-nine in 1686—a big gang for a Potomac planter at this early date. Fitzhugh bought no more slaves after this and did not need to, for his slaves increased naturally. There were fifty-one on the estate when it was inventoried after Fitzhugh's death in 1703. Thus he built a force of the same size as Cary Helyar's, but in thirty years, not three. In all, Fitzhugh may have spent £300 or £400 to acquire his labor gang; he could not afford Helyar's £1,200 investment, but he had time on his side, if not

254

money. William Fitzhugh had come to the Chesapeake to stay, and he left three sons to develop the family property. He himself had achieved considerable comfort: he built a house, bought a carriage, and imported English furniture and silver engraved with the family coat of arms. Just before he died he ordered some canvas, paints, and picture frames, so that a local artist could attempt the family portraits.[20] After William Fitzhugh died, his family went on to flourish. By the time of the Revolution there were four Fitzhughs among the wealthiest one hundred Virginians. Among them they owned seven hundred slaves.

Moving into the eighteenth century, let us consider a second pair of planters, far richer than Helyar and Fitzhugh, and fully established. Our man from Barbados is Christopher Codrington, owner of magnificent estates in Antigua as well as Barbados, and governor of the Leeward Islands. Codrington retired to England, and when he died in 1710 he left a generous endowment to All Souls College in Oxford, but he also felt rather bad about the slaves he held in the West Indies, and so he bequeathed his Barbados property—the finest estate on the island—to the Society for the Propagation of the Gospel, a missionary organization of the Church of England. Codrington intended the S. P. G. to establish a school in Barbados where blacks could be Christianized and educated. This was too daring a concept for the time. The S. P. G. school, when eventually established, was for white boys, not blacks. Only in the twentieth century has Codrington College fulfilled the founder's purpose; it is now an Anglican seminary attended by black candidates for the priesthood. Meanwhile, the S. P. G. continued to operate Codrington's sugar estate, and it kept such full records that we can tell all too plainly what went on. The birth and death registers show that one slave was born for every six who died; hence the S. P. G. kept buying new slaves. One of the overseers branded SOCIETY on the breast of every Codrington slave to identify runaways. At length, around 1760, when the cost of African imports was becoming prohibitive, the managers of Codrington made an interesting discovery. By

feeding the slaves better and working them less, they converted a naturally declining population into a naturally increasing one. Such was progress at Codrington estate.[21]

The Chesapeake equivalent to Codrington is Nomini
Hall, owned and operated by one of Virginia's richest
planters, Robert Carter. Far from leaving management to the
S. P. G., Carter handled all aspects of estate management
personally, as is shown by his long series of daybooks. When
he inherited the estate from his father in 1749, he already
had a couple of hundred slaves; by 1791 he had over five
hundred, an enlargement through natural increase. Robert
Carter had an imperious way with his fellow planters. He
once wrote to William Byrd III, one of the biggest operators
on the James River, announcing that he was prepared to buy
Byrd's entire wheat crop of 8,000 bushels, and that he was
sending down his schooner to pick up the first boatload. If
Carter treated Byrd this way, one may guess how he dealt
with his slaves. But in July 1776, a British fleet appeared
near Nomini Hall on the Potomac, and Carter found it necessary to assemble his black people and give them a litle
speech. "Do any of ye dislike your present condition of life,
and do wish to enter into Lord Dunmore's service?" he
asked. The black people faithfully answered, "We do not
wish to enter into Lord Dunmore's service to fight against
the white people of the 13 united provinces—but we all fully
intend to serve you our master." Such was the American
Revolution at Nomini Hall.[22]

However, this is not the full story, for Carter did much to
incite significant change among his slaves. During the Revolutionary War he converted from Anglicanism to the Baptist
church, and in his new enthusiasm he sponsored frequent,
ecstatic Baptist meetings on his estate, in which the Nomini
Hall slaves participated. Carter describes in his daybooks
how the blacks quaked and sang out and how some of them
were whipped by their overseers for coming to Baptist meetings. After the Revolution, Carter obviously came to feel that
slavery ill consorted with egalitarian revivalism, and he laid
plans for the manumission of his Nomini Hall slave force. In

1791 he devised a very complicated schedule, spreading the manumission process over twenty years, and starting with the oldest slaves, so that most of the ablest workers would continue to be enslaved until the age of thirty-five. Carter's manumission efforts should not be belittled; he tried harder than any other major Chesapeake planter, and certainly far harder than Christopher Codrington in Barbados. But it turned out that Carter's sons rejected the arrangement, which deprived them of much of their property, and most of the blacks who were manumitted during Robert Carter's lifetime seem to have been reenslaved shortly after his death. Slavery in the Chesapeake, as in the Caribbean, was not easily eradicated.

To move from Codrington and Carter to our final pair of case studies—Joseph Foster Barham's Mesopotamia estate in Jamaica and John Tayloe's Mount Airy estate on the Rappahannock in Virginia—is, in an important sense, to move backwards. Barham and Tayloe were humane masters, but they had fewer doubts about the efficacy of slavery than Codrington and Carter. Slaveholders shortly before Emancipation, they expressed above all the tenacity of the system. Joseph Foster Barham was an absentee planter who had spent one brief tour of duty on his Jamaican estate. He supported a Moravian mission at Mesopotamia, and as a member of Parliament he even joined Wilberforce in denouncing the slave trade. But when the Mesopotamia slaves, despite his humanitarian management, stubbornly continued to die faster than they were born, Barham laid the blame on their loose style of life and not on his slave regimen. John Tayloe, like Robert Carter before him, was a Northern Neck Virginian in personal charge of his estate, but Tayloe could also be construed as a semiabsentee, for he spent half his time in Washington, D.C., at his elegant town residence, the Octagon House. Furthermore, Tayloe had no interest in Carter's manumission scheme, for he had seven sons to provide for. Tayloe owned hundreds of slaves, but he freed only one, his body servant named Archy.

The chief reason for dwelling on Barham's Mesopotamia

and on Tayloe's Mount Airy is that both slave masters happened to keep wonderfully full records. Every year they made their overseers record the name, age, occupation, and state of health of each black man, woman, and child. By means of these annual inventories one can reconstruct the life histories of some thousand individuals on each estate, often from birth to death. Since the mothers of all young children are identified, and sometimes husbands and wives, one can also figure out a good deal about family relationships. The findings are enlightening, but they are also deeply depressing.[23]

At Mesopotamia, as on other Jamaican estates, the slave population was continuing to decline naturally in the early nineteenth century, despite considerable efforts to improve child care and to lighten the adult workload. Most of the Mesopotamia mothers had small families, irregularly spaced, and a great many of the women had no living children at all. The Mesopotamia women were certainly overworked, but they seem also to have been underfed, and because of semi-starvation some of them appear to have been infertile, incapable of ovulation or menstruation. The males on the estate were generally in poorer health than the females, and this too must have limited procreation. Whatever the reasons, the Mesopotamia slaves continued to decrease naturally until Emancipation, at which point the Jamaican black population began at last to grow.

At Mount Airy, as on other Chesapeake estates, the picture is far more encouraging. Tayloe's records show that slave births regularly outnumbered slave deaths. Many more women bore children than in Jamaica, and many more mothers had large families. There is plentiful evidence that the Mount Airy food supply was much more ample than that at Mesopotamia, and the work regime was less oppressive. Many of the Mount Airy women were domestics or cloth-workers, rather than field laborers. Many of the Mount Airy men held craft jobs. The Mount Airy children entered the work force several years later than children at Mesopotamia. Work logs for the Tayloe estate suggest a leisurely pace: four slave masons took two weeks to build a cottage chimney, and after their handiwork collapsed they spent another two weeks putting it up again. But if Tayloe did not overwork his slaves, he was ruthless about moving them from one plantation quarter to another or selling them off the estate. Over a fifty-year period, 1808 to 1861, 654 of the 976 slaves who lived at Mount Airy were either sold or moved. And distances could be great: 144 Mount Airy slaves were sent 800 miles away to open up new Tayloe cotton plantations in Alabama. The general pattern was to sell or move young boys and girls at about twelve or fourteen years old. Hence children of working age were routinely separated from their parents. Wives were less frequently separated from husbands.

Thus, while most of the evidence we have argues that slavery in the Chesapeake was far less traumatic than slavery in the Caribbean, the system was still brutal enough. This fact leads me to reflect once more upon Morgan's thesis about the symbiotic relationship between slavery and freedom. Is it really valid to argue that Americans only came to appreciate freedom because they were slaveholders? That the most ardent republicans and egalitarians were slaveholders? Is it really true that Virginia slaveholders had a more optimistic and vigorous conception of free institutions than the non-slaveholding New Englanders or Pennsylvanians? The argument, if correct, is surely bothersome—and it seems to be that the argument is fundamentally incorrect.

As I see the situation, American whites of all sorts, southern slaveholders and northern nonslaveholders, were evolving a more generous concept of human freedom and of human equality in the eighteenth century than political practitioners had ever worked out before. But no one, Thomas Jefferson included, had arrived at a very full expression of human liberty as of 1776. If Jefferson was ahead of most of his peers, it was not because of his slaveholding, but because of his individual genius. I would stress that all of the people we have been talking about—Englishmen in England, Englishmen in the Caribbean, Englishmen in the Chesapeake, and Englishmen who became Americans during the course of the seventeenth and eighteenth centuries—lived within the traditional European social order, a world divided between masters and servants. Those Englishmen who came to America modified this traditional order, but they did not overthrow it. They inherited a British concept of representative government which insisted upon active political participation, but which limited this participation to specially qualified persons. The liberty of voting was not conceived as a liberty open to all adults; it was a privilege that distinguished some adults from others. In seventeenth-century England, less than 5 percent of the people (or less than 20 percent of the adult males) shared the political liberty of voting for Parliament. Needless to say, if they were not landowners from the upper strata of society, they were dominated by that group. The seventeenth-century Puritans who came to New England brought with them a new definition of liberty and equality in religious terms, but again, New England's liberty was confined to the saintly few, limited to people especially favored by God. Puritan participatory politics did not extend to non-Puritans. At the close of the seventeenth century, John Locke articulated a belief in the sanctity of life, liberty, and property, and the right to rebellion in order to achieve these ends, all supported by his philosophy of natural rights. But for Locke, life and liberty were rooted in property. He was really only concerned with liberty for those in a position to enjoy it, and he offered nothing tangible to the propertyless bottom half of society.[24]

The leading Caribbean planters, slaveholders all, were especially insistent on "popular liberties" through representative government. But the assemblies in the sugar islands represented only the big planters. They had no interest in liberty for their slaves, nor even in liberty for the small planters. Institutionally the island governments closely resembled the North American mainland governments. The island assemblies petitioned the crown and harassed their royal governors as heartily as the Virginia and Maryland assemblies. But the islanders' belief in British freedom was exceptionally elitist. Just as their social structure was more rigid and hierarchical than those in England or North America, so their value system was narrower. In the Caribbean I see no special appreciation of freedom through slaveholding. Quite the contrary.

In the Chesapeake, especially during the revolutionary period, we find a noticeably broader political system. Suffrage qualifications were generous if one did not happen to be a woman, a servant, or a slave. I doubt that Jefferson was as bothered as we think he ought to be by announcing that all men are created equal when he personally held a large number of slaves. Slavery was a subject Jefferson avoided talking about, possibly because he was embarrassed, but more likely because he simply was not socialized to thinking he had to ponder this topic deeply. We are all familiar with Jefferson's remark that the whole commerce between master and slave is a perpetual exercise of the most boisterous passions. Jefferson was no fan of boisterous passion, and one might well suppose that he would endeavor to create a political system to control such outbursts, a system that would actively intervene on behalf of the hapless slave against the master. But of course Jefferson wanted no such political system. For him, as for Locke, natural rights only mattered for people fit to use them. Being fit for liberty himself, Jefferson wanted as few restrictions on his own liberty as possible. He had a self-serving concept of liberty, and in twentieth-century terms an incomplete concept. How could he be expected to have anything more?

Anyone who joins the throngs of tourists who visit Monticello or Mount Vernon must sense the psychic gulf between 1776 and the present. These Chesapeake plantation houses seem small places to us today, because we expect public shrines to accommodate large crowds. But Monticello and Mount Vernon were designed as private places, centers of hospitality to be sure, but hospitality for a restricted few, the Chesapeake gentry. There were indeed public places in eighteenth-century Virginia and Maryland—courthouses, taverns, racecourses, and churches—where the rich and the poor, masters, servants, and slaves, could and did mix together. But the colonial Chesapeake plantation house was the emblem of

261

an aristocratic society. At Mount Vernon one sees how master and slaves lived apart, Washington in his handsome house facing the Potomac and the blacks in their humble cabins to the rear. At Jefferson's elegant mountaintop retreat, the plantation fields and the slave quarters are a thousand feet below, out of sight, out of mind. Monticello is a thirty-five-room mansion, inoperable without a staff of servants, but Jefferson so designed the place as to hide the service area almost completely. His domestic blacks worked underground, in subterranean kitchens, cellars, dairies, and laundry rooms, as segregated from their master's world as if they were attendants to an English aristocrat or a Caribbean sugar nabob.

So when we honor the Chesapeake planters for their revolutionary republicanism, as we should, and when we condemn the Caribbean planters for their exploitation and irresponsibility, as we also should, it is important to remember that both of these groups shared one very basic thing: a social system made up of masters and workers, of the privileged and the unprivileged. There is no social concept today equivalent to the term "unprivileged." The term "underprivileged" is quite different, for it refers to members of society who have been denied economic, social, or political rights belonging to all men. The "unprivileged" members of the Chesapeake and Caribbean societies could claim no such rights. In both of these regions they were black slaves, and in both regions the slaveholders found no way of abandoning slavery, no way of extending privileged status to their slaves, and no way of reconciling freedom with slavery. So they concentrated on freedom for themselves. By the close of the eighteenth century, many slaveholders considered this arrangement objectionable. Christopher Codrington and Joseph Foster Barham tried religious instruction. Robert Carter tried manumission, but this was a solution too radical for his fellow Virginians, and even Carter scarcely questioned the need for a large class of dependent, servile workers. When Barham condemned the slave trade and considered how to end slavery for the blacks at Mesopotamia, his solution was to import coolie labor from China.

Freedom remained tied to privilege in the Chesapeake and Caribbean, as elsewhere in the western world, until the traditional master-servant relationship gradually eroded during the course of the nineteenth and twentieth centuries. Through industrialism, postindustrialism, consumerism, and hucksterism, the so-called modernization process has greatly leveled our social system. New forms of oppression have replaced the old, and social divisions have by no means been entirely eradicated, so that we still find it impossible to define community goals without reference to income, class, ethnicity, and sex. Our current definitions of equality, democracy, and republicanism, associated as they tend to be with an entire population rather than with a privileged cadre of white adult males, are far broader than in 1776, but also far more confused and contradictory. No convention of modern American wise men could conceivably frame a set of political objectives with the clarity, creativity, idealism, and innocence of the American revolutionary leaders. Much that we value in the world of 1776 was lost with the erosion of the social system upon which that world was based. But it will not do to sentimentalize the lost world of 1776. If the Founders' political achievement looks so attractive, it is mainly because they made no effort to tackle social problems which we consider it mandatory to confront. If the ambiance at Monticello looks so attractive, it was achieved at what we consider to be intolerable social costs. And though the slogans embedded in the Declaration of Independence look comfortable and familiar, our reading of the message has changed profoundly in two hundred years. "Life, liberty, and the pursuit of happiness": the meaning is very different from what it was in Jefferson's era of masters, servants, and slaves.

NOTES

1. Ebenezer Cook, *The Sot-weed Factor: Or, a Voyage to Maryland. A Satyr* (London, 1708), p. 2; Robert Beverley, *The History and Present State of Virginia* (London, 1705), Bk. 4, chap. 9.

2. Ralph Emmett Fall, ed., *The Diary of Robert Rose: A View of Virginia by a Scottish Colonial Parson, 1746–1751* (Verona, Va., 1977).

3. Richard Pares, *Yankees and Creoles: The Trade between North America and the West Indies before the American Revolution* (Cambridge, Mass., 1956), p. 3.

4. Edmund S. Morgan, *American Slavery—American Freedom: The Ordeal of Colonial Virginia* (New York, 1975).

5. For fuller discussion of the role of servants in seventeenth-century England, see Peter Laslett, *The World We Have Lost: England before the Industrial Age* (New York, 1965), esp. chaps. 1–3.

6. For fuller treatment of the seventeenth-century servant migration, see Abbot E. Smith, *Colonists in Bondage: White Servitude and Convict Labor in America, 1607–1776* (Chapel Hill, N.C., 1947); Mildred Campbell, "Social Origins of Some Early Americans," in James Morton Smith, ed., *Seventeenth-Century America* (Chapel Hill, N.C., 1959), pp. 63–89; and David W. Galenson, " 'Middling People' or 'Common Sort'? The Social Origins of Some Early Americans Reexamined." *William and Mary Quarterly*, ser. 3, 35 (1978): 499–524.

7. Morgan, *American Slavery—American Freedom*, chaps. 13–14.

8. See the essays by Carr, Menard, Walsh, and Jordan in Aubrey C. Land, Lois Green Carr, and Edward C. Papenfuse, eds., *Law, Society and Politics in Early Maryland* (Baltimore, 1977); Russell R. Menard, "From Servant to Freeholder: Status Mobility and Property Accumulation in Seventeenth-Century Maryland," *William and Mary Quarterly* [hereafter *WMQ*], ser. 3, 30 (1973):37–64; Lois Green Carr and David William Jordan, *Maryland's Revolution of Government, 1689–1692* (Ithaca, N.Y., 1974).

9. Richard S. Dunn, *Sugar and Slaves: The Rise of the Planter Class in the English West Indies, 1624–1713* (Chapel Hill, N.C., 1972), pp. 6, 69, 120, 156.

10. For fuller discussion of the Caribbean sugar boom, see Carl and Roberta Bridenbaugh, *No Peace beyond the Line: The English in the Caribbean, 1624–1690* (New York, 1972), chap. 3.

11. Dunn, *Sugar and Slaves*, chap. 3.

12. Nathaniel Bacon's inventory is in CO 5/1371/219–250, Public Record Office, London.

13. U.S. Bureau of the Census, *Heads of Families at the First Cen-*

sus of the United States taken in the Year 1790. Records of the State Enumerations: Maryland (Washington, D.C., 1908).

14. Winthrop D. Jordan, *White over Black: American Attitudes Toward the Negro, 1550–1812* (Chapel Hill, N.C., 1968), pt. 2 passim.

15. Wesley Frank Craven, *White, Red, and Black: The Seventeenth-Century Virginian* (Charlottesville, Va., 1971), passim, esp. p. 17.

16. Elizabeth Donnan, ed., *Documents Illustrative of the History of the Slave Trade to America*, 4 vols. (Washington, D.C., 1930–35), 4:100–102, 185, 187. For fuller discussion of early Chesapeake slavery, see Russell R. Menard, "The Maryland Slave Population, 1658 to 1730: A Demographic Profile of Blacks in Four Counties," *WMQ*, ser. 3, 32 (1975):29–54; Allan Kulikoff, "The Origins of Afro-American Society in Tidewater Maryland and Virginia, 1700 to 1790," ibid., 35 (1978):226–59; and Gerald W. Mullin, *Flight and Rebellion: Slave Resistance in Eighteenth-Century Virginia* (New York, 1972).

17. For fuller discussion of the Atlantic slave trade ca. 1675–1725, see K. G. Davies, *The Royal African Company* (London, 1957), and Philip D. Curtin, *The Atlantic Slave Trade: A Census* (Madison, Wis., 1969), chaps. 4–5.

18. Compare U.S. Bureau of the Census, *Negro Population, 1790–1915* (Washington, D.C., 1918), pp. 45–57, with George W. Roberts, *The Population of Jamaica* (Cambridge, 1957), pp. 35–43, 65.

19. J. Harry Bennett, "Cary Helyar, Merchant and Planter of Seventeenth-Century Jamaica," *WMQ*, ser. 3, 21 (1964):53–76; and Dunn, *Sugar and Slaves*, 212–23.

20. Richard B. Davis, ed., *William Fitzhugh and His Chesapeake World, 1676–1701* (Chapel Hill, N.C., 1963).

21. J. Harry Bennett, *Bondsmen and Bishops: Slavery and Apprenticeship on the Codrington Plantations of Barbados, 1710–1838* (Berkeley, 1958).

22. For sources for this and the following paragraph, see Louis Morton, *Robert Carter of Nomini Hall* (Williamsburg, Va., 1941); Robert Carter Letterbooks, 14 July 1772; 13 July 1776; 5 April–6 September 1778, Duke University Library, Durham, North Carolina.

23. Richard S. Dunn, "A Tale of Two Plantations: Slave Life in

265

Mesopotamia in Jamaica and Mount Airy in Virginia, 1799 to 1828," *WMQ*, ser. 3, 34 (1977):32–65.

24. For fuller commentary on the psychological implications of life within the traditional social order, see Richard S. Dunn, *The Age of Religious Wars, 1559–1715*, 2d ed. (New York, 1979), chap. 3.

EARLY MAPS OF THE CHESAPEAKE BAY AREA: THEIR RELATION TO SETTLEMENT AND SOCIETY

William P. Cumming

My theme was expressed 350 years ago by Captain John Smith. "For as Geographie without History," Smith wrote in the fifth book of his *Generall history*, "seemeth a carkasse without motion, so History without Geographie wandreth as a vagrant without a certain habitation."[1] Early maps, spare of detail and often incorrect as they are, are among the most valuable historical documents. They show what was known or believed about the land at different periods, the extent and limitations of knowledge at various times in the past. It is often as important to know what was believed wrongly as rightly; such geographical ignorance and errors explain actions that would otherwise be unintelligible. Early maps also show significant changes in geography that would not be known without them, such as inlets along the coast that have disappeared or changed (like those on the Carolina Outer Banks); the location of early settlements or towns that have vanished (like the Indian villages on John Smith's map of Virginia that have enabled archeologists to pinpoint successful digs for artifacts); and early boundary lines or trading routes that wars or commercial changes have erased. They give the history of the settlement of the land, often naming

267

individual settlers, and they sometimes explain the reasons for the names given places. And often they are works of art, reflecting changing styles and ranging from the imagination with which John White or Guillaume Le Testu or Lopo Homem peopled the sea with monsters and the land with strange creatures to the clear scientific accuracy of the maps of today.

Immediately urgent and imperative was the need of charts for explorers, who had to know what lay before them as they crossed the trackless ocean and reached an unknown shore; for colonizers who wished to find suitable terrain; for settlers who wanted to know possible opportunities and viable locations; and later for ship's captains and traders who had to avoid shoals and rocks in reaching ports and landings. For such purposes, however, early charts were often inadequate, misleading, ambiguous, or generally unavailable because they remained in manuscript. One can dismiss quickly the first charts of the North Atlantic coast, as they show no demonstrable knowledge of the Chesapeake. Juan de la Cosa's world map of 1500 apparently shows Cabot's 1497 exploration along Newfoundland or the Maritime Provinces; the stylized cusps below may record some unknown voyage or be the imagined continent of Asia.[2] Martin Waldseemüller's great 1507 world map is even more ambiguous,[3] although it was followed by many other early sixteenth-century maps with elaborate coastal nomenclature, as Waldseemüller's Carta Marina of 1516 and Ptolemy's *Geographia* of 1513.[4] All of these were derived from some earlier manuscript prototype made in Portugal or Spain.

The earliest documented voyage along the North American coast was that of Giovanni da Verrazzano in 1524. Although Verrazzano missed the Chesapeake Bay entirely, possibly because as a cautious navigator he stayed too far out to sea to observe the entrance, he and the maps of his voyage influenced profoundly the beliefs, motivations, and actions of later explorers and of the early colonists in Virginia, their sponsors in England, and their governors in the province. King Francis of France sent Verrazzano, an Italian navigator and merchant, with orders to find a westward sea passage to the Orient. As Verrazzano coasted along the Carolina Outer Banks, he saw over them to Pamlico Sound, and wrote, "We . . . found there an isthmus one mile wide and about two hundred miles long, in which we could see the eastern sea [Pacific Ocean] from the ship. This isthmus was named . . . Verazanio." Here was born the geographical misconception of Verrazzano's Sea, a great arm of the Pacific narrowly separated from the Atlantic, which quickly appeared on many maps, including one by Verrazzano's brother Gerolamo in 1529 (now in the Vatican).[5]

Several of these Verrazzano-type maps found their way to England. The so-called Harleian map, of uncertain provenance, has a strait at Santa Elena almost identical with that in John White's general manuscript map, and in the King's Library was one, now lost, presented to Henry VIII by Verrazzano himself. Sailing north for another fifty leagues and completely missing the entrance to the Chesapeake, Verrazzano landed with twenty men somewhere on the Eastern Shore; he gave a vivid account of this first recorded glimpse of the Virginia region and its inhabitants. It was, he wrote, "a beautiful land and full of great forests. . . . We saw there many vines growing wild . . . wild roses, violets, and lilies, and many kinds of berries and fragrant flowers." They found an old woman and a young woman, about eighteen to twenty years of age and very beautiful and tall, with four little girls and a boy. They tried to capture the young woman, but it was impossible because of the loud cries she uttered. Evidently dismayed, they seized the little boy and retreated to the ship. Then Verrazzano sailed on to discover New York harbor, which they called "Santa Margarita," and the land there, which they called "Angoleme." Eventually reaching Maine or the Newfoundland coast, they turned eastward and reached France on 8 July 1524.

With the surge of interest in England in westward exploration and colonization at end of the sixteenth century, several maps were produced showing the Verrazzano Sea that excited and directed expeditions searching for a shorter route than Cape Horn to the Orient: Michael Lok's map of 1582, published in Hakluyt's *Divers voyages,* and a polar map of Sir Humphrey Gilbert's, made by Queen Elizabeth's famous and influential court physician, alchemist, and astrologer, Dr. John Dee of Mortlake, in 1582.[6] The belief in Verrazzano's Sea apparently also influenced the location of Sir Walter Ralegh's Roanoke colony on the Carolina coast. John White's general manuscript map shows a strait to a great lake or body of water,[7] and Ralph Lane, the first governor, made an expedition of over 130 miles up the Roanoke River searching for a route to the Pacific. The colonists left at Roanoke vanished; but when Jamestown was founded in 1607, Captain Christopher Newport was ordered to search for three things: the survivors of the lost Roanoke colony, gold, and a westward passage to the South Sea. Newport failed to discover any of them. But hope continued, as is shown by a map by John Farrer, an officer of the Virginia Company, which was drawn in 1650 and published the next year. It continued to be reprinted, with changes and additions, for a score of years. Farrer claims that after crossing the Blue Ridge it would take only ten days' journey to reach Drake's New Albion on the Pacific. Farrer's original manuscript and the first state of the printed map show a strait leading from Hudson's River to the Pacific, and another from the St. Lawrence in Canada. In later states of the map the strait is closed.[8]

In 1670 Sir William Berkeley, governor of Virginia, sent a young German physician and traveler, Dr. John Lederer, on three expeditions westward. Lederer reached the Blue Ridge but could not see the Pacific, as his map shows. But he believed in Verrazzano's Sea, writing, "the Indian Ocean does stretch an Arm or Bay from California into the Continent as far as the Apalataean Mountains, answerable to the Gulfs of Florida and Mexico on this side." He did, however, put a lake with no westward limit on his map, noting, "How far this lake extends Westerly, or where it ends, I could neither learn nor guess." His opinion that the Pacific would have an arm corresponding to the Gulf of Mexico conformed with palindromatic theories of the time, in which parallel or

270

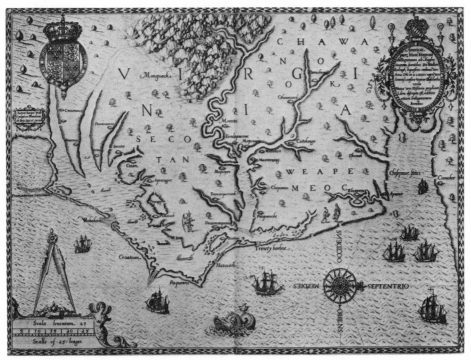

Fig. 1. "Americæ pars, Nunc Virginia dicta," 1590. After John White in Theodor de Bry, *America*, pt. 1 (Frankfurt, 1590). *Courtesy of the John Carter Brown Library*

271

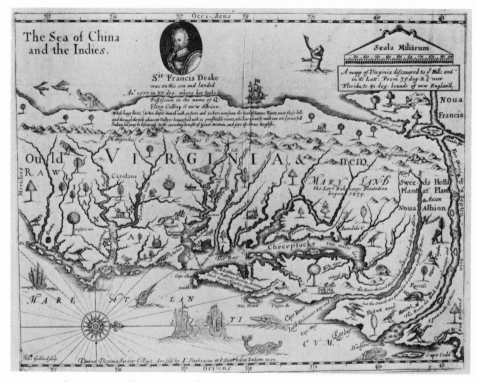

Fig. 2. John Farrer, "A mapp of Virginia," 1651. Fourth state, ca. 1654. *Courtesy of the John Carter Brown Library*

compensatory physical features balanced each other. Lederer further supported his view by recounting an incident that occurred near Clarksville, Virginia, on his second expedition. An embassy of six Rickohockan Indians arrived, and that evening they were entertained by the local chief at a festive ball. Suddenly the room was darkened, and the ambassador and his five retainers were barbarously murdered. Lederer was so frightened that he left without ceremony, but not before asking where the Rickohockans lived. Just beyond the Appalachian Mountains, he was told, "seated upon a Land, as they term it, of Great Waves; by which I suppose they mean the Sea-shore."[9] This was a clear misinterpretation of Indian sign language: Lederer mistook the Indians' hand motions for waves instead of hills.

Lederer's map was accepted by John Locke, philosopher and secretary to the lords proprietors of Carolina, and was used by John Ogilby, the royal geographer, in the "First Lords Proprietors' Map" of Carolina in 1672;[10] the Lederer information was included in later maps for nearly eighty years. The chief result of Lederer's narrative and map, however, was that he opened the fur trade with the Cherokees. William Byrd wrote that along the great Indian trading path, as it was called later, trading caravans of a hundred horses used to ply, each carrying one hundred to one hundred and fifty pounds of wares. Lederer reopened a flourishing fur trade that had almost died after the Indian insurrection. Here we see a direct connection between an explorer and mapmaker and Virginian trade and shipping.

Thus, for over a hundred and fifty years, Verrazzano's mistaken interpretation of the North Carolina sound which he saw over the Outer Banks from the masthead of his ship lured and deluded generations of explorers and European geographers. It is a classic example of the origin and continuation of a geographical misconception, for the hope and belief in a short route to the Pacific continued into the early eighteenth century (cf. Governor Spotswood and the Knights of the Golden Horseshoe in 1715).

To turn from this excursus on the fruitless search for a

westward passage or short overland route to the wealth of the
East back to the actual discovery of the Chesapeake Bay and
its delineation on early maps, it is necessary to examine a
Spanish voyage along the coast in 1525, the year after Verrazzano's expedition. The earliest record of the discovery—in
fact, the only contemporary document actually recording and
proving it—is Juan Vespucci's world chart of 1526, now in
the Hispanic Society in New York.[11] Early in 1525, Lucas
Vásquez de Ayllón, a wealthy auditor of San Domingo, sent
his pilot, Pedro de Quexós, to find a suitable place to settle a
colony on what is now the Carolina coast, a territory that the
king of Spain had granted Ayllón in a çedula of 1523. The
king had ordered Ayllón to explore the coast thoroughly for a
possible westward passage. The results of Quexós's 1525 expedition were reported in Seville and were entered on the
world map of 1526 by Juan Vespucci, nephew of Amerigo,
then examining royal pilot of the Hydrographic Office. The
coastline ends with the northern limits of Quexós's voyage at
Bahía de Santa María; the explorations of a Portuguese in the
Spanish service, Esteban Gómez, along the New England
coast later in the same year had not yet been reported in
Seville. The names given by Quexós—Santa Elena, Cape
Trafalgar, and so on—remained on Spanish maps for over two
hundred years.

The entire coast north of Florida on Vespucci's map runs
approximately east-west at 40° N., but there can be little
doubt that "Baya de Santa María" and "Cabo de Santa María"
represent the first cartographic and documentary record of
the discovery of the Chesapeake. Three years later, Diogo
Ribeiro made a famous world map, now in the Vatican Library, in which the reports of the Quexós and the Gómez
discoveries in New England were carefully assessed and delineated.[12] The shallow, wide bay is placed below 35° N.,
with a double series of islands across it. This raises the possibility, even the probability, that Ribeiro is portraying the
Outer Banks with the numerous smaller islands within the
Sounds. The river at the north end of the bay may, in this
case, be the Chesapeake.

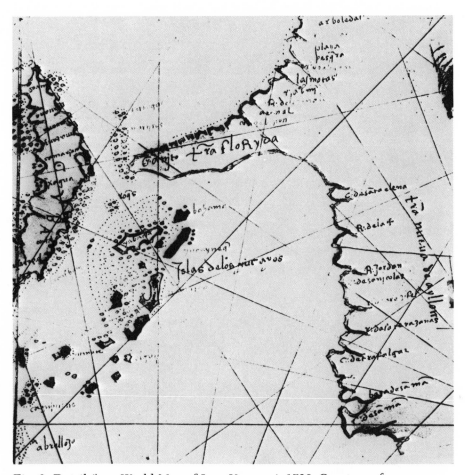

Fig. 3. Detail from World Map of Juan Vespucci, 1526. *Courtesy of the Hispanic Society of America, New York*

275

Fig. 4. Detail from World Map of Diogo Ribeiro, 1529. *Courtesy of the John Carter Brown Library*

Seven years later, in 1536 or 1537, Alonso de Chaves, then the royal cosmographer of Spain and later the pilot major, made a careful tabulation of all the known discoveries in his "Quatripartitum Opus," an important work which has unfortunately never been published. The folio on the southeast coast has the earliest surviving description of the Chesapeake, the Bahía de Santa María.

St. Mary's Bay is on the north coast at 36½°.
It is to the north of Cape Trafalgar a distance of 20 leagues.
It is to the southeast of St. John a distance of 20 leagues.
It is a great bay with many islands with the entrance of two
    rivers, the one of espirito santo, and the other Rio Salado.
The River espirito santo in the north coast is 36½°.
It is within the Bay of Santa Maria to the southeast.
The Rio Salado in north coast is 37°.
It is within the Bay of Santa Maria to the north.[13]

Evidently the Rio Salado ("Salt River") refers to the main body of Chesapeake Bay extending north.

The Spanish-type maps were copied widely, with beautiful embellishments and often with additional information, by European geographers: examples are by Pierre Desceliers (1550); in an anonymous atlas in The Hague (about 1538); by Le Testu (made for Admiral Coligny in 1555); and by Homem (1558).[14]

A more immediately pertinent problem arises from the evident confusion in Chaves and many later Spanish charts between the North Carolina sounds and Chesapeake Bay, or their identification as one bay filled with many islands, as one sees in the Ribeiro chart. Chaves clearly identifies Trafalgar with present-day Cape Lookout by his description, and says that the entrance to Santa María is twenty leagues north, the actual distance to Ocracoke Inlet. The sketch map sent to London from the Roanoke colony in 1585 has at the entrance to Ocracoke Inlet "the port of Saynt Maris wher we arivid first."[15] The error may have been caused by a Spanish-type map owned by Simon Fernandez, pilot of the flagship, preserved in a copy made by Dr. John Dee.[16] The entrance to Santa María is at 35°20′ N., a few miles south of Ocracoke.

277

Lane apparently thought the Roanoke River was the Spanish Rio Salado, and went up it 130 miles in a vain attempt to find a way to the Pacific.

Another Roanoke colony land expedition reached the true Baya de Santa María in the winter of 1585–86 and saw the wide entrance, but gave no indication of knowing how far north the bay went, as John White's map shows. De Bry's engraving of 1590 gives the name "Chesepiooc Sinus" to it.[17] This, the first cartographical appearance of that name, derived from an Indian tribe living near the south shore on Lynnhaven River. "Chesapeake Bay" soon appeared on other maps, as on Wytfliet's 1597 map, and has been the name ever since.[18]

After the Ayllón and Gómez explorations, over a third of a century passed without known voyages and activity along the coast. Spanish energy was directed toward conquering Central and South America; Spain's motto and belief were expressed by Peter Martyr in his *Decades*. "It is towards the south, not towards the frozen north that those who seek fortune should bend their way; for everything at the equator is rich."[19] But after 1560, the tempo quickened. Ships sent out about 1561 by Angel Villafañe or Pedro Menéndez de Avilés entered Chesapeake Bay and captured a young Indian. After an unsuccessful attempt to return him to his home in 1566, Avilés, the ambitious empire builder of Florida, sent expeditions into Chesapeake Bay in 1570, 1571, and 1572. Later, in 1588, Captain Vicente Gonzales explored the Chesapeake to its northern limits.[20] Meanwhile, to Spain's anger and perturbation, French and English pirates, privateers, traders, and explorers were ranging the coast, although no reports of their entrance into the Baya de Santa María are recorded.

When the Jamestown colonists arrived in 1607, it is very probable that they already knew some of the geographical features in the bay to look for and to expect. It is also probable that they had no better charts to direct them than the Spanish maps showing St. Mary's Bay and the White maps. The written documents collected and edited by David B. Quinn and Philip L. Barbour, although lacking positive evi-

278

dence, indicate the probability of information gathered from one or more of several sources. These sources may have included reports of recent voyages along the coast by English ships (Samuel Mace, Captain Newport); stories by survivors of the 1585 Lane expedition; accounts from Spanish deserters or captured prisoners; or even information from some Virginia Indians, although the "Virginians" mentioned as being in London in 1603 may not have come from the Chesapeake area. There is no reference in all the early reports from Jamestown to charts of the bay or to Indians brought back with them from London. Any directions the colonists had upon arrival were presumably verbal, not cartographical.[21]

The earliest known chart of the Chesapeake sent back to England was by Robert Tindall, gunner to Prince Henry, heir apparent to the throne, on 22 June 1607; this is no longer extant, but a copy dated 1608, a "draughte of Virginia," is in the British Museum.[22] Tindall accompanied Newport on his first expedition to Powhatan's village at the falls of the James River in May, soon after settling at Jamestown. Tindall's chart includes the James and York rivers, but shows little knowledge to the north.

A roughly drawn outline chart of the area had been sent to London from Jamestown early in 1608. It is known as "the Zúñiga chart," because Pedro de Zúñiga, the Spanish ambassador to England, obtained a copy of it which he sent to Spain by or before September 1608.[23] Philip Barbour argues convincingly that Captain John Smith drew it before his first expedition up the bay in June 1608. Only the area around the James and York rivers and the lower bay are the result of actual exploration. To the south, legends refer to the search for survivors of the Roanoke colony made early that year; to the north, the Chesapeake ends with the Potomac River. The geography and Indian villages are apparently the result of attempting to interpret half-understood information gleaned from the Indians. Belief is still strong in the nearness of the South Sea (Pacific) derived from Indian tales; a legend at the head of the James River states, "Hear the salt water beatethe into the river amongst theis rocks, being the south sea."

Smith wrote in his *True relation* (1608) that an Indian pris-
oner of Powhatan told them this. The phraseology is curi-
ously similar to what Lane heard before he went up the Roanoke River. There is another reference to cannibal Indians
living "upon this seay" on the map above the head of the
Rappahannock; across the west of the map is drawn the
shoreline of the "South Sea." Barbour thinks Smith sent a
copy of this map to Henry Hudson, who was then in London,
and that it may have been one of the factors in Hudson's 1609
voyage, in which he discovered the Hudson River while
searching for a westward passage.

The so-called Virginia map, now in the University of
Texas Library, appears to derive from the first half of 1608
also, since it has the same four rivers in present-day North
Carolina, the Chesapeake stops at the Potomac, and the shore
of the South Sea is drawn west of the mountains.[24] It lacks
the important legends on the Zúñiga map, however, although
more Indian villages, unnamed, are drawn on the Potomac.

It was not until nearly a year after the expedition up the
James River under Captain Newport that Smith made the first
of his two famous voyages of exploration up the Chesapeake.
Leaving Cape Henry on 2 June 1608 in a clumsy two-ton
barge with mast and sail, accompanied by fifteen colonists, he
crossed to the Delmarva peninsula and carefully explored the
bays, inlets, and larger rivers. After ascending Nanticoke
River to its head, he crossed to the mainland and sailed up the
broad Potomac to about present-day Georgetown. He reached
an Indian mine nine miles from the river but found it value-
less. However, "the abundance of fish" in the river was "so
thicke with their heads above the water that for want of nets,
(our barge driving amongst them), we attempted to catch them
with a frying pan, but we found it a bad instrument to catch
fish with." Returning, they came to the Toppahanock (Rappahannock) River, where Captain John Smith got out of the
barge and caught fish in shoal water with his sword, but nearly
died from a stingaree that drove its poisonous whiplike tail an
inch and a half into his arm.[25]

Smith set out in the same barge, with twelve men, on his

second voyage of exploration of the Chesapeake within a few days after his return. He explored the bay north of the Potomac River to the Susquehanna River, examining and recording the islands, coves, inlets, and rivers. The Susquehannock Indians, who lived two days' journey up, came down the river to see him. They were giant men, according to Smith and his companions—as depicted in the figure on his map—and had iron hatchets and knives purchased from Indian tribes dwelling further north, who presumably had purchased them from French fur traders. This is the first record of foreign trading goods reaching the Chesapeake Bay, evidence of the far-ranging commercial activity of fur-trading Indians. The party also explored the west bank on their return, examining the Patapsco River to the present site of Baltimore, the Patuxent, and the Rappahannock before returning to Jamestown on 7 September 1608. Smith's nine weeks of exploration were extraordinary, not only because of the extent and accuracy of his geographical observations, but also because of his skill as navigator and leader.

In 1612 Smith's "Map of Virginia" was published in a book of that title.[26] It is difficult to overestimate the influence and importance of this map; it was the prototype of Virginia maps for over sixty years. Careful study of its details and history has been undertaken by many scholars, such as P. L. Phillips, Ben C. McCary, and others: Coolie Verner has made an exhaustive carto-bibliographical tabulation of the twelve states of the original plate of the map and its European derivatives, with meticulous examination of additions, omissions, and errors.[27] Little can be added to what has already been written. The original plate by William Hole is a beautiful example of the engraver's art, although details make it overcrowded. There are 10 Indian tribes and 166 villages listed, 32 English names to geographical features, and 17 to rivers.[28]

Smith's map of 1612, directly and through its use by other mapmakers, must have had a wide and continued effect on the development of settlements on Chesapeake Bay. It was not only the most accurate and detailed map of any comparable area on the North Atlantic coast of America until the

Fig. 5. John Smith, "Virginia," 1612. John Smith, *A map of Virginia* (Oxford, 1612). Tenth state, ca. 1624.

last quarter of the century, it was also the most available one for the area throughout the century. It revealed to European geographers, colonial promoters, and prospective settlers a huge inland sea, 180 miles long, varying in width from 25 miles at the mouth to 10 miles at 110 miles to the north. Even more significant in its development by the English was the dendritic pattern of its navigable tributaries, stretching like the branches of a tree throughout a vast tidewater area, shown roughly by the crosses on Smith's map that indicated the limits of his explorations by water. Land transportation and communication could not depend on nonexistent roads. Water routes, unimpeded by dense forests and impassable swamps, were already open to navigation and exploitation by settlers and traders. These geographical features had an important bearing on the later development of the colony.

The dissemination of the information on Smith's map through and in the productions of other mapmakers affords an excellent example of sixteenth-century cartographical activity. The center of geographical publishing during this period was in the Netherlands, where the firms of Hondius, Blaeu, Jansson, Visscher, and others produced charts, maps, and atlases of exceptional quality. It was the Golden Age of Dutch cartography; the maps produced from 1570 to 1670 in Antwerp and Amsterdam have never been surpassed, as R. V. Tooley writes, "for accuracy according to the knowledge of their time, magnificence of presentation, and richness of decoration."[29] Reports of new discoveries and explorations were gathered, correlated, and incorporated in new maps; on the plates unknown areas were filled, with great artistry, by animals, trees, and depictions of human habitations appropriate to the region. Competition was vigorous between rival firms, who often followed or plagiarized each other's productions. Sometimes old plates were purchased or inherited by mapmakers who erased the earlier engraved cartouche for a changed title or merely added a new imprint. Within a decade after Smith's delineation of Chesapeake Bay, it was incorporated in maps and charts of Dutch geographers and mapmakers.

Fig. 6. Detail from Jan Jansson, "Nova Belgica et Anglia Nova,"
1636. *The Beinecke Rare Book and Manuscript Library, Yale
University*

The first such derivative copy of Smith's map, "Nova Virginiae Tabula," was made by Jodocus Hondius, Jr., in Amsterdam about 1618. The Hondius map was somewhat larger than the Smith prototype, but was simplified with the omission of some names and details. It, rather than Smith's original, was copied by several other publishers.[30] Smith's name appears as author on none of these nor on charts of larger areas that incorporated his discoveries. Even before Hondius's derivative of 1618, W. J. Blaeu's general navigational chart of the Atlantic Ocean and its bordering coasts, "Paaskaart van Guinea, Brazilien en West Indien" (ca. 1617), included Smith's conception, although necessarily much simplified. Blaeu's work was in turn followed by a series of other "West Indische Paskaerts" throughout the rest of the century, often with small variations and additions, but these maps were limited to the North Atlantic coasts and the Caribbean.[31]

More detailed use of Smith's work than was possible on the Dutch marine charts is found on Johann de Laet's map of New England, New Netherland, and Virginia (1630)[32] and in the magnificently engraved and designed charts of Sir Robert Dudley's *Dell' Arcano del Mare* (Florence, 1646–48).[33] Dudley was an experienced and knowledgeable seaman; his is the first marine atlas to use Mercator's projection for its charts. Coolie Verner calls his "Virginia Vecchia è Nuova" one of the best and least-known maps of Virginia in the seventeenth century.[34] It is the first to give York River its present name; because it is a navigational chart, however, all topography back of the shoreline is omitted.

About 1650 Jan Jansson, who had married a daughter of Jodocus Hondius and had become a rival of Blaeu, published "Belgii Novi, Angliae Novae et Partis Virginiae Novissima Delineatio," which was the prototype of an important family of maps.[35] Thanks to the engraver's skill, it included most of Smith's geography and nomenclature, although the map extends from the mouth of the Chesapeake to northern New England. Chesapeake Bay, however, tilts northwestward from its mouth, making the Delmarva peninsula unduly large. The Susquehanna River extends correctly north to

285

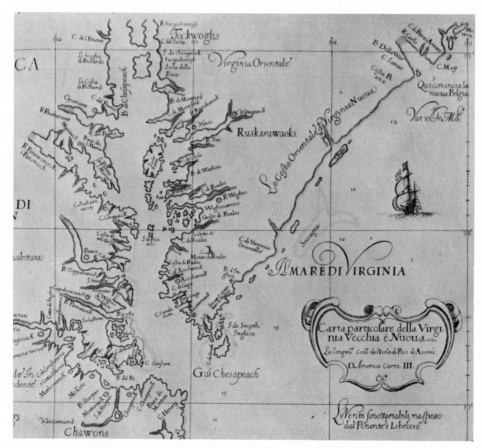

Fig. 7. Detail of "Virginia Vecchia è Nuoua," 1647. Robert Dudley,
Dell arcano del mare, 3 (1661), no. 101. *The Beinecke Rare Book
and Manuscript Library, Yale University*

within a few miles of the Mohawk River in New York. Along it are seventeen Indian tribal and village names, new information gained from explorers of Virginia and Maryland or from Dutch *boschlopers* of New Amsterdam. The map is charmingly decorated with numerous New World animals and two fortified Indian villages, probably copied from W. J. Blaeu's "Nova Belgica et Anglia Nova," published in 1640.

Although Smith's map, with its many derivatives, continued to be the best and most available chart for prospective settlers for many years, a few other maps were published. Soon after the charting of Maryland in 1633 appeared "Noua Terrae-Mariae tabula," in a 1635 promotional pamphlet entitled *A relation of Maryland: together with a map of the country*.[36] Engraved by T. Cecil, it is usually called "Lord Baltimore's map." It has none of the accuracy, abundance of detail, or craftsmanship in execution of Smith's map. E. B. Mathews states that if the author knew the Smith map, it was only from memory.[37] But it is the first map of Maryland, the first to give their present names to Delaware Bay, the James River (except on Tindall's manuscript map), the Rappahannock River (Smith gives this name to a river on the Eastern Shore), and several landmarks on the Potomac. St. Mary's, the first settlement and capital of Maryland, appears on the "Patowmeck flu" for the first time. This map also marked the boundaries of Maryland as claimed under its charter; it was used in several disputes over boundary lines. The most important and widely used derivative of the Lord Baltimore map is "Nova Terræ Marie Tabula" in *America*, published in 1671 by John Ogilby, the royal geographer. Very few of Captain Smith's names on his maps of Virginia and Old Virginia, Indian names and the names of friends, survived here or are in use at the present time.

John Farrer's manuscript map of 1650 and the 1651 printed map have already been mentioned; they have many more details and place names than Lord Baltimore's map.[38] Several appear for the first time, as Eastern Shore, Henrico City (on the James River in Virginia), Anandale C[ounty], and the Elk River in Maryland. Names of rivers are sometimes

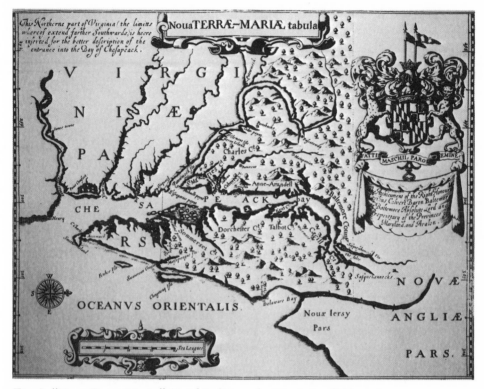

Fig. 8. "Noua Terræ-Mariæ" (Lord Baltimore's Map). *A relation of Maryland* (London, 1635). This revised version from John Ogilby, *Brittania* (1671). *Courtesy of the Maryland Hall of Records*

288

misplaced. Yet Farrer knew Virginia firsthand, and not only as deputy treasurer of the Virginia Company after 1619; he made several visits to the colony, one of the last with Captain Thomas Willoughby in 1635.[39] Virginia, his spinster daughter, added details and changes to four later states of the map; she inserted charming little pictures of trees and animals native to the region.

Farrer's "A Mapp of Virginia discovered to ye Falls" shows how little knowledge of the interior beyond the coastal plain had been gained by exploration since Smith's time. As on Smith's map, "the hills" (the Blue Ridge) lie not far beyond "the falls" (Richmond, Virginia). A short distance beyond the hills lay Drake's New Albion on the Pacific. Farrer, with Governor William Berkeley and others, believed that the wealth of the Indies could be transported "from the head of Jeames River," "to the exceeding benefit of Great Britain and al true English."

In 1666, appeared, crudely designed and engraved, "A Landskip of the Province of Maryland. Or the Lord Baltimors Plantation neere Virginia by Geo. Alsop Gent:" in a small booklet by the same author titled *Character of the Province of Maryland*.[40] Alsop was apparently an easygoing, fairly well-to-do but fractious young man who had been shipped off as a redemptioner to Maryland, where he arrived early in 1659. Both his booklet and his map are the result of six years' firsthand observation of the country, its animals and produce, and its inhabitants, Indian and European. The map is interesting chiefly in showing the names by then commonly accepted for the rivers. But the width and shorelines of the bay and drawing of the rivers is evidently stylized and careless. The Elk River, for example, is too far south on the Eastern Shore; the bay's width is undifferentiated. Alsop probably knew Smith's map even if he did not follow its geographical details; the animals and Indians may have been inspired by Virginia Farrer's *Virginia*. Though carelessly written, his comments are often perceptive and fascinating; he gives, however, little topographical information.

In 1673 appeared the second great seventeenth-century

map of the Chesapeake Bay area, Augustine Herrman's (Augustus Heerman's) "Virginia and Maryland." Like Smith's map, it has been the subject of careful and scholarly study: by E. B. Mathews (1898), P. L. Phillips (1911), L. C. Wroth (1930), W. W. Ristow (1972), J. B. Black (1975), and E. M. Sanchez-Saavedra (1975).[41] Both maps were unexcelled in their time for any other large area in the North American colonies. Herrman's was the basic prototype for other maps of the area until well into the eighteenth century, although, after the usage of European mapmakers, plagiarisms or revised copies of Smith's continued to appear.

Herrman, born about 1623 in Prague, early entered the service of the Dutch West India Company and by 1650 had established his own trading firm in New Amsterdam.[42] Soon he was one of the leading merchants and citizens of that city. He traveled on diplomatic missions for Governor Stuyvesant, who sent him to Maryland in 1659 as ambassador to Governor Fendall at St. Mary's concerning boundary disputes. In October of that year he wrote to Stuyvesant, "But first of all the South River [Delaware River] and the Virginias, with all lands and hills between both, ought to be laid down on an exact scale as to longitude and latitude." Lord Baltimore was also interested in having a map of his province, and by 14 January 1660 had made Herrman a "denizen" of Maryland, because "For our satisfaction and the bennefitt of Trade [he] hath drawne a Mapp of all the Rivers Creekes and Harbours thereunto belonging." For the next ten years, in addition to his business and magisterial responsibilities in both New Amsterdam and Maryland, he continued his surveys, extending them into Virginia. In 1662 he was granted full citizenship papers in Maryland, and was soon building his manor house on "Bohemia Manor," six thousand acres on both sides of the Elk River, granted him for "making the Mapp of this province" of Maryland.[43]

How or when Herrman acquired his undoubted competency as a surveyor is not known, but by 1670 he had completed his surveys of Maryland and Virginia. He then began plotting, drafting, and ornamenting his final manuscript ver-

290

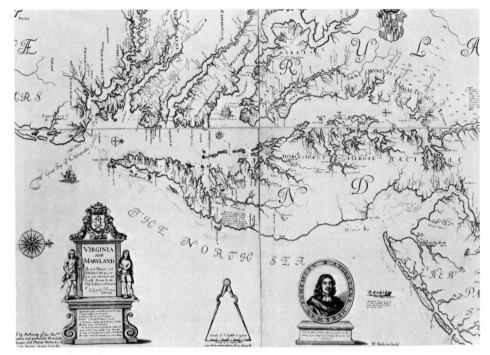

Fig. 9. Detail from Augustine Herrman, "Virginia and Maryland,"
1673. *Courtesy of the John Carter Brown Library*

sion. In 1673 William Faithorne, a London engraver, prepared the plate, which was sold by John Seller, hydrographer to the king. The exact and meticulous Herrman was not satisfied with the result, reportedly commenting that it was "slobbered over by the engraver Faithorne defiling the prints by many errors."[44] The map, however, is a superior achievement, measuring over two and a half by three feet, on four sheets, with handsome—even ornate—embellishments.

Herrman probably surveyed personally the shores of Chesapeake Bay and the rivers, creeks, and bays immediately adjacent, including Virginia. Very few soundings are entered for the lower bay, but the soundings for James River up to the falls, the Potomac up to the great bend, Elk River to Bohemia Manor, the Delaware River up to Schuylkill River, and many tributaries and creeks on both sides of the bay as well as on the rivers are given. Probably he obtained many of these soundings from local pilots. Hundreds of symbols on both banks of rivers indicate the location of houses, but the names of the owners are conspicuously absent except for a half-dozen or so important plantations or manors in Maryland, such as the Governor's Manor near St. Mary's, Baltimore Manor, Anne Arundel Manor, and Herrman's own Bohemia Manor. The hills to the interior away from the bay are not as well delineated as on Smith's map. When one compares the two, one is impressed by Smith's acute geographical sense, the result of less than ten weeks' voyaging, in comparison to the ten years Herrman spent in preparation.

The Public Record Office and the Blaythwayt Atlas in the John Carter Brown Library each have two manuscript maps on vellum, one of Virginia and one of Maryland. Derived from Herrman's surveys, they were apparently drawn and colored by some craftsman of the Thames School of chart makers. Jeannette Black suggests, on the basis of available evidence, that they were made in 1677. She further deduces that all four manuscripts were copied from a map or maps no longer extant, taken to London by Lord Calvert in 1669. Additions on the printed map, and correct spellings of names on the manuscripts that appear in obviously garbled form on the printed version, indicate that the manuscripts derive from an earlier source. She thinks that the copyist's latitude errors on the Maryland copy in the Public Record Office, in which the narrowness of the sheepskin forced an incorrect raising of the fortieth parallel, may have caused a later dispute by William Penn over the location of the Maryland-Pennsylvania boundary and thus have historical significance.[45]

Herrman's four-sheet map was too large for wide distribution or practical everyday use. The earliest derivative map may be the "Virginia and Maryland" in Speed's *Atlas* of 1676, a simplified revision following Smith's geography but using Herrman's toponymy.[46] In 1689, in the first edition of *The English Pilot: The Fourth Book,* John Thornton and William Fisher included a chart labeled "Virginia. Maryland. Pennsylvania, East & West New Jersey."[47] This was a close copy of Herrman's map for the Chesapeake, even to house symbols along the rivers. It added numerous soundings for navigation and extended the area to include New Jersey and the recently established Philadelphia between the Delaware and Schuylkill rivers. In later editions of the *Fourth Book* the soundings in Chesapeake and Delaware bays were revised and added to. Between 1690 and 1696 a large French map, "Carte Particulière de Virginie, Maryland, Pennsylvanie, La Nouvelle Iarsey . . . chez P. Mortier," based on Herrman and the *Fourth Book* chart, was published. This handsomely engraved map was the work of Nicolas Sanson or A. H. Jaillot; Peter Mortier published their atlases. The last important derivative of Herrman was John Senex's "A New Map of Virginia Mary-Land and the Improved Parts of Pennsylvania & New Jersey . . . 1719," which was included in his popular folio, *New General Atlas of the World* (London, 1721).[48] The Senex map has a few additional county names and settlements, but it lacks the fine craftsmanship of the Herrman engraving and omits numerous details and names of the prototype.

Two important maps dominate the eighteenth-century cartography of the region before the Revolution: Hoxton's chart of the Chesapeake (1735) and the Fry-Jefferson "Vir-

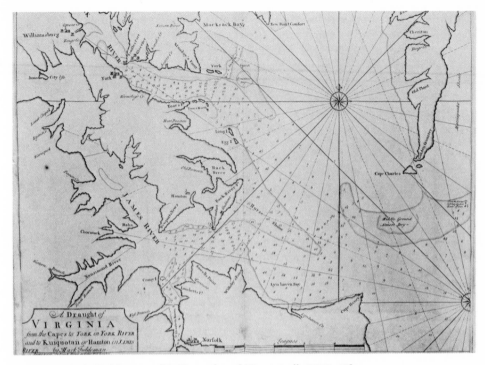

Fig. 10. Mark Tiddeman, "A Draught of Virginia," 1729. *The English Pilot: The Fourth Book* (London, 1729). *Courtesy of the John Carter Brown Library*

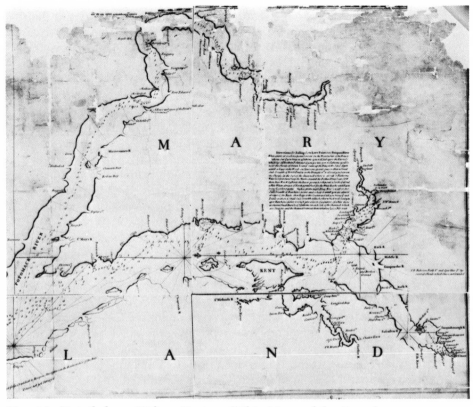

Fig. 11. Detail from Walter Hoxton, "This Mapp of the Bay of Chesepeack," 1735. *Courtesy of the Maryland Historical Society, Baltimore*

ginia" (1751 [1753]). Hoxton's was the first good chart of the Chesapeake emphasizing marine rather than topographic features; an experienced seaman and practical navigator himself, he crowded his chart with navigational advice and information, important boons to shippers, traders, and settlers along the riverfronts. "This Mapp of the Bay of Chesapeack, with the Rivers Potomack, Potapsco, North East, and part of Chester" was engraved and published in London by B. Betts in 1735. Hoxton had made twenty-three transatlantic voyages from England to Maryland. The chief historical importance of the chart is that in one of his long legends he made a table of the course, strength, and limits of the Gulf Stream northwest from Virginia, based on his years of observation. In this he anticipated the work of Benjamin Franklin and William Gerard de Brahm in his emphasis on its significance in voyages across the Atlantic to and from Virginia. "It is impossible to write on the subject of American contributions to navigation," wrote Lawrence C. Wroth, "without mentioning this large and detailed chart."[49] He had accumulated a wealth of soundings up the bay and several rivers, whereas before a ship's captain had to enter on charts his own navigational directions and soundings, knowledge gained tediously and often dangerously. Fewer than half a dozen of Hoxton's charts have survived, and they are almost illegible from hard use.

Before long, information from Hoxton's chart was incorporated in English and French charts. It was not until 1776 that a carefully revised copy was made, Anthony Smith's "New and Accurate Chart of the Bay of Chesapeake," with added legends, soundings, and corrections because of erosion or change of shorelines. Smith was an experienced pilot of many years at St. Mary's, the old capital of Maryland. The chart, expertly engraved for Smith by the publishing firm of Thomas Jefferys (who had died in 1771), was included in *The North American Pilot* (1777).[50]

Joshua Fry and Peter Jefferson's "Map of the Inhabited part of Virginia containing the whole Province of Maryland Drawn ... in 1751" [1753] is the finest map of the two provinces produced in the colonial period.[51] For the first time the interior between the fall line and the Blue Ridge is shown with details of its topography and settlements. In a revision published in 1755, the authors added extensively to the information beyond the Blue Ridge, largely furnished by the Indian agent and explorer Christopher Gist, and made many other small changes on all four sheets. It and all subsequent states and editions are easily distinguished by Captain J. Dalrymple's table of distance between settlements, given in the upper left sheet, and by the addition of "most" to the title: "A Map of the most Inhabited part of Virginia and Maryland." The map shows little hydrographic interest. There are no soundings. The bay area and Eastern Shore derive chiefly from Hoxton 1735 and, possibly indirectly and to a lesser degree, from Herrman 1673; the shoreline contours are simplified, however, and less exact. But the names of the owners of many plantations are given along the rivers and in the interior for the first time on any map of the region.[52] The 1755 edition, also for the first time, adds roads or routes in use in both provinces; the road from Edenton, North Carolina, through Williamsburg to Maryland and on to Pennsylvania indicates that land transportation and travel were possible. As early travelers' diaries show, these routes were seldom more than tracks that avoided swamps and cleared some of the removable obstacles; water transportation was preferable when possible.

Lewis Evans included Virginia in his "General Map of the British Colonies . . . 1755." He states that he followed Hoxton 1735 and Fry and Jefferson for his map south of Pennsylvania, but that he found numerous errors north of the Potomac and in the shape of the upper bay, which he corrected on his map and described in his *Analysis*, printed the same year.[53] These surveyed corrections included extending the latitude of the Potomac west of "the great Bent" ten or twelve miles, changing the width of the Delaware peninsula at the Neck, and correcting the bay from Annapolis to the Head of Elk. Evans and Anthony Smith, in his revision of the Hoxton chart in 1776, made the only substantial contributions to the colonial configuration of the bay after 1735.

297

It is difficult or impossible to obtain exact or unambiguous proof of the relationship of maps and charts of the
Chesapeake Bay to its settlement and society or of their influence, and it is dangerous to draw conclusions. But that the
clear and visual cartographic delineation of this great bay was
available to nearly any interested settler or merchant after
1612 is unquestionable. Within the capes, stretching northwest for nearly 180 miles from its mouth, was a body of water
open to 2,000 miles of navigation up innumerable rivers,
tributaries, smaller coves, and bays. No such terrain was
known to Europeans; arable land, rich forests, and waters
teeming with a multitude of edible sea life were available in
apparently inexhaustible quantity. No roads, cleared, built,
and maintained at great expense of labor and time, were necessary. Transportation was open and free; ships from Europe
could and did sail directly to the landings of individual plantation owners, there to load the heavy hogsheads of tobacco
rolled down to the wharves. Rolling thousand-pound hogsheads along roads any distance, it was found, damaged the
tobacco. It was better as well as more convenient to grow the
crop on plantations near navigable water. Tobacco was easy
to grow and sell; exchange for European goods could be
made from ships' stores at a grower's own or at a London
factor's landing, to which the hogsheads could be transported
in private boats and barges when the grower had less access
to water. Yet transatlantic ships of the colonial period could
ascend the James for a hundred miles; similarly the deep
channels of the Rappahannock and the Potomac extended far
upstream.[54]

The lack of detailed charts for the multitude of waterways necessitated local pilots who knew the local channels,
shoals, sandbanks, and occasional reefs. Many must have
kept their own logs or charts; if so, very few have survived.
Small boats, barges, ferries, or other craft, however, were
plentiful; no plantation could be without one. It is difficult
now to realize how common local transportation by water
was until the end of the first quarter of this century. As a boy
leaving for school, the present writer would take the regular

overnight packet from Newport News to Richmond, where the boat would dock the next morning. Still more popular and generally used was the voyage between Norfolk-Old Point Comfort and Washington, on one of two competing shiplines. The fare was the same; the competition was in the dinner served. Those incredible seafood dinners for a dollar remain memorable!

In examining the maps and charts of the period, however, one is frequently more aware of their misconceptions and deficiencies than their achievements and aids. Verrazzano's map spawned a family of maps that raised false hopes and frustrated undertakings; they continued throughout the early period to emphasize Virginia as a way station and middleman for the wealth of the Orient, rather than to aid in developing supporting settlements and a colonial society.

The lack of adequate charting of the Chesapeake for safe navigation is surprising, for other provinces did much better at an earlier stage. The Cape Fear River and its approaches were charted in 1662 with soundings of the channel and sandbanks before any permanent settlement was made; a map of about 1684 in the British Museum shows rather elaborate depth soundings of the inlets to and best channels for shipping in Pamlico and Albemarle sounds, and this map was drawn before any but a few scattered individuals had arrived. Ogilby's map of Carolina (1672) has an inset into Charleston Harbor made before Charleston had moved to Oyster Point, and the surveyor general of Carolina, John Culpeper, made a draft of the Ashley and Cooper rivers in 1671 with a note saying that soundings had already been sent to the lords proprietors. This draft was followed in Gascoyne's map.[55] None of the early surveyors general of Virginia and Maryland, as far as is known, was interested in, or perhaps capable of, a marine chart. The early backers of the Virginia colony were evidently unwilling to undergo the expense of surveys or of their publication; those had to be undertaken by individuals, if at all.

Even more surprising is the absence of the names of the owners of plantations or landings in the two colonies. The location of landowners along the rivers would have been an obvious service to navigators and others; it would also have resulted in purchase of the maps by many whose names appeared. The maps of several other colonies provided this information. Holme's "Improved Part of Pensilvania" appeared in 1687 and, much elaborated, about 1720. Ten years after Carolina was settled, Gascoyne's 1682 map listed the location of 31 landowners, which increased in printed maps to 250 itemized locations and names within a quarter of a century after Carolina's founding.[56] This disparity can be explained partly by the very nature of Virginia's settlement and social pattern. No large town, no important port, developed because, as one correspondent to the *London Magazine* wrote in 1749, "'tis the Blessing of this Country ... that the Planters can deliver their Commodities at their own Back doors, as the whole Colony is interflow'd by the most navigable Rivers in the World."[57]

During the colonial period Virginia and Maryland had no large mercantile or industrial population centers. Yet, in the achievements of the Virginians John Smith, Fry, and Jefferson, and of the Marylanders Herrman and Hoxton, these provinces produced four maps extraordinary for their time and purpose that were not surpassed elsewhere in the British American colonies.

NOTES

1. Captain John Smith, *A generall history of Virginia* (London, 1624), Bk. 5, in *The Travels and Works of Captain John Smith*, ed. E. Arber and A. G. Bradley, 2 vols. (Edinburgh, 1910), 2:625.

2. W. P. Cumming, R. A. Skelton, and D. B. Quinn, *The Discovery of North America* (London, 1971 and New York, 1972), p. 36. Whenever possible, the notes to this essay refer to readily available reproductions of the maps and charts under discussion; however, many maps are too large for clear reproduction of details when reduced to the size of a book page. There are

many reproductions with critical commentary of early sixteenth-century world maps. For full-scale photographic reproductions of twelve important early maps, see E. L. Stevenson, *Maps Illustrating Early Discovery and Exploration in America* (New Brunswick, N.J., 1903). For lists of chief critical commentaries and reproductions, see Woodbury Lowery, *A Descriptive List of Maps of the Spanish Possessions* (Washington, D.C., 1912); and Public Archives of Canada, *Sixteenth Century Maps Relating to Canada* (Ottawa, 1956); I. N. P. Stokes, *The Iconography of Manhattan-Island*, 6 vols. (New York, 1915–28), vol. 2; S. E. Morison, *The European Discovery of America: The Northern Voyages* (New York, 1971), with critical analysis of recent writers at the end of chapters. For discussion of early cartographical representations of Chesapeake Bay with simple line drawings, see C. M. Lewis and A. J. Loomie, *The Spanish Jesuit Mission in Virginia, 1570–1572* (Chapel Hill, N.C., 1953), pp. 252–69.

3. W. P. Cumming, *Southeast in Early Maps*, 2d ed. (Chapel Hill, N.C., 1962), pl. 1.
4. Cumming, Skelton, and Quinn, *Discovery*, p. 66, pl. 65.
5. Lawrence C. Wroth, *The Voyages of Giovanni da Verrazzano, 1524–1528* (New Haven, Conn., 1970), pp. 135–37 and pl. 20; Cumming, Skelton, and Quinn, *Discovery*, p. 71 and Harleian map (color), pp. 149–50.
6. Wroth, *Verrazzano*, pls. 3, 4, 35; Cumming, *Southeast*, pl. 8.
7. Cumming, *Southeast*, pl. 11. Fig. 1 is the printed version of 1590.
8. Ibid., pp. 141–42, pl. 29. Fig. 2 shows the strait closed.
9. Ibid., pl. 36; Douglas L. Rights and W. P. Cumming, eds., *The Discoveries of John Lederer* (Charlottesville, Va., 1958), pp. 37–38.
10. Cumming, *Southeast*, pl. 37.
11. Ibid., pl. 2. See fig. 3.
12. Ibid., pl. 4 (detail of southeast); Cumming, Skelton, and Quinn, *Discovery*, pp. 106–7. See fig. 4.
13. Photocopies of original in author's possession.
14. Cumming, Skelton, and Quinn, *Discovery*, pls. 139, 140, 141.
15. Cumming, *Southeast*, pl. 10.
16. Cotton Roll XIII. 48, Dept. of Manuscripts, British Library, London; cf. Cumming, Skelton, and Quinn, *Discovery*, pp. 278–79.
17. Cumming, *Southeast*, pls. 12, 14.

301

18. Ibid., pl. 17.
19. Peter Martyr, *De Novo Orbe,* trans. F. A. MacNutt, 2 vols. (New York, 1912), 2:419.
20. Lewis and Loomie, *Mission,* contains the best discussion of these expeditions.
21. David B. Quinn, *England and the Discovery of North America 1481–1620* (New York, 1974), pp. 403–52; and " 'Virginians' on the Thames, in 1603," *Terrae Incognitae* 2 (1970):7–14.
22. Philip L. Barbour, *The Jamestown Voyages under the First Charter, 1606–1609,* 2 vols. Hakluyt Society, ser. 2, vols. 136, 137 (Cambridge, 1969), 1:104–6; line drawing reproduced 1:105; Cumming, Skelton, and Quinn, *Discovery,* p. 236 (color).
23. Barbour, *Jamestown Voyages,* 1:238–40, reproduced opposite p. 235; Alexander Brown, *The Genesis of the United States,* 2 vols. (Boston, 1890), 1:84. Brown suggests that it was sent to England by Captain Francis Nelson and was intended to illustrate Captain John Smith's *True relation.*
24. H. P. Kraus, *Monumenta Cartographica,* Cat. 124, no. 128 (New York, 1969), pp. 43–46; Quinn, *England and the Discovery of America,* p. 461, suggests a date for it of late 1608 or early 1609. It is now in the University of Texas Library, Austin, Texas; it is reproduced in David B. Quinn, ed., *New American World,* 5 vols. (New York, 1979), vol. 5, fig. 108.
25. John Smith, *A map of Virginia* (Oxford, 1612), pp. 29–36.
26. Barbour, *Jamestown Voyages,* 2:321–464 (text of *A map of Virginia [1612]*), reproduced opposite p. 374; Coolie Verner, *Smith's "Virginia" and Its Derivatives,* Map Collectors' Series No. 45 (London, 1968), with reproductions of various states and derivatives. See fig. 5.
27. P. L. Phillips, "Virginia Cartography," Smithsonian Institution Miscellaneous Collections 37 (Washington, D.C., 1896); Ben C. McCary, *John Smith's Map of Virginia,* Jamestown 350th Anniversary Historical Booklets No. 3 (Williamsburg, Va., 1957); Verner, *Smith's "Virginia";* "The First Maps of Virginia," *Virginia Magazine of History and Biography* [hereafter *VMHB*] 58 (January 1950):3–15; and "Maps of Virginia in Mercator's Lesser Atlases," *Imago Mundi* 17 (1963):45–61.
28. The so-called Velasco map, which antedates Smith (1612), but records detailed information gained on his voyages up the Chesapeake, is a large (almost 3 by 4 feet) anonymous chart of the North American coast from Cape Fear to Labrador. Now in

the Archivo General de Simancas (Estado 2588/25, M.P.y.I.1), it was sent to Spain by Don Alonso Velasco, ambassador of the king of Spain to James I, with the information that it was copied from a map made by a surveyor sent to America by James. It is a composite of information gathered from various sources, oral or written, with names not recorded on any earlier map. Its chief importance probably lies in its northern half, with details derived from recent English voyages along the New England coast. The southern half is also of interest. South of Chesapeake Bay are names that may have been furnished by Thomas Harriot or from reports of the search for survivors of the Roanoke colony by the Jamestown colonists; on rivers flowing into the Chesapeake are forty-four numbered names of Indian settlements, with seventeen other names entered on the Eastern shore and far up the Susquehanna River. Many of these are not on the Smith 1612 map, but William Hole may have had the original of the Velasco map before him together with Smith's own draft when he engraved the 1612 map. See Brown, *Genesis of the United States,* 1:455–61, with a line drawing opposite p. 456; Brown suggests that Robert Tindall or Nathaniel Powell may have been the draftsman. Cumming, Skelton, and Quinn, *Discovery,* pp. 266–67 (color); references in Cumming, *Southeast,* p. 132.

29. R. V. Tooley, *Maps and Map-Makers* (London, 1949), p. 29.
30. The plate of Hondius's derivative copy of Smith's "Virginia" was acquired by W. J. Blaeu about 1629, after Hondius's death, and was included with changes of imprint in the atlases of Blaeu (1630 to 1667), De Wit (1680?), Visscher (1717?), and Covens and Mortier (1761?) for nearly a century and a half. Hondius also produced a smaller copy of Smith, engraved like his first plate by his uncle Pieter ven der Keere, which appeared in twelve editions of the Mercator-Hondius *Atlas Minor* from 1628 to 1636. In 1628 Theodore de Bry issued another derivative for vol. 13 of his *Grand Voyages.* In 1633 Heinrick, the brother of Jodocus Hondius, Jr., produced a finely engraved derivative, "Nova Virginiae Tabula," that appeared in thirty-seven editions of the Mercator-Hondius atlas until 1666, and with a Schenk-Valk imprint from 1680 to 1710. In 1636 Ralph Hall engraved a poor copy of Smith's map, simplified and distorted, but with a number of new names and charming details of deer, panther, wild boar, hunting scenes, and Indian vignettes

from the White-De Bry engravings. This was made for Wye
Saltonstall's Englished edition of the Mercator-Hondius atlas.
In 1671–73 a close copy of the Mercator-Hondius derivative,
smaller but more elaborately decorated, appeared in the En-
glish, Dutch, and German editions of *America,* published by
Ogilby, Montanus, and Dapper; this same plate was bought by
Pieter van der Aa and published with numerous decorative
changes in his *Galerie agréable du monde* in 1729. See Verner,
Smith's "Virginia."

31. The *West Indische Paskaerts* of Jacob Aerts Colom (1632–40),
    Anthony Jacobsz (after 1643), Henrick Doncker (1659), Pieter
    Goos (ca. 1660), Jacobus Robyn (1680), Johannes Loots (ca.
    1700), and Johannes Keulen (ca. 1720) are often found in at-
    lases. They were also printed separately, sometimes on vellum
    for hard shipboard use. They were widely used, especially by
    navigators of the Dutch East India Company and Dutch West
    India Company ships. See Stokes, *Iconography of Manhattan-
    Island,* 2:137ff., with several reproductions.

32. "Nova Anglia, Novum Belgium et Virginia" appeared in De
    Laet's influential *Beschrijvinghe van West-India* (Leyden,
    1630). A copy of this map, exact except for careless engraver's
    errors in transcribing names, was made by Jan Jansson in 1636
    and thereafter appeared in several of his atlases and his editions
    of Mercator (fig. 6). See Justin Winsor, *Narrative and Critical
    History of America,* 8 vols. (Boston, 1884–89), 3:126, which re-
    produces the Virginia detail of De Laet's map. Stokes, *Iconog-
    raphy,* 2:141, 144–45, gives a careful comparison of the De
    Laet-Jansson maps, pls. 31A and B.

33. Dudley's "Carta seconda Generale del America" is the first en-
    graved chart to give depth soundings in the bay. Another chart,
    "Florida è Virginia," extends south to Cape Canaveral. See
    Cumming, *Southeast,* pp. 136, 145–46, pls. 27, 28; Stokes, *Ico-
    nography,* vol. 2, pl. 37 ("Carta seconda Generale del Amer-
    ica"). Lowery, *Descriptive List,* pp. 123–28, and P. L. Phillips,
    List of Atlases in the Library of Congress (Washington, D.C.,
    1909–   ), 1:203–16 have extensive comments on Dudley's *Ar-
    cano.* See fig. 7.

34. Verner, "First Maps of Virginia," p. 9.

35. The best-known version of this series was made about 1655 by
    Nicholas Janz Visscher; his "Novi Belgii Novæque Angliæ"
    adds at the bottom a view of "Nieuw Amsterdam," replaced on

later states by the "Restituo" view. Other states of the same plate and new engraved plates were issued with the imprint of Justus Dankerts (1655), Hugo Allard (1656), Montanus-Ogilby (1671), Carolus Allard, Joachim Ottens, Reinier, and Joshua Ottens. The Chesapeake-Susquehanna area remains virtually unchanged on all of these versions of the Jansson-Visscher series. See Tony Campbell, *New Light on the Jansson-Visscher Maps of New England,* Map Collectors' Series No. 24 (London, 1965); Stokes, *Iconography,* vol. 1, pls. 7a-b, 7A, with accompanying descriptions.

36. C. C. Hall, ed., *Narratives of Early Maryland, 1633–1684* (New York, 1910), pp. 63–112, frontispiece. See fig. 8.
37. E. B. Mathews, *Maps and Map-makers of Maryland* (Baltimore, 1898), p. 360.
38. See n. 8 above and fig. 2; Cumming, Skelton, and Quinn, *Discovery,* p. 268 (Farrer MS), p. 269 (Farrer map, 4th state); Coolie Verner, "The Several States of the Farrer Map of Virginia," *Studies in Bibliography: Papers of the Bibliographical Society of the University of Virginia* 3 (1950–51):281–84; Cumming, *Southeast,* pp. 140–42 for references.
39. Mrs. Louis C. Bulkley, "The Parentage of Captain William Farrer, Councillor of Virginia," *VMHB* 50 (1942):355–56.
40. Hall, ed., *Narratives of Early Maryland,* pp. 355–92 (text); Mathews, *Maps and Map-makers,* pp. 365–68, reproduced p. 366.
41. Mathews, *Maps and Map-makers,* pp. 368–86, with geographical analysis; P. L. Phillips, *The Rare Map of Virginia and Maryland by Augustine Herrman: A Bibliographical Account* (Washington, D.C., 1911), with biographical data; *Annual Report,* John Carter Brown Library (by L. C. Wroth) (1930), pp. 10–15; W. W. Ristow, "Augustine Herrman's Map of Virginia and Maryland," *A la Carte* (Washington, D.C., 1972), pp. 96–101; Jeannette B. Black, *The Blathwayt Atlas,* vol. 2, *Commentary* (Providence, R.I., 1975), pp. 109–18; E. M. Sanchez-Saavedra, *A Description of the Country: Virginia's Cartographers and Their Maps, 1607–1881* (Richmond, Va., 1975), pp. 15–24. The British Museum and the John Carter Brown Library have published facsimiles of their copies of the map. Fig. 9 is a detail.
42. Paul G. Burton, "The Age of Augustine Herrman," *New York Genealogical and Biographical Record* 78 (1947):130–31. Herrman's birthdate has usually been given as in 1605 or 1621; on

the basis of a deposition in the Accomac County, Virginia, records that Herrman signed on 27 May 1667, stating his age to be "about 44 years," and of a notation in his will, Burton concludes that 1723 is a more probable date. For a carefully documented summary of Herrman's life, including arguments for a birthdate in 1621 and for his having been the agent for the Dutch trading firm of Gabry and Sons in New Amsterdam, see Dieter Cunz, *The Maryland Germans* (Princeton, N.J., 1948), pp. 12–26, and Appendix 1.

43. William Hand Browne et al., eds., *Archives of Maryland*, 73 vols. to date (Baltimore, 1883–   ), 1:462.
44. Quoted in Ristow, "Augustine Herrman's Map," p. 99.
45. Black, *Commentary*, pp. 114–18.
46. Verner, *Smith's "Virginia"*, p. 38, pl. 13.
47. Coolie Verner, *A Carto-Bibliographical Study of "The English Pilot the Fourth Book," with Special References to the Charts of Virginia* (Charlottesville, Va., 1960), pp. 33–40, gives the changes made in different states and plates of the map. Coolie Verner, ed., *The English Pilot: The Fourth Book, 1689* (Amsterdam, 1967) reproduces the first plate, first state. In the 1729 edition of *The English Pilot: The Fourth Book* a new chart of the lower Chesapeake was added: "A Draught of Virginia from the Capes to York, and York river . . . by Mark Tiddeman." See Verner, *Carto-bibliographical Study of "The English Pilot"*, pp. 51–61, with reproductions of several states. The *Tartar*, on which Tiddeman was master, made detailed soundings of the lower bay between June 1725 and May 1728. The *Fourth Book* continued to publish its "Virginia, Maryland . . . " basically unchanged for over a hundred years, until 1794. It was the first marine atlas of North American waters prepared, engraved, and published in England. Despite its crudities of engraving and increasing obsolescence, it became known as the American seaman's Bible. For comments on its contributions and deficiencies, see W. P. Cumming, *British Maps of Colonial America* (Chicago, 1974), pp. 39–45 passim. A rare undated engraved chart, a derivative of Herrman's map but with a somewhat larger area (K. Mar. VII.21, Map Library, British Library), has the title "A New Map of Virginia, Maryland, Pennsylvania, New Jersey Parts of New York and Carolina . . . Sold by T. Page . . . Tower-Hill." Thomas Page became associated with Richard Mount by 1702; his chart may have been published some time

between 1685 and 1702. The same large, four-sheet chart with the same title but with the imprint changed to "T. Page: & W. and R. Mount" appeared about 1725–28. It has been attributed to John Thornton by Coolie Verner (Douglas W. Marshall, ed., *Research Catalog of Maps of America to 1860 in the William L. Clements Library*, 4 vols. [Ann Arbor, Mich., 1972], 4:376).

48. Sanchez-Saavedra, *Description of the Country*, pp. 15–24, pl. 2 (Senex 1719, in accompanying folder). A reduced version of Herrman's map by Herman Moll was published in J. Oldmixon, *The British Empire in America* (London, 1708) and in editions of Moll's *Atlas Geographicus* (London, 1717) and *Atlas Minor* (London, 1729). Herrman is also used in the two finest general maps of North America published in the first half of the eighteenth century: Moll's "Dominions" (1715) and the twenty-sheet Henry Popple, "The British Empire in America" (1733).

49. L. C. Wroth, *Some American Contributions to the Art of Navigation 1519–1802* (Providence, R.I., 1947), p. 19; Wroth's booklet is a valuable pioneer work on the subject. A. R. Middleton, *Tobacco Coast: A Maritime History of Chesapeake Bay in the Colonial Era* (Newport News, Va., 1953), pp. 73–77, has an informative analysis of Hoxton's chart and the revision by Anthony Smith in 1776. See fig. 10.

50. In 1750 Mount and Page reprinted Hoxton's chart but did not include it in editions of the *Fourth Book*. Anthony Smith's revised chart of 1776 was engraved in a four-sheet French edition by George Louis Le Rouge, the French royal hydrographer, for his *Pilote américain septentrionale*, "Carte de la Baie de Chesapeake ... 1778." In the same year he reduced this to a large one-sheet form for Sartine, minister of the navy. Sanchez-Saavedra, *Description of the Country*, pp. 35–44, examines the history of the Hoxton chart and reproduces the Sartine copy (pl. 4). Although earlier charts and maps draw the course of the Gulf Stream through and beyond the Straits of Florida (see, for example, Moll's "North Part of America" [1720]: "The only Passage of the Gallions for Spain"), the first printed chart to delineate its course and width is Benjamin Franklin's great four-sheet chart of the Atlantic Ocean, based on information furnished him by his cousin Timothy Folger, a Nantucket sea captain, and published by Mount and Page about 1769–70. Three copies have recently been located: two are in the Bibliothèque nationale, Paris, and one in the Naval Library, London. See Philip R.

L. Richardson, "Benjamin Franklin and Timothy Folger's First Printed Chart of the Gulf Stream," *Science* 207 (1980) :643–45, with reproduction. In 1772 W. G. de Brahm published a chart of the Gulf Stream with a hydrographic table of notes made on a transatlantic voyage in 1771; cf. a reprint of *The Atlantic Pilot*, ed. Louis De Vorsey (Gainesville, Fla., 1974) and De Vorsey, "Pioneer Charting of the Gulf Stream: The Contributions of Benjamin Franklin and William Gerard De Brahm," *Imago Mundi* 28 (1976):105–20, with reproductions.

51. *The Fry and Jefferson Map of Virginia and Maryland: Facsimiles of the 1754 and 1794 Printings* (Charlottesville, Va., 1966); Coolie Verner, "The Fry and Jefferson Map," *Imago Mundi* 21 (1967):70–94, has the best carto-bibliography of the different states and editions; P. L. Phillips, *Virginia Cartography* (1896) and "Some Early Maps of Virginia and the Makers," *VMHB* 15 (1907):71–81; see Cumming, *Southeast*, pp. 219–21, for the 1753 date for the first edition.

52. Some towns were very slow to appear on maps. Williamsburg, the site of the college, was designated as the provincial capital in 1699, where Middle Plantation had been established for many years. Middle Plantation does not appear on any map. The name and location of Williamsburg is given on Tiddeman's "Draught of Virginia from the Capes to York" in *The English Pilot* of 1737, but it first appeared on a general map of the province in the first edition of Fry and Jefferson [1753]. Baltimore on the Patapsco first appeared on Thomas Pownall's 1776 revision of Lewis Evans's "Middle British Colonies," long after 1729–30, when the commissioners appointed by the Maryland legislature chose the present location, bought it, and had the street plans of "Baltimore Town" laid out. On the Hoxton 1735 chart, on which the Patapsco River has been carefully depth-sounded, "Baltimore Iron Work" appears at "Ferry Branch" (above present-day Middle Branch, not at the site of Baltimore on North West Branch); this has been dropped from the Smith 1776 revision, which, however, retains "Branche Ferry." On the Fry and Jefferson map of 1755 is "New T.," a small later settlement that developed at Jones Falls. "Baltimore Towne" (established 1669) appears on the Herrman map of 1673 and on subsequent maps for over a century, but it is on Bush River, near the mouth of the Susquehanna. It was an earlier attempt to establish a port, apparently failing because of silt and the shallow-

ness of the river. By 1757, Baltimore on the Patapsco had twenty-five houses and stores, including a brewery, and by the end of the colonial period its population was nearly 7,000—but it was entered on no map (J. W. Reps, *Tidewater Towns: City Planning in Colonial Virginia and Maryland* [Charlottesville, Va., 1972], pp. 141–43, 281–84).

53. Reprinted in L. H. Gipson, *Lewis Evans* (Philadelphia, 1939), pp. 148–49, with facsimiles of the Evans maps; also quoted in Thomas Pownall, *A Topographical Description*, ed. Lois Mulkearn (Pittsburgh, 1949), pp. 20–21, with a reproduction of Pownall's "Map of the Middle British Colonies . . . 1776." Probably the most notable Virginian mapmaker of all is Dr. John Mitchell, whose "Map of the British Colonies in North America . . . 1755" was used by the peace commissioners in drawing the boundaries of the new republic and has been used in international and interstate boundary disputes ever since as an authoritative document (E. and D. S. Berkeley, *Dr. John Mitchell: The Man Who Made the Map* [Chapel Hill, N.C., 1974], pp. 175–213). But although his home was at Urbanna near the Chesapeake on the Rappahannock River and he had access to the records in the Board of Trade in London, the purpose of the map and its small scale prevented it from making any significant new contribution to the cartography of the bay area. John Henry's "New and Accurate Map of Virginia" (1770), though it is often underestimated for its information and for Henry's surveys of the western counties, lacks value for Chesapeake Bay. The Chesapeake is not shown above the Potomac, and the lower part is poorer than the Fry-Jefferson map (*The John Henry County Map of Virginia*, intro. by Louis B. Wright [Charlottesville, Va., 1977], facsimile).

54. Middleton, *Tobacco Coast*, treats comprehensively the geography and maritime history of the bay.

55. Cumming, *Southeast*, pp. 146, 148, 151, pls. 37, 39, 41.

56. Ibid., pp. 159, 162–163, 166, pls. 39, 42.

57. "Observations in Several Voyages and Travels in America," *London Magazine*, July 1746; reprinted in *William and Mary Quarterly*, ser. 1, 15 (1907):147. In 1657 Anthony Langston had given several reasons for the lack of towns in Virginia, which he deplored; the colonists had settled "up and down by these famous rivers . . . in a stragling distracted Condition"; there was little industry "for want of Iron, and steel"; and "every man

309

builds in the midst of his own Land . . . that his great Grand-child may be sure not to want Land." He might have added that the policies of the British government opposed the growth of industries that would compete with English manufactured goods (*William and Mary Quarterly*, ser. 2, 1 [1921]:101–2). Norfolk and Annapolis were thriving shipbuilding ports for chandlers' produce and maritime trade, but their population was small in relation to that of the two colonies that comprised a third of the inhabitants of British America at the time of the Revolution.

INDEX

Italic page references indicate illustrations.

313

317

318

327

328

David B. Quinn was educated at Queen's University, Belfast (B.A., 1931; D. Lit., 1958) and King's College of the University of London (Ph.D., 1934). After serving as lecturer at University College, Southampton, and senior lecturer at Queen's University, Belfast, he became professor of history at the University College of Swansea in 1944. In 1957, he was named the Andrew Geddes and John Rankin Professor of Modern History at the University of Liverpool, a chair he held until his retirement from the university in 1976. He is currently visiting professor at St. Mary's College of Maryland.

Professor Quinn has published extensively in the fields of Elizabethan history and the history of North American colonization; among the many books of which he is author or editor are the recent *North America from Earliest Discovery to First Settlements* (1977) and *New American World* (with A. M. Quinn and S. Hiller, 5 vols., 1979). He also serves on the editorial board of *Terrae Incognitae*, published annually for the Society for the History of Discoveries by Wayne State University Press.

The manuscript was edited for publication by Sherwyn T. Carr. The index was prepared by Alison M. Quinn. The book was designed by Mary Primeau. The typeface for the text is Mergenthaler's VIP Caledonia, based on a design by W. A. Dwiggins in 1938. The display type is Letraset's Hunter.

The text is printed on 60 lb. Glatfelter offset paper. The book is bound in Holliston Mills' Kingston Natural Finish cloth over binder's boards.

Manufactured in the United States of America.